The Lord's Song in a Foreign Land

The Psalms as Prayer

Thomas Peter Wahl

A Liturgical Press Book

THE LITURGICAL PRESS
Collegeville, Minnesota

Cover design by David Manahan, O.S.B. "David the Prophet," Chartres Cathedral, ca. 1150.

1	2	3	4	5	6	7	8

Library of Congress Cataloging-in-Publication Data

Wahl, Thomas Peter.
    The Lord's song in a foreign land : the Psalms as prayer / Thomas Peter Wahl.
        p.   cm.
    Includes bibliographical references.
    ISBN 0-8146-2086-8 (alk. paper)
    1. Bible.   O.T.   Psalms—Devotional literature.   2. Devotional calendars.   3. Prayer—Biblical teaching.   I. Title.
    BS1430.4.W34   1998
    223'.2077—dc21   97-47370
                                                                CIP

To my brothers
in Collegeville and Tokyo

Contents

Introduction.   1

First Week   5

Second Week 67

Third Week 127

Fourth Week. 169

Index 209

Index of Psalms. 213

Introduction

To pray is to lay our hearts open to God, to lay down our lives before God in praise and petition, in the total giving of self into God's hands. But in that case, the matter out of which prayer is made is our own experience: we thank God for what God has done for us, we repent of what we have done or failed to do, we praise God for the glory that we have seen reflected in creation or manifested in God's works, whether that be in the story of Jesus Christ or in the valor or compassion of one who has been touched by Christ.

It may seem odd, then, that the core of the prayer which we do as Christians, at least in the Liturgy of the Hours, is drawn from a body of texts that were largely composed in the Iron Age! The life and thought of that period are distant from our experience, whether we think of the ancients' high mortality rate or the technology of warfare, of their lack of a conception of a useful afterlife or our scientific knowledge, which alienates us from their naive marveling at the processes of nature.[1]

And yet, the psalms do have a compelling grip on us. We do find expressed in them feelings of joy and grief, of fear and anger, with which we seem to identify; we seem to find in them a reflection of our own aspirations and complaints, our own gratitude and shame. Christians—and for that matter Jews, who are no more inhabitants of the Iron Age than we are—have always instinctively prayed the psalms as metaphors of their own experience.

The following reflections on psalms are an attempt to explore how Christians can honestly make these ancient prayers their own in a way that recognizes the cultural, intellectual, and moral gap between Israel[2] and us. The

---

1. We can, however, experience marvel in a more sophisticated way!
2. I use the term "Israel" to refer not only to the United Kingdom of the tenth century and the Northern Kingdom of the divided monarchy but also to the one people of both

canonical psalms always lent themselves to use in a variety of analogous circumstances through their employment of general or metaphorical language.

In the Roman Catholic *Book of Blessings*[3] there is a service for "a victim of crime or oppression." The rite allows for different choices of biblical readings to fit the circumstances, but the actual prayer of blessing is fixed:

> Lord God, your own Son was delivered into the hands of the wicked, yet he prayed for his persecutors and overcame hatred with the blood of the cross. Relieve the suffering of N.; grant him/her peace of mind and a renewed faith in your protection and care. Protect us all from the violence of others, keep us safe from the weapons of hate, and restore to us the tranquility of peace. We ask this through Christ our Lord.

The concrete content of various expressions in the prayer will differ from one occasion to another, depending on whether it is prayed for one whose home has been burglarized, for one who has suffered rape, for the people of a neighborhood who can get no help from City Hall against drug pushers, or for a minority community experiencing overt discrimination. It is not only the prayer "Relieve the suffering . . ." that will express different experiences but even the allusion to the "Son [who] was delivered into the hands of the wicked."

Something similar was true of the psalms, almost all of which were originally intended for the use of different persons on various similar occasions. Thus, in a psalm for recovery from illness, the language describing the patient's suffering is vivid, but more metaphorical than literal:

> Your arrows have sunk deep in me;
> your hand has come down upon me.
> Through your anger all my body is sick;
> through my sin, there is no health in my limbs. . . .
> My wounds are foul and festering. . . .
> All my frame burns with fever,
> all my body is sick. . . .
> My heart throbs, my strength is spent;
> the very light has gone from my eyes.
>   (Ps 38:3-4, 6, 8, 11)

---

kingdoms, Israel and Judah, and even, like Ezekiel and the sayings of Jesus, to their successors in Judah and the Jewish people.

3. Prepared by the International Committee on English in the Liturgy (Collegeville, Minn.: The Liturgical Press, 1989) 145.

The purpose is evidently to make the prayer usable no matter what the illness: tuberculosis, pneumonia, cancer, congestive heart failure, a wound or whatever. Similarly, a prayer for the enthronement of the king was preserved to be used at the ceremony for each succeeding king to proclaim the continuation of Yahweh's sanctioning of the Davidic line.

Even by the time the psalms were collected, such prayers had been used again for new but analogous situations not envisioned in their composition. Thus, the thanksgiving for recovery from sickness, Psalm 30, had been used in the rededication of the Temple after its desecration by Antiochus IV Epiphanes, and the royal Psalms 2 and 110 were understood to allude to the messianic restoration of the royalty. Our metaphorical praying of the psalms, then, stands in deep continuity with biblical usage.

We will look at the psalms for Morning and Evening Prayer of the Liturgy of the Hours. For each day of the four-week cycle an essay will examine how at least one psalm can provide the matter for our prayer. For all the other psalms we will provide a psalm prayer based on the same kind of reading, reflecting the analogy of our experience to that of Israel.

We normally quote the inclusive-language version of the Grail Psalms.[4] It is close to the psalter of the Liturgy of the Hours but avoids gender-specific language for human beings. Despite—or perhaps aided by—the discipline of phrasing the English to fit a specific theory of the rhythm of Hebrew poetry, the translators of the Grail version have regularly chosen an apt word or phrase, providing something that sounds English with a moderately formal but consistently vigorous tone, while respecting the intelligence of the reader in preserving the cultural distance of the original. If they are a bit cavalier in their treatment of the Hebrew text, e.g., by adding words imagined to have been lost in the manuscript tradition, they are not much more frequently off the mark than most standard English translations are. And the inclusive-language version of the Grail generally avoids outright boorish adaptations, though one might wish that the revisers had even more consistently allowed rhythmic principles to suggest bolder recasting of a phrase.

---

4. *The Psalms: An Inclusive Language Version Based on the Grail Translation from the Hebrew* (Chicago: GIA Publications, 1993).

FIRST WEEK

PSALM 141:1-9   EVE OF FIRST SUNDAY

(140) 141. An evening prayer for protection

1   I have called to you, LORD; hasten to help me!
    Hear my voice when I cry to you.
2   Let my prayer arise before you like incense,
    the raising of my hands like an evening oblation.

3   Set, O LORD, a guard over my mouth;
    keep watch, O Lord, at the door of my lips!
4   Do not turn my heart to things that are wrong,
    to evil deeds with those who are sinners.

    Never allow me to share in their feasting.
5   If the upright strike or reprove me it is kindness;
    but let the oil of the wicked not anoint my head.
    Let my prayer be ever against their malice.

6   Their leaders were thrown down by the side of the rock;
    then they understood that my words were kind.
7   As a millstone is shattered to pieces on the ground,
    so their bones were strewn at the mouth of the grave.

8   To you, LORD God, my eyes are turned;
    in you I take refuge; spare my soul!
9   From the trap they have laid for me keep me safe;
    keep me from the snares of those who do evil.

[10 Let the wicked fall into the traps they have set
    whilst I pursue my way unharmed.]

5

Usually lament psalms are very earthy: "Save my life!" "Destroy my enemies!" The ancients, after all, had no conception of a useful afterlife: if God was to do something for them, it must be here and now; if God was to display his justice against the unjust, it must be done at once. In that world, Psalm 141 shows a remarkable ethical sensitivity. Not that those who prayed it had a more spiritual conception of life than their contemporaries or had any belief in rewards or punishment beyond death, but their prayer had a stronger moral sense than is found in most psalms: "Keep me from sin, from evil company"; "Better to be rebuked by the just than to be favored by sinners."

Like all other psalms, this one was meant for repeated use by a variety of persons. This particular psalm could be prayed by anyone seeking relief from enemies (v. 9), whether they were creditors trying to take one's landholding or old foes in a family feud or enemies in battle. In Jeremiah 20:7-12 the prophet makes such a prayer against political opponents who consider his message treasonous and seek to kill him.

Now, there are many other psalms to pray against one's enemies; why did some Israelites choose this one? Doubtless the reason is that this psalm plays on a whole set of themes that were common among persons formed by wisdom traditions: avoiding sin, especially in speech; shunning evil company; thinking of prayer as a kind of sacrifice; paradoxically treasuring deserved rebukes; seeing temptation under the image of traps; and expecting sinners to be destroyed in their own traps. It is true, we have here a petition against one's enemies.[5] But there was more for those who were trained to look within, who were alert against their own foolishness rather than blaming all their ills on others. This in part makes the psalm easier than many for the modern person to pray.[6]

The psalm wishes:

Let my prayer come before you like incense,
the raising of my hands like an evening oblation.

5. Verse 10, "Let the wicked fall into the traps they have set," a phrase omitted in the Liturgy of the Hours, which suppresses all prayers and wishes against one's enemies as inappropriate to Christian prayer.

6. But note verses 6-7, which are so obscure and probably corrupt as to be quite unintelligible in context. I would not recommend breaking your head trying to make sense of them, though you might find the richness of their imagery fruitful for your prayer if you don't always require neat reasoning. I once thought that it would be clever to compose a musical setting in which each voice would sing a different possible translation of these verses.

Those who prayed thus knew and revered the Temple ceremonies, knew the pleasure that Yahweh took in the sweet smell of the daily sacrifices.[7] Prayer was not a substitute for the ceremonies but did have the same ability to please Yahweh. (Compare Sirach 35:1-3 and 4-11ff. for a well-nuanced understanding of the relationship of ethical life to the prescribed cult.) The psalm was taken up by Christians as one of the oldest Vespers psalms, appropriately accompanying the incense offering. The earlier Church saw this offering more realistically as a sacrifice than do we, who are more likely to think of incense as we think of flowers and song and candles, as an overflowing of the reverence and joy with which we approach God.

In any event, to pray this psalm along with our offering of incense is to acknowledge the relative character of our ceremonies, which call for a heart conformed to what we do. In fact, the Israelite incense offering had a better claim to please God than does ours, for Israel's evening sacrifice was the cult which Yahweh himself had established for his people, but this can hardly be said of our incense. For there is only one sacrifice that the Christian recognizes as having independent value—the sacrifice of the Cross. Our worship, our gift of self, is taken up to participate in that sacrifice. For the Christian, then, to think of the "evening oblation" as the sacrifice of the Cross is not an arbitrary allegory but a deep expression of faith. These prayers can become ours only if they can express our experience, our needs, our faith.

Nor are the petitions appropriate only for the ancient Israelite. Schooled by the Pauline gospel, the Christian knows that deliverance from sin (vv. 3-5) is not just a question of strength of character or strength of will; it is only God who can make our hearts pure, keep our lips from arrogance, violence, and deceit.

The final verses (8-10) are a prayer for one's life. The psalm, after all, was not to be prayed against petty annoyances but against persons bent on destroying one's life. The last verse ("Let the wicked fall into the traps they have set . . .") has been omitted from the Liturgy of the Hours in accordance with a policy of suppressing petitions for the destruction of one's foes. But even here we see that these petitions were meant not so much for revenge as to free the petitioner from danger, for the last words of the psalm indicate why the enemy should be destroyed: "whilst I pursue my way unharmed."[8]

---

7. Moderns, of course, would probably be revolted by the smell of burning suet and flesh, but if you grew up being told that it was a sweet smell, you would like it. Those of us, at least, who prize Camembert cheese should understand such social construction of reality.

8. Admittedly the Hebrew of verse 10 is more obscure than the English but does seem to indicate some such purpose.

There will be times when Christians must recognize clearly the enemies from whom we pray to be protected. We pray, for instance, for deliverance from those who would subvert our children, those Christians who by their lives or doctrine or discipline make Christ's body unrecognizable in the Church, from persons who may be generous but whose generosity comes with strings attached and in fact becomes a call not to preach the gospel. But even when we cannot recognize, perhaps especially when we cannot recognize those against whom we must cry for protection, we know that our struggle is not ultimately against flesh and blood but against principalities and powers in the high places!

PSALM 142   EVE OF FIRST SUNDAY

(141) 142. The prayer of one deserted by friends

2   With all my voice I cry to you, LORD,
    with all my voice I entreat you, LORD.
3   I pour out my trouble before you;
    I tell you all my distress
4   while my spirit faints within me.
    But you, O Lord, know my path.

On the way where I shall walk
    they have hidden a snare to entrap me.
5   Look on my right and see:
    there is no one who takes my part.
    I have no means of escape,
    not one who cares for my soul.

6   I cry to you, O LORD.
    I have said: "You are my refuge,
    all I have in the land of the living."
7   Listen, then, to my cry
    for I am in the depths of distress.

Rescue me from those who pursue me
    for they are stronger than I.
8   Bring my soul out of this prison
    and then I shall praise your name.
    Around me the just will assemble
    because of your goodness to me.

God, we have heard the voice of your Son crying from the depths of distress with no one to take his part, and we confess that though he died, you delivered him from the prison of death and so gave us hope. Gathered around him, in his name we give you thanks for his resurrection and for the pledge of our own deliverance.

PSALM 63:2-9   MORNING FIRST SUNDAY

(62) 63. Longing for God

> 2   O God, you are my God, for you I long;
>   for you my soul is thirsting.
>   My body pines for you
>   like a dry, weary land without water.
> 3   So I gaze on you in the sanctuary
>   to see your strength and your glory.
>
> 4   For your love is better than life,
>   my lips will speak your praise.
> 5   So I will bless you all my life,
>   in your name I will lift up my hands.
> 6   My soul shall be filled as with a banquet,
>   my mouth shall praise you with joy.
>
> 7   On my bed I remember you.
>   On you I muse through the night
> 8   for you have been my help;
>   in the shadow of your wings I rejoice.
> 9   My soul clings to you;
>   your right hand holds me fast.
>
> [10 Those who seek to destroy my life
>   shall go down to the depths of the earth.
> 11 They shall be put into the power of the sword
>   and left as the prey of the jackals.
> 12 But the king shall rejoice in God;
>   (all who swear by God shall be blessed,)
>   for the mouth of liars shall be silenced.]

No mystical meditation was this! No expression of spiritual longing for God. Rather, the ancient Israelite was engaged in the life-preserving enterprise of finding protection from enemies.[9] Like other psalms, this one was

9. This purpose of the psalm was recognized by the ancient Jewish scholars who gave titles to the psalm (found in most translations but not in the New English Bible or in the Liturgy of the Hours). Assuming as they did that the psalms were prayers actually prayed

composed to be used repeatedly by different persons in similar circumstances, apparently at first by any Israelite but then later adapted for the king (v. 12: "But the king shall rejoice in God"). We no longer recognize the original use of the psalm in the Liturgy of the Hours, as the last three verses have been omitted because they gloat over the death of the enemies:

> Those who seek to destroy my life
> shall go down to the depths of the earth.
> They shall be put into the power of the sword
> and left as the prey of jackals.
> But the king shall rejoice in God;
> all that swear by him shall be blessed,
> for the mouth of liars shall be silenced.

Still, the psalm is not so much a petition for the destruction of the enemies as it is a protestation of loyalty to the God who is capable of destroying them.

Verses 2-3 express one's intense longing for God to show his presence by intervening in one's troubles. One's yearning is for God not somehow in himself but in his saving action. And in fact verse 4 alludes to the "love-*hesed*" that prompts such action, that *hesed* which is "better than life." This saying, however, is a paradox, if not an outright hyperbole, since the ancient with no conception of useful life beyond the tomb could hardly imagine God's *hesed* as active if it did not preserve the petitioner's life. After all, the whole point of one's psalm is to get God to help, and so one says what must be said to convince God; it wouldn't do to say, "Only my life is better than your mercy"!

Confident that God will spare one's life, one vows (v. 5) to praise God with that life.[10] This psalm transforms a motif of the vow of sacrifice. For instance, the petitioner in Psalm 22:27 vows a sacrifice by declaring that the poor will eat and have their fill (at the sacrificial banquet; cf. Deut 16:11, 14; 26:12); this motif is then spiritualized in Psalm 69:32-33, where the poor will rejoice more in the psalm of praise than they would in sacrificial food (!). And now in this psalm the claim is made that one will find the praise of Yahweh as filling as the sacrificial banquet (v. 6). Verses 7-9 further develop the theme

---

by King David, they tried to determine from the text itself when he had said these words. According to the title they gave it, the psalm dates from "when he was in the desert of Judah," that is, when Saul was trying to kill him. Their assumption of Davidic authorship was, of course, faulty, but they correctly thought of the psalm as a prayer for a person whose life was at risk from an enemy.

10. In the Hebrew "in my life" (Grail version: "all my life") is the means or locus of praise rather than the duration.

of rejoicing in God's help, and verses 10-12 give the reason for one's joy, namely, the destruction of one's enemies.

That's what the psalm meant to the ancient Israelite. But you are not an ancient Israelite. How do you pray the psalm? The psalm becomes your prayer only as it expresses your experience, re-formed in the matrix of your faith. It is for this reason that the Liturgy of the Hours strikes off verses 10-12, considering it inappropriate for Christians to wish for the destruction of their enemies or to gloat over it. Although this mutilation of the psalm is defensible for pastoral reasons—what can be a good source of prayer for the sophisticated Christian could become a source of confusion at best for others—still, as we have seen, it is not only in the attitude toward the enemy that Psalm 63 is foreign to our experience.[11] Behind the psalm's attitude toward enemies is a different understanding of both God and self.

Still, the psalm was always meant to be adaptable: the "I" of the psalm changed with each performance, as it was prayed by or for a different Israelite. For one person the enemies were creditors and the like-minded wealthy judges who were endangering her inheritance or threatening to make slaves of her children; for another they were debtors whose delays in paying their debts threatened to ruin him; for a third they represented an unknown person suspected of alienating a spouse. When the king prayed it, the enemies became no longer those of the individual Israelite but the enemies of the nation. And so as we make the psalm express our own concerns, we are in a profound sense following the intention of those who originally used the psalm.

The enemies may be persons you perceive as hindering the gospel, or someone you see as threatening your life, or those who support social structures that undermine your human dignity—indeed, you may hear the psalm as a prayer of the exploited against yourself! Or finally the enemies may be those profound forces that subvert the order of creation, urging violence, exploitation, self-indulgence, the forces that our ancestors identified as Satan and his legions.

However, the psalm itself is not a prayer against the enemies but an expression of trust in God, who delivers me from my enemies. This is seen especially in the version of the Liturgy of the Hours, which omits the last three verses. In the psalm we express our confidence—not just love but confidence;

---

11. I rather like what the Sisters at St. Benedict's Monastery in St. Joseph, Minnesota, have done: in their Office book they print the prayers against the enemies in small type but do not pray them aloud. Thus, while the message is clear that we have trouble with these passages, those who have come to terms with the trouble have the text available for their reflection.

therefore the reference is specifically to God as the one who acts, to God as Savior. While our prayer need not always be specifically Christological, it is hard to see how a Christian could ponder long on God as Savior without adverting to our experience of salvation in Jesus.

The psalm reminds me of the prayer of an eleventh-century monk, Othlo, which never fails to move me. He prayed out of the bitterness of his struggle of faith, "O Almighty, if any such there be, and if you are all-present, as I have often read in many books, show me, I pray, who you are and what you can do, delivering me at once from my present peril, for I can no longer bear these temptations." Othlo tells us that never again was he tormented with doubts against faith.[12] A psalm like Psalm 63 could also have had a role in expressing Othlo's distress, yearning, and need.

Yes, and as the prayer becomes your own, it is your exigencies, your attitudes, that express themselves in every line, every phrase. There is no real need to get lost in speculation about how much the ancient Israelite actually longed for God, for now the words about thirsting for God come to express your need, whether experienced with overpowering intensity or affirmed only by force of the will against the pride of self-sufficiency.

Merciful God, out of the desert of my vacuousness, in the howling wilderness of my sin and rebellion, I thirst for you to reveal your power, to deliver me. I pray not only for myself. In my voice hear the prayer even of those who do not know their need, the inarticulate groanings of powerless parents in Latin America, of a drug abuser in my city, of one who grows weary in the pursuit of pleasure. Show forth your power, deliver us, and we will rejoice in the shadow of your wings, singing your praises day and night!

PSALM 149   MORNING FIRST SUNDAY

149. Praise to the God of victories

¹   Alleluia!

Sing a new song to the LORD,
Sing praise in the assembly of the faithful.
²   Let Israel rejoice in its Maker,
let Zion's people exult in their king.
³   Let them praise God's name with dancing
and make music with timbrel and harp.

---

12. PL 146:53.

⁴ For the L<small>ORD</small> takes delight in his people,
and crowns the poor with salvation.
⁵ Let the faithful rejoice in their glory,
shout for joy and take their rest.
⁶ Let the praise of God be on their lips
and a two-edged sword in their hand,

⁷ to deal out vengeance to the nations
and punishment on all the peoples;
⁸ to bind their kings in chains
and their nobles in fetters of iron;
⁹ to carry out the sentence pre-ordained:
this honor is for all God's faithful.

Alleluia!

Give to the hearts of your faithful, God, deep joy in your love. Open our lips to exult in you as our King, and arm us to join in your battle to liberate us and our world from the tyranny of the Prince of Darkness. We ask this in Jesus' name and for his sake.

PSALM 110:1-5, 7   EVENING EVERY SUNDAY

(109) 110. The Lord and the chosen king

¹ The L<small>ORD</small>'s revelation to my Master:
"Sit on my right;
your foes I will put beneath you feet."

² The L<small>ORD</small> will wield from Zion
your scepter of power;
rule in the midst of all your foes.

³ A prince from the day of your birth
on the holy mountains;
from the womb before the dawn I begot you.

⁴ The L<small>ORD</small> has sworn an oath and will not change.
"You are a priest for ever,
a priest like Melchizedek of old."

* * * * *

⁵ The Master standing at your right hand
will shatter rulers in the day of wrath,

[⁶   Will judge all the nations,
    will heap high the bodies;
    heads shall be scattered far and wide.]

⁷   He shall drink from the stream by the wayside,
    will stand with head held high.

The text of Psalm 110 is chaotic. That means that ancient scribes made so many mistakes in copying or translating the text that scholars even disagree simply about what words are supposed to be read. For instance, in most Hebrew manuscripts verse 3 reads obscurely:

Your people are voluntariness on the day of your might
in holy splendor¹³ from the womb of dawn.
Yours is the dew of your youth.

The old Jewish Greek translation (the Septuagint) reads:

With you is nobility on the day of your might.
In the splendor of the sanctuary
from the womb before the dawn
I begot you.

Hard as it may be to believe, except for the absence of the words "yours is the dew," the Greek presupposes exactly the same Hebrew letters as the Hebrew except for the vowels, which were after all not recorded in writing for the first thousand years after the psalms were written. For example, the ancient Jews who translated into Greek pronounced the Hebrew letters *yldtyk,* something like *yelidtîka*—"I begot you,"¹⁴ while the later rabbis who preserved the Hebrew text pronounced the same letters *yaldutêka*—"your youth."¹⁵

Well, if the scholars disagree, the people who translated the psalms for prayer had to make a choice, and our prayer will reflect that choice. In this case they served us well, following generally the old Greek tradition, which

13. Many Hebrew manuscripts and some ancient translations here read "on the holy mountains," a reading followed by the Liturgy of the Hours.

14. As did also several Hebrew manuscripts and the informants of Origen, whose transliteration in Greek characters seems to reflect a similar verb.

15. As a matter of fact, even if the phrase was originally prayed more like the rabbinical reading, the development reflected in the Septuagint and other ancient witnesses is not necessarily devoid of all authority. After all, the whole story of the development of the Bible is one of reinterpretation of older tales, sayings, and texts. At what point in this process do we decide that further changes cease to have any canonical character?

corresponds to the similar royal Psalm 2:7. It is likely that it was the rabbis who chose a reading that least lent itself to counter a polemical Christian interpretation. (Note, it may well be that both readings were meant to cover up some unacceptable mythology presupposed by the original!)

Like Psalm 2, this psalm was used in royal ceremonies, perhaps at the king's coronation. It strongly reflects Egyptian royal language in seeing the king as son of the God and in its emphasis on the king's power to destroy his enemies. As such it was meant to impress its hearers with the message that with Yahweh's support the king is invincible—don't even think of rebelling! A song like this would have been part of the royal ceremony of the great kings like David, Hezekiah, and Josiah. It was also surely part of the ceremonial of a Manasseh, who sponsored the corruption of Israel's worship, and a Jehoiakim, who persecuted Jeremiah for preaching Yahweh's condemnatory word! The royal cult could undergird a king's program of piety and justice; it could just as well support impiety and exploitation. And, as perhaps in all government since some bully first invented the crown, there was more of exploitation than of justice in Israel's story.

Hearing such psalms proclaimed repeatedly of kings who proved false to the promise, some Israelites began to suspect that this oracle referred to another king to come; for when a righteous king like Hezekiah was followed by a criminal like Manasseh, they came to expect a king whose reign of peace and justice would not be subverted by another. During the Exile the old hymns were preserved to be held in readiness for the restoration, so that they would have the right ceremonies for a new coronation. But as the years of foreign domination stretched on, the old hymns with their hyperbolic visions of universal and unending reign, of perfect justice and fertility, were heard ever more as literal prophecies for the future.

Jesus and his disciples were heirs to this Jewish expectation. And, while Jesus was hesitant to identify himself as this messiah, after Pentecost his disciples had no such hesitation. In his life, teaching, death, and resurrection they had experienced such liberating, creative power that they seized whatever images they could from the Scriptures of the First Testament to identify who and what this Jesus was. Identifying Jesus as the great expected King, they heard all the royal psalms as singing the mystery of God in Jesus the Christ.

We cannot be sure how the psalm was originally used or just what was meant by its various parts, maybe in part because the text was changed when it was no longer used in the royal court but was heard as messianic promise. For instance, it is not clear that it was the king who was originally addressed in verse 4, "You are a priest forever," though evidently the Letter to the Hebrews did take this verse as spoken to the King and so to Christ. Nor can we be sure who was the "Master"[16] and who the "you" of verse 5 (i.e., which is Yahweh, which the king—cf. verse 1, where "my lord/master" is at Yahweh's "right hand"), or who it is that drinks from the stream.

But to pray this psalm, the Christian is not dependent on the mistaken supposition of the earliest Christians that the psalm was a prediction of Christ at the time of its composition. Rather, the structures of God's relationship with God's people, kingship and priesthood—divine fatherhood, protection, legitimation—as these things were recognized by Israel, remain the very matrix of the reality of God's world, never more fully realized than in Jesus, in whom all reality reaches its fulfillment.

When we pray this psalm, we will surely celebrate in it the One whom we recognize as King. In Christ we find those things that were the glory of Israel's king realized even more fully than in Hezekiah or David. He is begotten of God before the dawn, and his enemies—above all through his resurrection and parousia—are made his footstool. "He must reign until he has put all his enemies under his feet. The last enemy to be destroyed is death" (1 Cor 15:25f., RSV). Even the promise of eternal priesthood, which may originally have been made to the Jerusalem priest rather than the king, will be heard (after Hebrews 5; 7) as addressed to Jesus. For the imagery which helps us to understand and express our experience in Christ is in no way limited to royal imagery.

We glory in this King, we rejoice in our subjection to Christ, which is already realized in part within the limits of our obedience to Christ, and which in its liberating fullness we expectantly await in the parousia. We exult in our paradoxical King, whose victory is won in his sacrifice, who offered only one sacrifice, but whose priesthood is eternal as that sacrifice is realized in sacrament and in the sacrificial life of his priestly people.

PSALM 114   EVENING FIRST SUNDAY

(113A) 114. The wonders of the Exodus:
the one true God

Alleluia!

When Israel came forth from Egypt,
Jacob's family from an alien people,
2 Judah became the Lord's temple,
Israel became God's kingdom.

---

16. The New American Bible follows some Hebrew manuscripts in reading "Master" as LORD, therefore as Yahweh.

3 The sea fled at the sight,
   the Jordan turned back on its course,
4 the mountains leapt like rams
   and the hills like yearling sheep.

5 Why was it, sea, that you fled,
   that you turned back, Jordan, on your course?
6 Mountains, that you leapt like rams;
   hills, like yearling sheep?

7 Tremble, O earth, before the LORD,
   in the presence of the God of Jacob,
8 who turns the rock into a pool
   and flint into a spring of water.

Rather than just announcing the importance of the Exodus, claiming that it proves God's ability to save, this poem lets us actually see for ourselves the deliverance of Israel and draw our own conclusions. There are few poems that show better the power of the Bible's imaginative use of concrete imagery.

The poem begins abstractly enough: The Exodus is the beginning of Israel's existence as the place of Yahweh's sanctuary and of God's rule (vv. 1-2). But then, as the story is retold, the telling imbues the message with extraordinary feeling. The sea (Exod 14) and the Jordan (Josh 3) are no longer things that the Lord manipulates; rather, they pulse with life. Like timid soldiers before a terrible adversary, they fear and take flight. The mountains (Judg 5:5; Exod 19:18; Ps 68:9) leap like frightened sheep. Immediately the psalm goes on to taunt the sea, the river, the mountains: What were you so scared of? And finally the psalm challenges all the earth: We've no reason to fear you; rather tremble, O earth, before Yahweh, who can certainly save us from you, who in the beginning even caused the rock to give us water (Exod 17:1-7; Num 20:2-13).[17]

There is, in fact, more to the poem than vivid imagery. When Yahweh faces down the sea and the river Jordan, he is confronting the powers of chaos. In the primordial days of Ugaritic myth, Baal in pitched combat defeats the god Yamm, or "Sea," who is also called "Judge River." In this psalm the deliverance of Israel from Egypt is depicted as the triumph over chaos,

---

17. Actually the Hebrew word for "leap" could connote pleasure (Qoh 3:4) as well as fear (cf. Ps 29:6), but in the context it seems to indicate the latter. Likewise, the word translated "tremble" in verse 7 could express either distress or delight; the verb refers either to writhing in pain or dancing for joy, but the context suggests distress. However, perhaps both verbs were chosen for their ambiguity!

which is accomplished by Yahweh rather than the Canaanite god Baal.[18] Nor need Yahweh stoop to actual combat with Yamm; the sight of Yahweh alone is enough to send Yamm off in flight!

The psalm was doubtless done at a festival, likely Passover. No matter that it doesn't really fit any of what we think of as the "typical" genres like hymn or psalm of confidence. It could, for instance, have been used in connection with some sort of dramatization of the saving acts, which would perhaps be highly stylized, like our Eucharist as a stylized representation of the Lord's Supper and even of the death and resurrection of Christ.

It is hard to overestimate the significance in Israel of the story of how Yahweh delivered the Hebrews from Egypt. It was retold generation after generation, always becoming new in the telling. It assured the first Israelites in the Land of Canaan that they had nothing to fear from the Canaanite military city states: the God who delivered us from Pharaoh will keep us from becoming slaves of the kings of Canaan. In the early kingdom it was a warning against arrogance: we were once slaves in Egypt; the land we now possess is God's gift to us, but let us not become oppressors like Pharaoh. To Jeroboam, who led the North in its rejection of the tyranny of Solomon and his son Rehoboam, the story symbolized his people's own deliverance from slavery to the southern kings.[19] Prophets and deuteronomic reformers used the old story to condemn their people's infidelity to the God who had rescued them from Egypt and given them their land. To Jews in exile it became a pledge that as Yahweh brought them out of Egypt, he will bring them up out of Babylon. For early Christian Jews the story became a model of liberation from both slavery to Rome and slavery to their hatred of Rome. The first Christians saw the death of Jesus as Exodus (Luke 9:31), for through it he led his people to freedom. And the song of deliverance by the saints of Revelation was the song of Moses as well as of the Lamb (Rev 15:2-4).

The tale of the God who delivers slaves from Egypt is always a dangerous one to tyrants. American slaveholders, who wanted their servants to learn Paul's exhortation to be obedient to their masters, were not pleased when their blacks discovered this story: "Go down, Moses, way down in Egypt's Land! Tell old Pharaoh to let my people go." The story gave unexpected energy to Latin American *comunidades de base,* which had begun as a movement

---

18. More about this on Psalm 93, morning of the Third Sunday.

19. The story of Jeroboam's conservative religious reforms have come to us only through hostile southern tradition (1 Kgs 12:26-33). When he set up bulls in the ancient Israelite sanctuaries of Dan and Bethel (surely as pedestals for Yahweh, like the cherubim in Jerusalem), the words he spoke at each place were good Passover theology: "Behold your God, who brought you out of Egypt!"

to teach lectors to read the Scripture lessons effectively at Mass. They came to recognize that their landowners, industrialists, and politicians were holding them in bondage—but also that God showed them the way to freedom if they were willing to take the risk to follow where God would lead.

Yes, the story has the power to transform people wherever they are held in bondage. And there is plenty of bondage to go around—economic exploitation, political repression, restriction of opportunities to women and persons of color, slavery to our lusts and to our greed, bondage to our old ideas, to the latest fad, even bondage to our need for power. Yes, we are all both oppressed and oppressors, tyrants and slaves. One time the psalm will give us hope, another time fear. And both the hope and the fear can be gifts of grace, for the bonds by which I hold another in slavery at the same time hold me captive. And the God who liberated the Hebrews would set us free from every kind of captivity.

PSALM 5:2-10, 12-13   MORNING FIRST MONDAY

5. Morning prayer

² To my words give ear, O LORD,
   give heed to my groaning.
³ Attend to the sound of my cries,
   my King and my God.

   It is you whom I invoke, ⁴ O LORD.
   In the morning you hear me;
   in the morning I offer you my prayer,
   watching and waiting.

⁵ You are no God who loves evil;
   no sinner is your guest.
⁶ The boastful shall not stand their ground
   before your face.

⁷ You hate all who do evil;
   you destroy all who lie.
   Deceitful and bloodthirsty people
   are hateful to you, LORD.

⁸ But I through the greatness of your love
   have access to your house.
   I bow down before your holy temple,
   filled with awe.

⁹ Lead me, LORD, in your justice,
because of those who lie in wait;
make clear your way before me.

¹⁰ No truth can be found in their mouths,
their heart is all mischief,
their throat a wide-open grave,
all honey their speech.

[¹¹ Declare them guilty, O God.
Let them fail in their designs.
Drive them out for their many offenses,
for they have defied you.]

¹² All those you protect shall be glad
and ring out their joy.
You shelter them; in you they rejoice,
those who love your name.

¹³ LORD, it is you who bless the upright:
you surround them with favor as with a shield.

Through baptism, through your gift of faith, God, I have access to your temple. Relying not on my righteousness but on your grace, I lay my life this morning in your hands, begging you to deliver me from the Enemy, yes, from self-deception and from my own unruly desires, that I may rejoice in your protection. I ask this in Jesus' name and for his sake.

PSALM 29   MORNING FIRST MONDAY

(28) 29. The glory of God seen in the storm

¹ O give the LORD, you children of God,
give the LORD glory and power;
² give the LORD the glory of his name.
Adore the LORD, resplendent and holy.

³ The LORD's voice resounding on the waters,
the LORD on the immensity of waters;
⁴ the voice of the LORD, full of power,
the voice of the LORD, full of splendor.

⁵ The LORD's voice shattering the cedars,
the LORD shatters the cedars of Lebanon,

⁶ makes Lebanon leap like a calf
   and Sirion like a young wild ox.

⁷ (The LORD's voice flashes flames of fire.)

⁸ The LORD's voice shaking the wilderness,
   the LORD shakes the wilderness of Kadesh;
⁹ The LORD's voice rending the oak tree
   and stripping the forest bare.

³ᵇ The God of glory thunders.
¹⁰ In his temple they all cry: "Glory!"
   The LORD sat enthroned over the flood;
   the LORD sits as king for ever.

¹¹ The LORD will give strength to his people,
   the LORD will bless his people with peace.

If the psalms as a whole are Iron Age prayers, Psalm 29 is a prayer of the Bronze Age, in its origin at least. Almost all the phrases or theological vocabulary of the psalm are paralleled in ancient Canaanite literature and would appropriately be addressed to the Canaanite Baal Haddad, god of weather and fertility. It is quite likely that this prayer was taken up and adapted by Israelites in the tenth century B.C.E., when Solomon was learning how to build a temple from Hyram, king of Tyre, and his experts. Think of it as something like the wholesale adoption by Catholics of Lutheran, Methodist, and Anglican hymnody since the 1960s to supply a woeful lack of hymns appropriate for vernacular liturgy. Evidently, a hymn or elements for a hymn were chosen that were thought appropriate to Yahweh, who was already associated with terrifying weather phenomena in the old stories about the occupation of the Land and about the Judges (Josh 10:11; Judg 5:21 [which surely describes the effects of a rain flood]; cf. the very old Ps 18:8-16).

In that context the "children of God" (v. 1; actually "children of the gods" in Hebrew) who were once called to praise Baal and now Yahweh, were the gods of the Canaanite pantheon, who are often so named in Canaanite literature. In the related Babylonian story of creation, when Marduk has conquered the great Sea Monster, the rest of the gods offer him praise. Early Israelites did not yet question the existence of gods other than Yahweh; they were forbidden by their covenant only to fear or serve them. Here they call on all the gods to praise, indeed to prostrate themselves (the "adore" of verse 2) before Yahweh.

The two principal elements of Hebrew "hymns" are the invitation of praise, which we have just seen, and reasons for praising. The reason for praise given in this hymn is the awe-inspiring power of Yahweh's thunderous voice over the weather, shaking the mountains and stripping the leaves of the forest.

For Israel, the thunder and lightning, the coming and departure of the storm, had no natural explanation. In fact, the Hebrews had no way even to question whether there could be a natural explanation. These mighty phenomena were beyond human understanding; they were the work of the God. For us, the changes of weather have quite a different meaning. Each evening we can see the satellite photos on television; we see the storm coming and we see the clearing. If God is to be behind the weather for us, God must be much farther, much more deeply behind it, as the One who calls into being the orderly chaos of creation!

But the psalm does not end with the weather phenomena. Impressive as the storm may be, the psalm will be complete only when it has addressed Israel: What has all this to do with Israel? The power of God in the storm calls forth the cry of "Glory!" from all, from gods and humans alike, in the Jerusalem Temple, where deeper than all appearances God sits enthroned upon the cosmic floods and is acknowledged as King. And that God, finally, is the God of Israel, who gives his people strength (usually a military term) and the blessings of *shalôm*, that is, peace and prosperity. In the context the reflection on God as the one whose thunder rocks the world becomes a kind of parable of the God who uses all this power in aiding Israel.

God remains the one who supports us. Though I might pray the psalm with a special élan after a violent storm, it takes more than that to make it last a lifetime. But whatever victory, whatever peace, whatever prosperity befalls me, my Church, my world, remains the work of the God whose thunderous voice makes the mountains leap and shatters the cedars. The election of a wise and compassionate pope, the defeat of an oppressive piece of legislation, the birth of a baby, the abandonment of self by which a friend gains control over an addiction—all these have a cosmic dimension and are the work of the God of Glory. The traditional use of the psalm for the feasts of apostles makes fundamental sense, for God's powerful word, the gospel, is the source of the blessings and victory that are at the center of our experience of God's love.

But whom do we address when we pray the psalm? Formally it was addressed to the gods of the pantheon, calling on them to worship Yahweh. We can hardly address these gods sincerely; it's hard enough for us to believe in one God. Some will want to address their brothers and sisters who in baptism are children of God, or to speak in imagination to all humanity, whom God has made "a little less than gods" (Ps 8:6). Perhaps we can stretch our imaginations still further.

Already for the early Jews who preserved the psalm after the Exile, the plurality of gods addressed in this psalm would have been problematic: the exponents of the Isaian tradition by the time of the Exile or a little later denied the very existence of other gods (Isa 44:6; 45:5, 14, 21). But at the same time, interest in the heavenly court of Yahweh was maturing. It is only after the Exile that the heavens proliferate with beings clearly subordinate to God, who engage night and day in the praise of God and the protection of God's people from their foes. It is with these heavenly beings, the cherubim and seraphim, the angels and archangels, the principalities and powers, that they identified all this heavenly host. And as for the expression "children of Elîm—gods," they identified "Elîm" with "Elohîm," a normal Israelite title of Yahweh, which, although plural in form, is always construed with singular verbs and adjectives.

We might do worse, even at the dawn of the third millennium. Surely we have problems with our old images, but it doesn't take wings, a halo, and a harp to make an angel. To live in a universe inhabited by angels is to acknowledge that God's world is more abundant in life than we can see, that God's love has overflowed in rich existences, who in turn abound in love for God and for all God's creatures. At Mass we join our voices with the angels and saints. Whenever we pray, even if we must pray alone, we are never alone but stand in that company, where the seraphim chant "Holy," the four living creatures cast themselves before the throne, and the elders offer their incense, crying, "To the One who sits on the throne and to the Lamb be blessing and honor and glory and might for ever and ever!" (Rev 5:13).

PSALM 11   EVENING FIRST MONDAY

(10) 11. The security of God's friends

1   In the LORD I have taken my refuge.
How can you say to my soul:
"Fly like a bird to its mountain.

2   See the wicked bracing their bow;
they are fixing their arrows on the string
to ambush the upright by stealth.

3   Foundations once destroyed, what can the just do?"

4   The LORD is in his holy temple,
the LORD, whose throne is in heaven;
whose eyes look down on the world;
whose gaze tests the people of the earth.

⁵   The LORD tests the just and the wicked,
    and hates the lover of violence;
⁶   sending fire and brimstone on the wicked,
    and a scorching wind as their lot.

⁷   The LORD is just and loves justice;
    the upright shall see God's face.

The ever-present enemies threaten with force far beyond your powers. What do you do? The psalm presents two possibilities, flight to the mountains or refuge with Yahweh, and chooses the latter. Like other psalms, this is surely not just a record of one person's struggle but a formula preserved to be used repeatedly, perhaps by the person who takes sanctuary in the Temple or the cities of refuge (Num 35; Deut 19:1-13; 1 Kgs 1:50-53; 2:28).

Two things would suggest such sanctuary as the proper context of this psalm: (1) the specific allusion in verse 4 to the Temple as the place from which Yahweh tests the wicked, and (2) the reference in verse 7 to the upright seeing the face of Yahweh, something that regularly takes place in the Temple. If the psalm is meant to be used by anyone taking refuge in the sanctuary, then the saying that is quoted ("Flee to the mountain," vv. 1c-3; the Hebrew reads "flee" rather than "fly"),[20] expresses not what the person praying has just heard but the typical alternative understanding of what to do in the circumstances.

In the ancient context, the flight to the mountains was not just a metaphor but a literal possibility. David fled to the wilderness from Saul (1 Sam 22ff.), and much later Mattathias fled to the mountains from the Hellenistic Syrians (1 Macc 2:27f.). But if you flee to the mountains, you lose all human community. You are on your own, you can trust no one, for the host who seems to protect you may, rather, turn you over to your enemy (1 Sam 23:6-13, 15-21). At best, you are thrown in with fugitive debtors and criminals who are ineligible for sanctuary. (David, more fortunate than most, has the company of his brothers as well as "every one who was in distress, and every one who was in debt, and every one who was discontented" [1 Sam 22:2, RSV].)

Psalm 11 rejects the alternative of flight to the wilderness, choosing instead to take refuge with Yahweh. For though the enemies actually do threaten "the upright" with bow and arrow, with ambush, though it is true

---

20. Some scholars would see only verse 1a as the quotation, with verses 2-3 as the psalmist's own complaint. In any event, the psalmist and the counselor disagree, not on what they observe, but on what to do about it.

that the one who prays is no match for their might ("What can the just do?"), the one who prays need not rely on his or her own strength but on Yahweh, who "is just and loves justice," who has the power and the will to distinguish between the upright and their wicked pursuers.

We, of course, do not have the institution of sanctuary. Even when someone does try to take sanctuary, as did draft resisters in the 1970s and Salvadoran refugees in the 1980s, the institution is not legally recognized. While such a person might appropriately use this psalm, it will no longer have the same meaning as it did in antiquity, for, as always, every change of circumstances inevitably brings a change in the meaning of a prayer, even though the words remain unchanged.

But what of the Christian in more settled circumstances? Can the psalm be prayed only by one whose life or liberty is at stake? Middle-class America may not be the norm of human life in this violent world, whether the battlefield be experienced as the exploitation of Central American campesinos or of American migrant workers, as the perils of the drug-infested ghetto or of ethnic conflict in the Middle East. But this essay, in fact, is more likely to be read by middle-class Americans, as it is written by one. Can we find honest ways to pray this psalm without rendering it trivial?

In the first place, in praying this psalm let us not forget those who in fact are in mortal danger. The prayer of Christians is a priestly prayer, laying before God the inarticulate groanings of all creation, speaking, crying, pleading the needs of those who do not have the words to speak. Reading the daily papers is a part of the priestly ministry of the Christian in order to become aware of those whose suffering for justice or whose denial of justice can evoke our prayer. At times we may even hear this prayer spoken against ourselves when we recognize our complicity or our acquiescence in injustice to others.

Each month, each year, the list changes; it would be of little use to provide what I perceive to be this month's innocent victims, but if you don't recognize what I'm talking about, you might ask yourself some serious questions about what your reading is, what you follow on television and radio. After all, traditionally the psalm was among those prayed on martyrs' feast days.

The psalm was also prayed on the feast of the Exaltation of the Holy Cross. As long as the psalm is not seen as a *prediction* of the passion, such a Christological reading is well justified. Jesus, like those who prayed the psalm, had to choose between flight from his foes (for flight it would be, even were he to escape them by calling his twelve legions of angels to defend him)[21] and flight to God. Christians believe, yes, the resurrection means that despite

21. Matt 26:53.

all appearances, Jesus' confidence in God was not misplaced, that even death did not triumph over him.

And it is in Jesus' experience that our own experiences of conflict, of discouragement, of temptation, lose their triviality. In us the cosmic conflict between Christ and the powers of darkness is realized. The early Christians saw truly that the Christian's struggle is with the demons, that it is only the power of God at work in them that can stave off defeat, and that the Christian's victory over the demons in that daily struggle is participation in the resurrection of Christ.

PSALM 15   EVENING FIRST MONDAY

(14) 15. Who can stand before the Lord?

¹ LORD, who shall be admitted to your tent
and dwell on your holy mountain?

² Those who walk without fault,
those who act with justice
and speak the truth from their hearts,
³ those who do not slander with their tongue,

those who do no wrong to their kindred,
who cast no slur on their neighbors,
⁴ who hold the godless in disdain,
but honor those who fear the LORD;

those who keep their word, come what may,
⁵ who take no interest on a loan
and accept no bribes against the innocent.
Such people will stand firm for ever.

We confess, God, that it was not our righteousness that brought us to Mount Zion, to the City of the living God, but the appeal of your love. Let your love so transform us that we may manifest that love to our brothers and sisters by deeds of justice and compassion, and by our joy and awe in your presence. We ask this in Jesus' name.

PSALM 24   MORNING FIRST TUESDAY

(23) 24. The Lord of glory

¹ The LORD's is the earth and its fullness,
the world and all its peoples.

2 It is God who set it on the seas;
who made it firm on the waters.

3 Who shall climb the mountain of the LORD?
Who shall stand in God's holy place?

4 Those with clean hands and pure heart,
who desire not worthless things,
(who have not sworn so as to deceive their neighbor.)

5 They shall receive blessings from the LORD
and reward from the God who saves them.

6 These are the ones who seek,
seek the face of the God of Jacob.

* * * * *

7 O gates, lift high your heads;
grow higher, ancient doors.
Let the king of glory enter!

8 Who is the king of glory?
The LORD, the mighty, the valiant,
the LORD, the valiant in war.

9 O gates, lift high your heads;
grow higher, ancient doors.
Let the king of glory enter!

10 Who is the king of glory?
The LORD of heavenly armies.
This is the king of glory.

Whether for temple or for synagogue, Psalm 24 represents some kind of liturgy, with parts for a variety of voices. Beginning with a confessional statement (vv. 1-2), the psalm continues with two little dialogues, one a kind of torah instruction (vv. 3-6), the other often described as a processional entrance liturgy. Just how the various parts functioned in an original liturgy is not clear, but what is obvious is the participation of more than one speaker. At least a question of verse 3 is answered in verse 4, and the questions of verses 8a and 10a on the one hand respond to exhortations of verses 7 and 9, and on the other hand are answered in verses 8bc and 10bc.

The confession of verses 1-2 is an acknowledgment that the earth belongs to Yahweh because he made it. It uses old motifs of Israelite thought, the use of building construction as an image for the creation of the earth and the idea that this world is built over great primordial waters.

What follows would seem to have been some sort of entrance rite (compare Psalm 15 and prophetic variations on the same theme in Isa 33:14-16 and Jer 7:2-7), in which the moral demands of Yahweh cult are proclaimed to prospective worshipers. Presumably at the Temple gate (Jer 7:2), someone representing the worshipers asks about the proper dispositions (v. 3; Ps 15:1; Isa 33:14). The appointed authority responds with criteria both positive (v. 4a; Ps 15:2, 4ab; Isa 33:15a; Jer 7:3b, 5) and negative (v. 4b-c; Ps 15:3, 4c-5; Isa 33:15b-e; Jer 7:4, 6) and the assurance that those who meet the criteria can safely "dwell" there (Ps 15:5b; Isa 33:16; Jer 7:3c, 7).[22] Verse 6 seems again to be the voice of the representative, affirming that these pilgrims are, in fact, such a generation that seeks Yahweh.

Verses 7-10 are generally considered to be a dialogue between Levites carrying the ark and the gatekeepers, perhaps the same persons who have just outlined the conditions for worshipers. The Levites demand that the gates be opened for the "king of glory." The gatekeepers ask, "Who is the king of glory?" And the Levites reply with military titles of Yahweh and finally the name "The LORD of armies—Yahweh Tsebaôt," a title especially associated with the ark of the covenant.[23]

Whatever may have been the ritual origins of this psalm or of its parts, by the time of Jesus it was prayed regularly in the Temple on the first day of the week, the first day of creation, because of the allusion to creation in verses 1-2;[24] at any rate, it had been quite emancipated from any dramatic processional use.

Even if we should use the psalm in procession, say for Palm Sunday, the meaning of the prayer will inevitably be altered by its new use. The mountain of the Lord, the holy place, the ancient doors are no longer the ones alluded to in the psalm. Nor can our understanding of the Lord valiant in war, of the Lord of armies, be simply what Israel envisioned. The story of God and of God's people has continued for a couple of thousand years since the psalm

22. The prophetic examples, of course, lack certain characteristics of the form. Jeremiah has no introductory question, and for neither is the place of secure dwelling the sanctuary—in Isaiah it is the safe "heights"; in Jeremiah, it is Jerusalem, though "this place" of verse 3 is ambiguous, since it can be a technical term for a sanctuary. However, just such variants from the typical genre are characteristic of prophetic forms, which are, after all, adaptations of familiar patterns of speech to make a radically new threat or promise. These prophets were certainly not the functionaries appointed to greet the Temple worshipers!

23. Others would question whether in fact the ark was ever used in procession after being deposited in Solomon's Temple. Rather, the dialogue would express dramatically the wish for a ritually induced theophany.

24. Rosh Hashanah (iv) 31a; Tamid (vii 4) 33b; cf. the psalm title in the Septuagint.

was first used. For Jews the picture of the King of military might is at least colored by millennia of exile—and now by the restoration of the state of Israel (and by whatever a Jew may think of the faithfulness of that state to God's purposes).

For Christians, all our attempts to understand God, all our ways of approaching God, are radically transformed by what we believe God to have done in Jesus Christ. God's kingship has no primary reference to Palestine, nor does God's military might have anything to do with the recovery of that land.[25] The claim that all the earth is the Lord's, then, takes on for us an even more universal meaning than it ever did, for God's reign is realized, at least in part, wherever the gospel has been heard, to whatever extent it has had an effect even on a non-Christian culture like that of India or of the People's Republic of China.[26] While the psalm's perspective remains true, all lands and all peoples, even should they repudiate Israel's God, still belong to God, who remains their Creator. Who is not subject to God in obedience will become subject in judgment.

"Clean hands and pure heart" (v. 4a): Just as the ancient had to flesh out the conditions demanded of the worshiper with all the demands of Moses and the prophets, we likewise will hear this as a call to do all we have learned from God's revelation in Jesus, who said that not those crying "Lord, Lord" will enter the kingdom of heaven, and who also offended the holy people by eating with prostitutes and collaborators.

The hour is coming, the Johannine Jesus told the woman at the well, when you will worship the Father neither on Mount Gerizim nor in Jerusalem but in spirit and in truth. All have access to the temple, for we are the temple of the living God (2 Cor 6:16; 1 Cor 3:16; 6:19); Jesus is our access to the worship of God (Letter to the Hebrews). But on the other hand, all earthly worship is rendered relative by the expectation of the heavenly liturgy (Rev 4–5) and the heavenly temple (Rev 11:19), yes, and of the final day when there shall be no temple in the City, for its temple is the Lord God the Almighty and the Lamb (Rev 21:22). If we are God's temple, it is we who lift up our heads in relief at his coming.[27]

---

25. The connection was, however, unfortunately attempted by the Crusaders.

26. For all its atrocities, for all its glaring failures to achieve all its ideals, those ideals (for instance, of using the nation's resources for all the people and not just for a powerful elite) show Communism to have had its origins in Christianity and so to be a specifically Christian heresy.

27. No part of the gate is known as the "head." It seems that the cry "Lift up your heads!" personalizes the gates, seeing the Lord's coming as restoring their honor (Judg 8:28; Zech 2:4 [1:21]; Job 10:15; Ps 83:3).

The Palm Sunday hymn is not fanciful in lauding Jesus as the divine King: "The King of Glory comes, the nation rejoices; open your gates before him, lift up your voices." We who call Jesus "Lord" confess that when he entered the Temple, it was God indeed who entered in; and we celebrate that entrance because it begins the week that shows us who God is, since it is in the passion and death of Jesus and in his resurrection that God's very self is most clearly revealed to us. We who join in that procession seek the purity of heart, not just to be spectators in the coming week, but through our own obedience to God to be sharers in the passion of him who was obedient unto death, in hopes that in the Last Day we may join him in the triumphal procession through the most ancient of gates.

PSALM 33   MORNING FIRST TUESDAY

(32) 33. Praise of God's providence

1   Ring out your joy to the LORD, O you just;
    for praise is fitting for loyal hearts.

2   Give thanks to the LORD upon the harp,
    with a ten-stringed lute play your songs.
3   Sing to the Lord a song that is new,
    play loudly, with all your skill.

4   For the word of the LORD is faithful
    and all his works done in truth.
5   The LORD loves justice and right
    and fills the earth with love.

6   By God's word the heavens were made,
    by the breath of his mouth all the stars.
7   God collects the waves of the ocean;
    and stores up the depths of the sea.

8   Let all the earth fear the LORD,
    all who live in the world stand in awe.
9   For God spoke; it came to be.
    God commanded; it sprang into being.

10 The LORD foils the designs of the nations,
    and defeats the plans of the peoples.
11 The counsel of the LORD stands forever,
    the plans of God's heart from age to age.

12 They are happy, whose God is the LORD,
   the people who are chosen as his own.
13 From the heavens the LORD looks forth
   and sees all the peoples of the earth.

14 From the heavenly dwelling God gazes
   on all the dwellers on the earth;
15 God who shapes the hearts of them all
   and considers all their deeds.

16 A king is not saved by his army,
   nor a warrior preserved by his strength.
17 A vain hope for safety is the horse;
   despite its power it cannot save.

18 The LORD looks on those who fear him,
   on those who hope in his love,
19 to rescue their souls from death,
   to keep them alive in famine.

20 Our soul is waiting for the LORD.
   The Lord is our help and our shield.
21 Our hearts find joy in the Lord.
   We trust in God's holy name.

22 May your love be upon us, O LORD,
   as we place all our hope in you.

Just and compassionate God, who subdue creation by your might and govern the nations, who have chosen us in Jesus to share in your election of the children of Israel, deliver us. Watch over your Church, ever prone to defend itself with the weapons of the world, and lead us rather to rely on your strength and the power of your word through Jesus Christ, our Lord.

PSALM 20   EVENING FIRST TUESDAY

(19) 20. A prayer before battle

2 May the LORD answer in time of trial;
   may the name of Jacob's God protect you.

3 May God send you help from the shrine
   and give you support from Zion;
4 remember all your offerings
   and receive your sacrifice with favor.

⁵ May God give you your heart's desire
  and fulfill every one of your plans.
⁶ May we ring out our joy at your victory
  and rejoice in the name of our God.
  May the LORD grant all your prayers.

⁷ I am sure now that the LORD
  will give victory to his anointed,
  will reply from his holy heaven
  with a mighty victorious hand.

⁸ Some trust in chariots or horses,
  but we in the name of the LORD.
⁹ They will collapse and fall,
  but we shall hold and stand firm.

¹⁰ Give victory to the king, O LORD,
  give answer on the day we call.

Most commentators see Psalm 20 as a blessing on a king before going into battle. But recently Erhard Gerstenberger has argued plausibly that it is a blessing by a family or by a local congregation on a member in distress, "reinforc[ing] these blessings with a fleeting glimpse of messianic expectation (v. 7)."[28] The Grail translation in the Liturgy of Hours presupposes the royal and military interpretation by translating the various forms of the root *y-sh-ʿ* with the very specific term "victory" rather than their more general meaning of "rescue" or "salvation." The central issue, of course, is whether the "you" of verses 2-6 was the same person as the "anointed/king" of verses 7 and 10.

The very fact that there can be this dispute about the original purpose of the psalm shows something important about the language of psalms: despite the concreteness of the imagery, the circumstance is indicated only very ambiguously. This is quite different from the prose prayers of the Bible, which will often make very explicit allusion to their circumstances. Abraham's servant, for instance, prays:

"O LORD, God of my master Abraham, please grant me success today . . . .
I am standing here by the spring of water, and the daughters of the men of
the townspeople are coming out to draw water. Let the girl to whom I shall
say, 'Please offer your jar that I may drink,' and who shall say, 'Drink, and I
will water your camels'—let her be the one whom you have appointed for

28. *Psalms: Part 1: With an Introduction to Cultic Poetry* (Grand Rapids, Mich.: Eerdmans, 1988) 103–105.

your servant Isaac. By this shall I know that you have shown steadfast love to my master" (Gen 24:12-14, RSV; cf. Num 11:11-15; 2 Sam 15:31; 1 Kgs 17:20, 21; 2 Kgs 19:15-19; etc.).

But the poetic prayers, the psalms, deliberately avoid such defining details as the naming of persons or the specific identification of troubles. It's rather like the difference between Baptist and Catholic prayers, whether you pray for "Brother Bob and Sister Sal and their healthy new baby" or for "these your servants." The psalms, like the prayers of the Catholic *Book of Blessings* or of the *Book of Common Prayer,* were meant to be used repeatedly, for different persons in various similar but not identical circumstances.

Even if Psalm 20 in its original form was meant as a prayer for the king going into battle, it was based on more general formulas of blessing, if not a fully developed prayer of blessing (vv. 2-6). And in any case, after the monarchy was suppressed, the final sayings about the king (vv. 7 and 10) were surely heard as alluding to the King to come, the Messiah.

We pray this psalm in continuity with the ancient Israelites. Like them, each time we pray the psalm we may address a different person with the "you" of the first several verses. The editors of the Liturgy of the Hours have provided helps for praying each psalm, a title and a Scripture or patristic quotation that suggests a Christian reading. While the title in the Liturgy of the Hours shows the military and royal understanding ("A prayer for the king's victory"), the quotation from Acts 2:21 ("Whoever calls upon the name of the Lord will be saved") suggests a universal application.

Seeing how ambiguous the text is regarding what is prayed for, you might pray it one week for your bishop, your prioress, another week for the president or Congress (does not Jesus tell us to pray for those who do us evil?!), or for a troublemaking dissident. Yet another week you might pray for someone who is having a serious operation or a student facing a critical decision in life. Who we pray for is limited only by the content of the prayer: a prayer for someone in some kind of danger ("time of trial" and "protect you" in verse 2, and "victory" [or "salvation"] in verses 6, 7, 10).

Of necessity much of the language of the psalm becomes metaphorical for the person who would pray it today, and that is probably as true for the Jew as for the Christian. The "offerings" of verse 4 are no longer animal sacrifices, and the anointed monarch of verses 7 and 10 is no longer a king reigning in Judah but is surely recognized by the Christian as the King whose decisive victory over death is renewed daily in his members in whatever ways they experience deliverance. The restrictive translation of "rescue" as "victory" in verses 6, 7 and 10 means that we will also use victory as a metaphor for deliverance from any threatening danger. And the Zion temple from which help comes (v. 3) becomes a metaphor for the heaven of verse 7, which is itself a metaphor for that inaccessible realm of otherness where God truly abides. It may be pretty hard in our world to find someone whose military security lies in chariots and horses (v. 8), but for ages to come those terms will do well enough to identify the ever-changing and ever-obsolescing armaments, yes, all the pitiful means by which human beings try to impose their plans and desires upon a resisting world.

Though our conception of how God intervenes to save may be vastly different from that of the ancients, still at the center of everything they were perfectly right: we cannot ultimately save ourselves. Even in passing an exam or saving a marriage, while we can fail on our own, success is pure gift; for everything, whether within ourselves or outside, by which we reach success is gift. How much more so is that final existential victory at the center of all reality, which we strive to name with the term "resurrection," God's work!

PSALM 21:2-8, 14 EVENING FIRST TUESDAY

(20) 21. Thanksgiving for victory

² O LORD, your strength gives joy to the king;
how your saving help makes him glad!
³ You have granted him his heart's desire;
you have not refused the prayer of his lips.

⁴ You came to meet him with the blessings of success;
you have set on his head a crown of pure gold.
⁵ He asked you for life and this you have given,
days that will last from age to age.

⁶ Your saving help has given him glory.
You have laid upon him majesty and splendor,
⁷ you have granted your blessings to him for ever.
You have made him rejoice with the joy of your presence.

⁸ The king has put his trust in the LORD;
through the mercy of the Most High he shall stand firm.
[⁹ His hand will seek and find all his foes,
his right hand find out those that hate him.

¹⁰ You will burn them like a blazing furnace
on the day when you appear.
And in anger the LORD shall destroy them;
fire will swallow them up.

¹¹ You will wipe out their offspring from the earth
　and their children from among its peoples.
¹² Though they plan evil against you,
　though they plot, they shall not prevail.

¹³ For you will force them to retreat;
　at them you will aim with your bow.]
¹⁴ O LORD, arise in your strength;
　we shall sing and praise your power.

With Psalm 20 transformed into a royal and military psalm, as a blessing that wished victory for the king, Psalm 21 may have been associated with it as a kind of companion piece, with its thanksgiving for the king's victory. The vocabulary of the two poems shows a fair bit of correspondence: "king" in 21:2, 8 and 20:10; "salvation," translated as "saving help" in 21:2, 6 and as "victory" in 20:2, 7, 10; "give him his heart's desire" in 21:3 and 20:5 (somewhat different expression); "might" in 21:14 and 20:7; Yahweh's "right hand" in 21:9 and 20:7.

The poem consists of two parts: a kind of thanksgiving in verses 2-7 and an expression of confidence in verses 8-13, with a conclusion in verse 14. The thanksgiving of verses 2-7 could come from a coronation ceremony, for in the list of benefits verse 4 refers to the crown, and verse 6 to the royal glory, majesty, and splendor. The other verses, 3, 5, and 7, allude to the "eternal" blessings God has promised in response to the king's prayers (cf. 1 Kgs 3:4-14, especially verse 13, where the requests normally expected of a king are named). Unlike other thanksgiving prayers, the speaker is not the one who has received the benefits: the king is spoken of in the third person. We must imagine a chanter giving thanks on behalf of the whole court for the divine benefits to the king.

Of the triumphant expression of confidence (vv. 8-13), all but verse 8 is suppressed in the Liturgy of the Hours in accord with the editorial policy of removing all expressions of desire for the death of enemies.[29] To expect the destruction of the king's enemies is a typical motif of royal prayers (Pss 2:12; 45:5-6; 110:5-6) and would be in place at a coronation. It is best to conceive of this expectation of constant victory as being among the reasons why the

---

29. Actually it is not clear whether these verses address Yahweh or the king, for some of the vocabulary is more appropriate to the one, some to the other. Is it Yahweh or the king who destroys his enemies? In any case, the king's enemies are assumed to be Yahweh's. Note that the Grail translation uses third-person forms in verse 9, whereas the Hebrew has the second person, as in verses 10-13.

king rejoices (v. 2). The last verse, with its allusion to God's "strength," brings us back to the first verse of the psalm, and the "sing and praise" is a motif that fits a thanksgiving song, being often found in the vow of the individual lament (Pss 13:6; 27:6; 57:8; 59:17; 144:9).

Fair enough, then. We've got (perhaps from the coronation ceremony) a prayer of thanksgiving on behalf of the king for the granting of royal majesty, the promise of eternal blessings, and the assurance of victory over his enemies. But that's quite another world from ours! How are you going to pray this in Cincinnati? Traditional uses of the psalm can be suggestive. It was used on Ascension Day with the antiphon "Be exalted, Lord, in your power; we shall sing and praise"; for the Exaltation of the Holy Cross: "The King is exalted on high, when the noble trophy of the Cross is adored by all Christians through the ages"; for the Common of One Martyr: "You have set on his head, O Lord, a crown of precious stones"; and for the Common of Confessors: "He asked you for life, and this you have given him, Lord. You have laid upon him majesty and splendor. . . ." The king in the psalm is thus identified as Christ[30] on some occasions and on others as those who share in God's majesty precisely by serving God or suffering for God like Christ and in union with Christ.

The psalm is certainly no messianic prophecy, though the ancient rabbis read it as such.[31] Even the New Testament never quotes it as alluding to Christ. Still, if we do pray the psalm in thanksgiving for the one who is our King, we find that phrase after phrase the prayer makes solid sense. As well it might, for the reason that Jesus is called King is that his role was seen as analogous to the role of the Israelite king, yes, as fulfilling beyond all expectation Israel's hope for the great King to come. "You have not refused his prayer . . . have set on his head a crown of pure gold . . . have given days that will last from age to age . . . have granted your blessings [in which even we share] to him for ever." And as for his enemies, "Though they plan evil against you, though they plot they shall not succeed." And since the whole Christian people is a royal priesthood, we can also pray the psalm in thanksgiving for any Christian, saint or sinner, man or woman, priest or layperson, whose anointing with chrism in baptism signifies sharing in Christ's kingship and is a pledge of divine help and victory in the lifelong combat with the forces of the Prince of Darkness.

Rise, O Lord, in your strength; for we shall sing and praise your power!

---

30. For while the antiphons quote words that are addressed to Yahweh in the last verse, they evidently identify "the Lord" as Christ (note the substitution of "King" for "Lord" in the antiphon for the feast of the Holy Cross).

31. Targum, and Talmud Sukkah 52a.

PSALM 36 MORNING FIRST WEDNESDAY

(35) 36. God's goodness: human malice

2   Sin whispers to sinners
in the depths of their hearts.
There is no fear of God
before their eyes.

3   They so flatter themselves in their minds
that they know not their guilt.
4   In their mouths are mischief and deceit.
All wisdom is gone.

5   They plot the defeat of goodness
as they lie in bed.
They have set their feet on evil ways,
they cling to what is evil.

* * * * *

6   Your love, LORD, reaches to heaven,
your truth to the skies.
7   Your justice is like God's mountain,
your judgements like the deep.

To mortals and beasts you give protection.
O LORD, 8 how precious is your love.
My God, the children of the earth
find refuge in the shelter of your wings.

9   They feast on the riches of your house;
they drink from the stream of your delight.
10   In you is the source of life
and in your light we see light.

11   Keep on loving those who know you,
doing justice for upright hearts.
12   Let the foot of the proud not crush me
nor the hand of the wicked cast me out.

13   See how the evildoers fall!
Flung down, they shall never arise.

Blessed Jesus, you are the Light of God shining in the world, the Fountain of all life. Enlighten my mind that I may understand the world aright.

Fill me with your life that I may have the strength and will to reject the enticements of sin and to live like you in generous obedience to the Father.

PSALM 47   MORNING FIRST WEDNESDAY

(46) 47. God, king of the world

² All peoples, clap your hands,
cry to God with shouts of joy!
³ For the LORD, the Most High, we must fear,
great king over all the earth.

⁴ God subdues peoples under us
and nations under our feet.
⁵ Our inheritance, our glory, is from God,
given to Jacob out of love.

⁶ God goes up with shouts of joy;
the LORD goes up with trumpet blast.
⁷ Sing praise for God, sing praise,
sing praise to our king, sing praise.

⁸ God is king of all the earth,
sing praise with all your skill.
⁹ God is king over the nations;
God reigns enthroned in holiness.

¹⁰ The leaders of the people are assembled
with the people of Abraham's God.
The rulers of the earth belong to God,
to God who reigns over all.

Festive celebration, this. Trumpets and processions, rhythmic clapping of hands and jubilant cries of the crowd. The psalm doubtless had its origin in cult, proclaiming in the sanctuary or the synagogal assembly what takes place in the unseen heavenly realm: the ascent of Yahweh to his royal throne.

Our age does not cause kings to flourish. Where we do have them, they don't rule. The queen of England and the emperor of Japan keep hands off the making of policy, so that when scandals erupt or policies fail, they can stand in all purity for the ideal of stable and just government, which is at best only frailly realized in the grubby world of parliaments and ministers. Our antipathy for monarchs who actually rule is well justified by the melancholy history of those who did, a long, sordid story of arrogance, exploitation, and folly.

Then what are we to make of a God who rules as a monarch? Every year in late November many a homilist takes to lamenting, at least privately, how hard it is to preach on Christ the King. Similarly, since the beginning of the twentieth century, numerous American theologians have sought to find an alternative to the imagery of God as King, in some cases envisioning God as a kind of a president rather a king—with plenty of checks and balances![32] Even so, while the pursuit of an expanding variety of images for God is a worthy goal, the image of God as monarch still has plenty of life in it.

Our images of God thrive as much on their dissimilarity to the secular models as on their correspondence. God is of an altogether other world: if God is indeed God, there is nothing to fear from God's rule. For God has no petty needs, no needs that could be fulfilled to our detriment. God has no failures of understanding or judgment: the Creator of the universe is not going to bungle innocently into harming us. Nor has God any lack of power: whatever God determines, God can accomplish. Not that we would foster a totally naive conception of this power. For God's omnipotence is defined, if not limited, by that which is possible and that which is good. Of course, God cannot create a rock so heavy that God cannot move it, just as God cannot commit a sin. To talk about such things is a game of language that is without meaning in the real world. And it may be that the whole realm of such impossibilities is much larger than we would suppose. Is it, for instance, a similar meaningless notion to speak of a world without disease? In any event, it is no great marvel that God should recognize good where we in our limited vision fail to see it.

But if God's power is not able or willing to do for us what we most want, where is the good news in proclaiming that God is King? If God will not see to it that no child dies of malnutrition, will not resolve social conflicts, or will not assure us that should peace once come, things will never fall back to where they were or to worse, what good is God's kingship? What kind of a king is it that can only sit by with compassion and love and watch us struggle?

But the psalms of the kingship of Yahweh are not about a God who can do everything we want, the King of a great paternalistic welfare state! They are about conflict and victory: "He subdues peoples under us and nations under our feet." The victories the ancient Israelites had in mind were those that of old brought the conquest of land from the Canaanites or from the Philistines, Ammonites, and Moabites under David or Jeroboam II and Uzziah. Even though those lands had long since been lost by the time this

---

32. See David Nicholls, "Federal Politics & Finite God: Images of God in United States Theology," *Modern Theology* 4 (1988) 373–400.

psalm was included in the collection of the psalter, those who preserved it had come to see in the victories more than the acquisition of real estate, far more than could be seen in the political failures of the time.

When we pray Psalm 47, we celebrate the King who leads us into battle and to victory. But "though we live in the flesh we do not conduct a carnal warfare, for the weapons of our warfare are not worldly, but have God's power to destroy strongholds" (2 Cor 10:3f.). The whole struggle of our Christian life is the battle to realize the kingdom of God. It is probably a harder battle than the violence of war, which despite its dangers is limited in time and in the demands it makes on the participants; the Christian's battle is for life and mobilizes every aspect of life.

Some Christians will, of course, feel uncomfortable with this and the many military images of the psalms. They seem to conflict with Jesus' teaching of love of enemies. But all such language becomes analogical as we use it, and analogy respects differences as well as similarities. Thus the weapons of our warfare are neither swords nor guns nor bombs. However, the military images do suggest the inevitability of conflict in the Christian life; the love demanded by the gospel entails more than being nice.

The weapons of the gospel have been powerful to extend the reign of God. Such things as our hospital system and universal education, secularized as they have become, are in fact founded on the work of men and especially of women who heard the call to care for the sick and to minister to the poor and those neglected by society. Whether in great ways or in small, every aspect of our obedience to the gospel promotes a world more humane, more enlightened, more open to hope. No matter that things will get worse again, that greed or neglect or hatred will crowd in again. At least for a time there was here some experience of the reign of God. And for those who did experience it, it meant all the difference between life and death.

There are other days and other psalms to express the anguish, the terror, and the pity of a world where the enemies prevail. They have their place, indeed pride of place in the psalter. But when we have the psalms of God's kingship, let us celebrate with all our hearts the Lord whose kingship repeatedly asserts itself in ever new manifestations, which are a pledge of the fullness of the kingdom that God is preparing in the world of the Resurrection.

PSALM 27   EVENING FIRST WEDNESDAY

(26) 27. Trust in time of affliction

¹   The LORD is my light and my help;
    whom shall I fear?

The LORD is the stronghold of my life;
before whom shall I shrink?

2 When evildoers draw near
to devour my flesh,
it is they, my enemies and foes,
who stumble and fall.

3 Though an army encamp against me
my heart would not fear.
Though war break out against me
even then would I trust.

4 There is one thing I ask of the LORD,
for this I long,
to live in the house of the LORD,
all the days of my life,
to savor the sweetness of the LORD,
to behold his temple.

5 For God makes me safe in his tent
in the day of evil.
God hides me in the shelter of his tent,
on a rock I am secure.

6 And now my head shall be raised
above my foes who surround me
and I shall offer within God's tent
a sacrifice of joy.

I will sing and make music for the LORD.

7 O LORD, hear my voice when I call;
have mercy and answer.
8 Of you my heart has spoken:
"Seek God's face."

It is your face, O LORD, that I seek;
9 hide not your face.
Dismiss not your servant in anger;
you have been my help.

Do not abandon or forsake me,
O God my help!
10 Though father and mother forsake me,
the LORD will receive me.

¹¹ Instruct me, LORD, in you way;
on an even path lead me.
When they lie in ambush ¹² protect me
from my enemies' greed.
False witnesses rise against me,
breathing out fury.

¹³ I am sure I shall see the LORD's goodness
in the land of the living.
¹⁴ In the LORD, hold firm and take heart.
Hope in the LORD!

We may well have here a psalm to be said on behalf of the person who takes refuge in the sanctuary or in a city of refuge, like Adonijah fleeing from Solomon after a failed coup (1 Kgs 1:50-53) or the person who has killed another by accident or in passion (Num 35).

The poem begins with the announcement that one is taking sanctuary, using poetic imagery that indicates what that means to the one who prays. Since the holy place where one takes refuge is the home of Yahweh, one's flight is not just a legal arrangement but refuge in God: one's protection comes from Yahweh (vv. 1-6). One then addresses Yahweh directly, asking for protection against one's enemies (vv. 7-12) and concluding with an expression of confidence (v. 13). A priest then gives reassurance in a variant on a popular formula (v. 14; cf. Deut 31:6, 7, 23; Josh 1:7, etc.; 1 Chr 22:13; 28:20).

It may well be that the sentiments and concepts of the psalm go well beyond those of the kind of person who first used it in antiquity—the poor devil whose axehead slipped off its handle, killing his neighbor, and who fled to the only safe place he knew, in terror of the vengeance that the neighbor's family were bound to bring upon him. But that was the very purpose of the psalms: the poem, probably spoken by a professional of the sanctuary,[33] would articulate on behalf of the worshiper what it was that the worshiper was doing and what requests he was making of God.

Even if the model of the fugitive we have just considered does not really fit those who first used this psalm, at least it illustrates the kind of dangers they faced, the violence from which they expected God's protection.[34]

---

33. Doubtless in expectation of a gift from the beneficiary.

34. An alternative understanding of the psalm is the prayer of a king before battle. At issue is whether verse 3 is to be understood literally or as a metaphor for the threatening dangers, as is verse 10 for the depth of abandonment.

As we pray the psalm, our task is not to reflect on the experience of the ancient Israelite. It is rather to find in our own life, in the lives of those for whom we pray, the place that corresponds to the experience of the ancients. As always with prayer against the enemies, when we pray it we may ask protection from the demonic legions arrayed against us. Whatever may be our conception of the personality of the forces of darkness, those of us who struggle with our darkest side are likely to find that the imagery of the great cosmic battle rings true to our experience: we sense God's work as help against enemies that are more powerful than we are.

But to speak of the battle with satanic forces is in no way an abdication of responsibility. The Christian can never claim helplessly that "the devil made me do it." Rather, this imagery is a way of recognizing that our moral struggle, with addiction perhaps or sloth or arrogance, is not just a private striving for perfection, not just a petty matter between me and God, but a participation in the age-old conflict between light and darkness.

At another time the prayer can articulate our experience in what we perceive as conflicts for the promotion of the kingdom of God. One could easily imagine this prayer as a comfort to a Père Marie-Joseph Lagrange, O.P., the great and very Catholic critical biblical scholar, when he was forced into voluntary exile in 1912–1913 from life and work in his beloved École Biblique because of malicious suspicions about his loyalty. Far be it from me to give any examples closer to our own day!

By way of intercession we could pray the psalm for persons we recognize as being in danger "for justice' sake," even though the person who risks life and future in pursuit of human rights might not recognize or acknowledge the whole faith expressed in this psalm. Our task is to articulate before God, like the temple priests of old, the meaning of what these persons are doing. We can plead before God that not a drop of water given to the thirsty will go without its reward.

In my own prayer I often see the allusions to the temple where one finds protection (vv. 4-6) as a way of speaking of my religious community, where (as Benedict says in his Rule) with the help of many brethren I learn the rudiments of the struggle against the demons. For the ancient, God's deliverance must come here and now if it is to come at all. We, however, cannot honestly pray out of such a supposition, for we believe that God's deliverance is not limited to what we perceive now with our eyes. Psalm 27, after all, was traditionally prayed in Jesus' name on Good Friday under the antiphon "false witnesses rise against me and iniquity has lied to itself."[35] Yet,

---

35. Following the Vulgate translation of verse 12.

for Jesus the way to deliverance led through the grave, as is implied in the Easter antiphon "I believe I shall see the Lord's goodness in the land of the living," the same antiphon, moreover, which is used in the Office for the Dead.

As always, the experience of Jesus is the foundational experience of Christ's members: what happened to Jesus is the pattern of what happens to us. As Jesus endured rejection and danger, so do we; as Jesus was protected by his Father, so are we. But if we are protected just as Jesus was, it means that we will also feel abandoned by God, that our protection will not keep us from dying but will rather bring us victory only through defeat, life springing as God's gift out of death.

PSALM 57   MORNING FIRST THURSDAY

(56) 57. In time of danger

> ² Have mercy on me, God, have mercy
> for in you my soul has taken refuge.
> In the shadow of your wings I take refuge
> till the storms of destruction pass by.
>
> ³ I call to you God the Most High,
> to you who have always been my help.
> ⁴ May you send from heaven and save me
> and shame those who assail me.
>
> O God, send your truth and your love.
>
> ⁵ My soul lies down among lions,
> who would devour us, one and all.
> Their teeth are spears and arrows,
> their tongue a sharpened sword.
>
> ⁶ O God, arise above the heavens;
> may your glory shine on earth!
>
> ⁷ They laid a snare for my steps,
> my soul was bowed down.
> They dug a pit in my path
> but fell in it themselves.
>
> ⁸ My heart is ready, O God,
> my heart is ready.
> I will sing, I will sing your praise.

⁹ Awake, my soul;
    awake, lyre and harp,
    I will awake the dawn.

¹⁰ I will thank you, Lord, among the peoples,
    among the nations I will praise you
¹¹ for your love reaches to the heavens
    and your truth to the skies.

¹² O God, arise above the heavens;
    may your glory shine on earth!

You came to the glory of resurrection, Jesus, through the experience of feeling betrayal, through the desperation of being pursued by the powerful. Comfort and strengthen your servants who suffer for their loyalty to you or who struggle desperately against the attacks of the demons.

This psalm, like most others, can be prayed now for self, now for others.

PSALM 48   MORNING FIRST THURSDAY

(47) 48. The invincible city of God

² The LORD is great and worthy to be praised
    in the city of our God,
    whose holy mountain ³ rises in beauty,
    the joy of all the earth.

Mount Zion, true pole of the earth,
    the Great King's city!
⁴ God, in the midst of its citadels,
    is known to be its stronghold.

⁵ For the kings assembled together,
    together they advanced.
⁶ They saw; at once they were astounded;
    dismayed, they fled in fear.

⁷ A trembling seized them there,
    like the pangs of birth.
⁸ By the east wind you have destroyed
    the ships of Tarshish.

⁹ As we have heard, so we have seen
    in the city of our God,

in the city of the LORD of hosts
which God upholds for ever.

10 God, we ponder your love
within your temple.
11 Your praise, O God, like your name
reaches the ends of the earth.

With justice your right hand is filled.
12 Mount Zion rejoices;
the people of Judah rejoice
at the sight of your judgements.

13 Walk through Zion, walk all round it;
count the number of its towers.
14 Review all its ramparts,
examine its castles,

that you may tell the next generation
15 that such is our God,
our God for ever and ever
will always lead us.

The burghers of Jerusalem were proud of their city, and this psalm shows it. The context of the psalm is clearly military: defense of the city against attack. The beauty of the city, the conviction that the city is "the joy of all the earth" is intimately related to its impregnability. For the practical Israelite, a beautiful city is a strong city; after all, in their world the whole purpose of a city is defense.

The city is strong, they reason, because Yahweh is one of them, dwelling like them in their city. It is, I suppose, a bit unfair to speak of the role of Yahweh in Jerusalem in any such egalitarian terms: Yahweh is not just one of the citizens but the transcendent Lord of the city, the very sight of whom can cast enemies into panic. It is, in fact, this terrible otherness that gives them confidence in Yahweh, who applies all this invincible power to the defense of Zion. Such confidence could, however, have its dark side. Jeremiah is forced to denounce those who rely on "the Temple of the Lord, the Temple of the Lord, the Temple of the Lord!" while oppressing widows, fatherless children, and alien residents (Jer 7:3-7).

The strength of the city is not proclaimed just in abstractions. At the center of the poem is a little narrative, first summarized in verse 4, "God, in the midst of its citadels, is known to be its stronghold," and then developed in verses 5-8. The kings attack Zion, but then (in the language of Holy War) fall into panic and flight at what they see, like the ships of Tarshish destroyed by an east wind.[36] "As we have heard, so we have seen" (v. 9): experience confirms doctrine, and leads in verses 10-12 to praise, addressed again to Yahweh in the second person.

In an exhortation that surely relates to a ritual procession, the congregation is called to walk around the city inspecting its fortifications "that you may tell the next generation that such is our God" (v. 14). Remarkably, it is through the defenses of the city that God is known! So the poem returns to where it began, not with self-satisfaction over the security of the city, but with the greatness of Yahweh.

The Christian of today can pray the psalm in rejoicing at the historical Jerusalem. However flawed that ancient city may have been, it is through Zion that in fact we have come to know our God. Isaiah and Micah have almost identical prophecies of days to come when the nations will come to Mount Zion, saying, "Come, let us go up to the mountain of the LORD, to the house of the God of Jacob; that he may teach us his ways and that we may walk in his paths" (Isa 2:3; Mic 4:2). In some way, in Christianity the Gentiles do come to know the God of the Jews, so that even the medieval Jewish thinker Maimonides could concede that Christianity, and likewise Islam (even though he thought them falsehoods), by making the revelation of Torah widely known "only served to clear the way for King Messiah, to prepare the whole world to worship God with one accord."[37]

Nevertheless, note that if we do pray the psalm this way, we are no longer praying it as it was originally meant. That was possible only in the Jerusalem of old with its Temple intact and the national enemies kept at bay. Any change in the social or political experience out of which a psalm is prayed or in the worldview of the one who prays it inevitably changes the meaning of the psalm as it is prayed. We can't play ancient Israelite, and if we did, our psalm would be a game, not a prayer.

As Christians, then, we may well pray the psalm in terms of those things in our life that best correspond to the Jerusalem of the psalm. The fortress in which I know God's presence as deliverer is Christ's body (John 2:19-21; Heb 12:18-24) and the Church (whether the local or the greater Church) in which I find that body realized (2 Cor 6:14–7:1), my own body (1 Cor 3:16-17;

---

36. A few Hebrew manuscripts surely reflect an earlier text in reading, "A trembling seized them there, like the pangs of birth, like the east wind that destroys the ships of Tarshish."

37. Mishneh Torah: Melakim v.xi.4, at least according to the manuscripts and some of the early editions. *Code of Maimonides: Book Fourteen, The Book of Judges*, trans. Abraham M. Hershman (New Haven: Yale University Press 1949) xxiii. Cf. Zeph 3:9.

6:19), or finally that New Jerusalem which John the Elder describes coming down from heaven (Rev 21) and which we await in hope. All these possibilities are suggested in the traditional liturgical use of the psalm for Christmas, Pentecost, the Common of Virgins, and the Dedication of a Church.

The Christian exultation in the Zion of the Church or of one's religious community, like that of the ancient Israelite, dare not be unconditional. Absolute praise, absolute adherence to any but God is idolatry. Zion is often enough murderer and whore (Isa 1:15; Hos 2:2; Rev 3:1-6, 14-22), even though God still works in her midst in word and sacrament. A Counter-Reformation commentator writes, regarding Hos 2:2 (in the Vulgate, "Rebuke your mother, rebuke her"), of the real need to criticize the Church while still loving her as a mother. Despite all the failure of compassion that I have known in the Church—and which I have myself committed in the Church's name—all the blindness to issues of justice, despite all the arrogance, greed, and exploitation, still it is in this same Church that I have been challenged by the gospel, that I have seen something of the living Christ in the lives and work and wisdom of men and women who have been touched by that gospel. It is in this Church that I have known pardon and love.

The enemies of the Church are not ultimately those states that persecute, those organizations that labor against its interests, those individuals who hate it, but the Prince of Darkness, who would totally co-opt it for his service, the Principalities and Powers who would see the gospel totally subverted. It is against this total perversion that the Church is invincibly protected. And I confess that this is so only because God is in the midst of it. It is not the excellence of the institution or the purity of its members, but the presence of God, for the institution has abundantly demonstrated its proneness to corruption, and we members are all flawed. It is only God's promise that gives me hope that "the gates of hell shall not prevail against it" (Matt 16:18). The hymn, after all, is finally the praise, not of Zion, but of the God who protects Zion. It begins and ends with God: "Great is the Lord and worthy to be praised."

PSALM 30   EVENING FIRST THURSDAY

(29) 30. Thanksgiving for recovery from sickness

2   I will praise you, LORD, you have rescued me
    and have not let my enemies rejoice over me.

3   O LORD, I cried to you for help
    and you, my God, have healed me.
4   O LORD, you have raised my soul from the dead,
    restored me to life from those who sink into the grave.

⁵ Sing psalms to the Lord, you faithful ones,
   give thanks to his holy name.
⁶ God's anger lasts a moment; God's favor all through life.
   At night there are tears, but joy comes with dawn.

⁷ I said to myself in my good fortune:
   "Nothing will ever disturb me."
⁸ Your favor had set me on a mountain fastness,
   then you hid your face and I was put to confusion.

⁹ To you, Lord, I cried,
   to my God I made appeal:
¹⁰ "What profit would my death be, my going to the grave?
   Can dust give you praise or proclaim your truth?"

¹¹ The Lord listened and had pity.
   The Lord came to my help.
¹² For me you have changed my mourning into dancing,
   you removed my sackcloth and clothed me with joy.
¹³ So my soul sings psalms to you unceasingly.
   O Lord my God, I will thank you for ever.

The Israelite who had come close to death but had, in fact, escaped, would come to the sanctuary to offer a thanksgiving sacrifice. A Levite or some such Temple functionary would offer to sing a thanksgiving song appropriate to the occasion. Such a song was Psalm 30. It would do for anyone who had been sick and recovered, no matter what the illness or injury; only verse 3 actually alludes to the sickness, "you, my God, have healed me." (Or is the idea of "healing" only a metaphor for deliverance from any kind of trouble?)

Like other prayers of this type, Psalm 30 consists essentially of an expression of the intention to praise (v. 2a) along with narrative explaining my reasons for praise (actually the story here is told three times, each time at greater length [vv. 2b, 3-4, 7-12]). The whole psalm is addressed to Yahweh in the second person, except for a little hymn in the middle (vv. 5-6) addressed to the bystanders, inviting them to praise God, not so much for what Yahweh did for myself as for what God is typically like and typically does for those who are in trouble.

The longest of the little narratives (vv. 7-12) best describes the deliverance for which I give thanks: I had been prospering and was grateful for it (vv. 7-8a),[38] but then Yahweh let disaster strike (v. 8b, threatening my life; cf. v. 4), so I prayed urgently for help (vv. 9-10), and Yahweh saved my life (vv. 11-12).

---

38. The phrase "Nothing will ever disturb me" surely is not arrogant boasting any more than in Pss 16:8; 62:3, 7. In the Hebrew the following line can be translated "Your favor

The urgency of the prayer is motivated especially by the old assumption that there is no hope in death, there is no useful afterlife; if I am not saved now, I am not saved at all. To convince Yahweh to intervene, I emphasize what he will lose by my death: "Can dust give you praise or proclaim your truth?"!

Now, although the psalm was originally meant to be available as a thanksgiving for any individual who had been saved from death, the ancient canonical title ("A song for the dedication of the House [= the Temple]),[39] shows that it was later reused as a thanksgiving for the deliverance of the whole Jewish people from destruction. When the Temple was restored and rededicated after the Exile, or more likely after the violent persecution of the Jews by Antiochus Epiphanes in the 160s before Christ, apparently they searched for a hymn to use for the celebration and chose this one. A happy choice, but in the process every phrase takes on new meaning.[40]

As the psalm was now reused, the "I" came to indicate the whole Jewish people rather than the individual worshiper. The deliverance from death was now deliverance from destruction as a people. "Can dust give you praise or proclaim your truth?" (v. 10). This motive for deliverance, used in the prayer in time of trouble, took on still more poignant meaning: it was not just that there would be one fewer worshiper if God failed to help, but that without the Jews there would be no one at all to sing God's praises! And the promise to praise God forever referred no longer just to the rest of one's life but to the generation upon generation through which God's whole people will continue to sing praise. The psalm, then, which had always been meant to be reused by a variety of persons to express their own experiences, was now adopted to express the analogous experience of a whole people. Something similar was done by early Christians who prayed the psalm to express the experience of

---

has set me on a mountain fastness" and so would be part of the prayer of acknowledgment that I made in my good fortune. One of the problems of the psalm is, therefore, just where to put the quotation mark that ends the prayer begun in verse 7. The best choice is the middle of verse 8.

39. These canonical titles, found in most standard translations at the head of many of the psalms, were supplied by ancient Jewish scholars to indicate traditional sources, early speculations about the origins of specific psalms. The Hebrew, Vulgate, and English-language Catholic tradition has counted such titles as verse 1 (and sometimes verse 2) of many psalms, a fact that accounts for discrepancies in verse numbering between the New American Bible and the Revised Standard Version.

40. Various rabbinic authors understood the psalm to contain allusions to the dedication of the Temple by Solomon, to the restoration of the Temple after the Exile, and again to the resolution of the Maccabean crisis (William G. Braude, *The Midrash on Psalms,* Yale Judaica Series XIII [New Haven: Yale University Press, 1959] 1:390f.).

Jesus in his passion and resurrection. While the New Testament does not apply the psalm to Christ, Origen is already doing so in the third century.[41]

While we cannot honestly use the psalm as an Old Testament *prophecy* of the resurrection of Christ, we can well pray it as a *prayer of thanksgiving* for his deliverance from death. As we do so, the unique character of that deliverance will affect the way we hear certain phrases. "You have raised my soul from the dead, restored me to life from those who sink into the grave" (v. 4): A report of protection against dying thus becomes a confession of the restoration of the dead Christ to life! This death of Christ and his resurrection is the matrix of all our experience as Christians.

We may at once recognize in our own life how God has delivered us from death: from some self-destroying hypocrisy or fear, some fatal sexual liaison, some addiction, from a preoccupation with self that failed to recognize our role in society. But if we fail to recognize that without Christ we are dead in sin, dead to hope, this says more about our failure of perception than about the realities of our condition! Not that the psalm can only be prayed about the pivotal events of the spiritual life. While the psalm might be somewhat hyperbolic as an expression of gratitude for recovery from a cold, it surely has not lost its appropriateness as thanksgiving for recovery from an injury or illness that threatened one's life!

Some days we will pray the psalm on behalf of another. Surely persons engaged in health care, pastoral ministry, counseling, or education will sometimes witness transformations that can only be described as a restoration of life from the dead. For it is the same God who once brought recovery to the imperiled Israelite of the Iron Age, who still gives all life, all hope, all healing, to whom, millennia hence, glory will still be given by generations who will look back with pity or amusement at our primitive—or our overly sophisticated—strivings to understand who we are over against this God. Yes, to this God be all thanksgiving and glory forever.

PSALM 32   EVENING FIRST THURSDAY

(31) 32. The joy of being forgiven

1   Happy those whose offense is forgiven,
        whose sin is remitted.
2   O happy those to whom the LORD

---

41. It may well be that the Massoretic correction of the reading of verse 4 was meant as a protection against Christian polemics based on the Septuagint translation of the older Hebrew text.

imputes no guilt,
in whose spirit is no guile.

³ I kept it secret and my frame was wasted.
I groaned all day long,
⁴ for night and day your hand
was heavy upon me.
Indeed my strength was dried up
as by the summer's heat.

⁵ But now I have acknowledged my sins;
my guilt I did not hide.
I said: "I will confess
my offense to the LORD."
And you, Lord, have forgiven
the guilt of my sin.

⁶ So let faithful people pray to you
in the time of need.
The floods of water may reach high
but they shall stand secure.
⁷ You are my hiding place, O Lord;
you save me from distress.
(You surround me with cries of deliverance.)

* * * * *

⁸ I will instruct you and teach you
the way you should go;
I will give you counsel
with my eye upon you.

⁹ Be not like horse and mule, unintelligent,
needing bridle and bit,
else they will not approach you.
¹⁰ Many sorrows have the wicked,
but those who trust in the LORD
are surounded with loving mercy.

* * * * *

¹¹ Rejoice, rejoice in the LORD,
exult, you just!
O come, ring out your joy,
all you upright of heart.

No need to hide my sins from you, God, for you know me as I am and pursue me with your love in all my offenses. Let me know the liberty of simple, honest acknowledgment of my sin, that I may exult in your pardon, with all who love you.

PSALM 51   MORNING EVERY FRIDAY

(50) 51. A prayer of contrition:
fourth psalm of repentance

3   Have mercy on me, God, in your kindness.
In your compassion blot out my offense.
4   O wash me more and more from my guilt
and cleanse me from my sin.

5   My offenses truly I know them;
my sin is always before me.
6   Against you, you alone, have I sinned;
what is evil in your sight I have done.

That you may be justified when you give sentence
and be without reproach when you judge,
7   O see, in guilt I was born,
a sinner was I conceived,

8   Indeed you love truth in the heart;
then in the secret of my heart teach me wisdom.
9   O purify me, then I shall be clean;
O wash me, I shall be whiter than snow.

10   Make me hear rejoicing and gladness
that the bones you have crushed may revive.
From my sins turn away your face
and blot out all my guilt.

12   A pure heart create for me, O God,
put a steadfast spirit within me.
13   Do not cast me away from your presence,
nor deprive me of your holy spirit.

14   Give me again the joy of your help;
with a spirit of fervor sustain me,
that I may teach transgressors your ways
and sinners may return to you.

¹⁶ O rescue me, God, my helper,
and my tongue shall ring out your goodness.
¹⁷ O Lord, open my lips
and my mouth shall declare your praise.

¹⁸ For in sacrifice you take no delight,
burnt offering from me you would refuse;
¹⁹ my sacrifice, a contrite spirit,
a humbled, contrite heart you will not spurn.

²⁰ In your goodness, show favor to Zion;
rebuild the walls of Jerusalem.
²¹ Then you will be pleased with lawful sacrifice,
(burnt offerings wholly consumed),
then you will be offered young bulls on your altar.

The ancient Israelite found sin terrifying. One could be killed for it. It's not just that God might be angry and punish one for sinning, but it seems that the sin in itself produces what Klaus Koch calls an "aura" of sin, a contagion of death and disaster, which will surely bring its dire consequences. And as always, for the Israelite death is final; there is no hope of any useful future life to mitigate it.[42]

Now, it was possible to avert the effects of a sin with a sin offering. While the descriptions of such offerings are available only from the late P document (Leviticus 4–7 and Numbers 15), they must roughly reflect earlier practice from the period of the kingdoms. One brings an offering and explains one's sin to the priest, who determines if the sacrifice can be accepted and who then does the sacrifice. He kills the animal, sprinkling its blood before God in the sanctuary and burns part of it. Afterward the priest and the other males of his house eat the cooked flesh of the sacrifice, which in our translations is called a "sin offering," but which in Hebrew is called simply a "sin." By consuming the "sin," the priests are able to neutralize the sin: it is especially characteristic of the priests that they alone are not harmed by the eating of the "sin" (cf. Hos 4:8).

But the trouble was that only the "unintentional" sin could be atoned for (Lev 4:2, 22, 27; 5:15, 18; and esp. Num 15:24-29), sins for which there were mitigating circumstances. Something premeditated could not be expiated. It would seem that Psalm 51 is a prayer for one whose sin cannot be atoned by sacrifice.[43] The ancient scholars who wrote the title of the psalm

42. *The Prophets,* vol. 1: *The Assyrian Period* (Philadelphia: Fortress Press, 1983) 23, 34.
43. For the verbs of verse 18, "For in sacrifice you take no delight, / burnt offering from me you would refuse," are often used to indicate God's willingness or unwillingness to accept

long after it was composed made an educated guess when they attributed the psalm to David after his sin with Bathsheba and his murder of her husband, a crime for which sacrifice could not have been accepted. David may not have prayed the psalm, but it would have been appropriate for one like him who had committed deliberate murder, and so could not atone with a sacrifice.

If I were an ancient Israelite, then, unable to have my sin forgiven by sacrifice, I must cast myself on God's mercy, unable to do anything for myself. I pray for nothing but forgiveness and present God with the strongest possible reasons to pardon me. Since there is no way to deceive God, I admit my guilt without reserve (vv. 5, 6, 7), unlike other psalms in which one can profess both guilt and innocence (Ps 38:2-19 but 21; Ps 40:13, cf. 7-11); and I acknowledge my guilt publicly so that if God acts against me, no one will accuse God of injustice (v. 6). I promise further to praise God when forgiven (vv. 16-17) and to instruct the ungodly (v. 15), warning them from my own experience, as is done in Psalm 32. Such an instruction based on experience could be a normal part of the thanksgiving service (Pss 32:8-10; 34:12-23).

But the psalm shows signs of alteration. The Jews of the early synagogue, finally acknowledging the prophetic interpretation of their exile as punishment for their sin, sought words to confess their guilt. What could be better than the moving words of this old psalm for the guiltiest of Israelite sinners? The only change they made was the addition of the last two verses (vv. 20-21), associating the restoration of Jerusalem with God's forgiveness and suggesting where God's interest lies by assuring God that they will be generous in sacrifices when the sanctuary is rebuilt.

But even the mere change of reference, the fact that the "I" of the psalm is now Israel, the Jewish people, has radically changed the psalm. No longer is the sin that of an individual who has committed murder or perjury; rather, it is the whole complex of faithlessness, greed, cruelty, the arrogance of generations, confessed now by the heirs, who have only in part been guilty of the sins. And forgiveness, should it be granted, must have a communal dimension—the restoration of their national life.

We pray this psalm as distant heirs to all who prayed it before us. The psalm becomes our prayer when through it we acknowledge our own sin, whether this be our own arrogance, injustice, cruelty, or that of our nation, our religious community, our Church. The language may sound pretty hyperbolic as an allusion to our petty offenses, especially to a generation which

---

a particular type of sacrifice or sacrifice in specific circumstances (Lev 1:4; Ps 119:108 [Grail's "homage" in Hebrew is a technical word for sacrifice]; Ezek 20:40f.; Hos 8:13; Mal 1:10, cf. 1:13).

sometimes won't even mention sin in the penitential rite of the Mass ("Let us reflect on any faults or shortcomings we may have committed," says the priest delicately). True enough, the sins confessed by the Israelite were among the gravest imaginable crimes. Nevertheless, for our prayer we can use only what we've got to work with. No need to dramatize.

At the end of François Mauriac's *The Woman of the Pharisees,* the cold, censorious Mme. Pian, who in her arrogant self-righteousness has destroyed the lives of several persons, undergoes a profound conversion; this proud woman is finally able to face up to the squalidness of her sin. But we recognize her spiritual maturity in that she doesn't have to dramatize her sins; she has come to realize that "it is useless to play the part of a proud servitor eager to impress his master by a show of readiness to repay his debts to the last farthing."[44]

And so, at best, it is with us. But how to recognize the monumental squalidness of our sin? No need to deny the good that is in us—only to be able also to recognize the sin that is ours. For each of us has enough to regret, to renounce, in a lifetime, if only we can open our imagination. Many of us have in the story of our past, if not in our present, the guilt of the manifold kinds of neglect, cruelty, exploitation that can be profoundly destructive to the life of a parent, a spouse, a friend, the people of a parish: the "sins of my youth," the bleeding conquests of middle age, yes, and the avarice that will not let go even in old age. It is not that I feed morbidly on my guilt but simply that this remains part of my story, which I neglect to my own peril. If it is truly past, already repented, rectified or unrectifiable, it still remains that mortal peril from which God's power and love has delivered me; to recall it imaginatively is to praise the God in whose deliverance I abide.

The psalm can also become my prayer for the deeply embedded sin that manifests itself in all my petty sins. Though the psalm was meant in its origins for the gravest of offenses, its words do not specify such gravity. Nor can I too easily dismiss as negligible the deep pain, the insecurity, the frustration, the sense of weariness I leave with others in my wake. Surely not that this is the whole story of our lives; there is in us and in our doings much of God's work, much love, generosity, compassion. Nor does this prayer for forgiveness become the whole staple of our prayer. We are given Psalm 51 once a week in the Liturgy of the Hours, on Fridays; the other six penitential psalms are scattered over the four-week cycle.[45]

44. Translated by Gerard Hopkins (New York: Henry Holt, 1946) 241.
45. Well, at night prayer Psalms 130 and 143 are also prayed weekly (Wednesdays and Tuesdays, respectively). The other four psalms traditionally listed as penitential are Psalms 6, 32, 38, and 102.

Taking up on the Jewish exilic adaptation of the psalm, we can make the psalm a communal confession, an acknowledgment of our guilt as a nation or church. This could be done, of course, in a self-righteous manner: I gloat at my own purity while acknowledging my opponents' obstruction of the gospel, the liberals' abdication of responsibility, or the conservatives' violations of human dignity. Our hearts are surely quite capable of twisting everything to feed our arrogance—that is the human condition. But it is also possible to make such a prayer with a sense of solidarity, a humility that recognizes our complicity, recognizes the limitations of our own position, acknowledges the same dynamic of sin at work in us as we see manifested in the arrogance, greed, intolerance, sloth, or hypocrisy of our nation, our religious community, our Church.

Denis the Carthusian marvels, "How little [did David think] what thousands and hundreds of thousands of sinners would learn repentance from this Psalm, who when they see Priests, highly educated, prepared with all the array of the world's learning, professing to give up themselves and their lives to the instruction and conversion of others, find them all so utterly [to] fail; because they speak not with the fire of the Holy Ghost, but so coldly, drily, wretchedly; instead of those sharp, penetrating, red-hot words, which they who have taken in hand to bring men from darkness to light . . . ought to have."[46] Yes, the old psalm has not lost the power to provide us with fiery words to acknowledge our guilt without excuses before God, to recognize God's power and desire to forgive, to restore and by doing so to give joy.

PSALM 100   MORNING FIRST AND THIRD FRIDAY

(99) 100. Praise to God, creator and shepherd

1   Cry out with joy to the LORD, all the earth.
2   Serve the LORD with gladness.
     Come before God, singing for joy.

3   Know that the LORD is God,
     Our Maker, to whom we belong.
     We are God's people, sheep of the flock.

4   Enter the gates with thanksgiving,
     God's courts with songs of praise.
     Give thanks to God and bless his name.

---

46. See J. M. Neale and R. F. Littledale, *A Commentary on the Psalms from Primitive and Medieval Writers,* vol. 2 (London: Joseph Masters, 1883²; reprinted New York: AMS Press, 1976) 202.

> ⁵   Indeed, how good is the LORD,
>   whose merciful love is eternal;
>   whose faithfulness lasts forever.

The psalm is an invitation to worship, apparently for use with a procession. The places mentioned in verse 4, "gates" and "courts," are parts of the Temple compound. Only the priests entered the roofed-in Temple building; the Israelites, like most ancient peoples, did their celebrations in the courtyard. And what a celebration it was! The words of verses 1-2, "cry out" and "sing for joy," both suggest quite a din—no perfunctory "memorial acclamation" this!

The whole ceremony was a jubilant affair, with processions and chants, trumpets and pipes and cymbals, vested celebrants (each with his own distinctive festal garment—no matched sets out of a church-goods catalog). Sacrifices were offered, and since most of them were not holocausts, it meant that there was meat to eat (hardly a daily occasion).[47] With this there would surely be the customary bread, olives, wine, fruits, sweetened cakes, and all that it takes to make merry. Even in the dry law books "rejoicing" is regularly associated with festivals (Lev 23:40; Deut 12:7, 12, 18; 2 Sam 6:12; 1 Kgs 1:40; 1 Chr 15:16; Ezra 3:12).

The psalm begins to define what all the merrymaking is about. Verses 3 and 5 give the reasons, reasons that all reverberate with language associated with Israel's covenant. "The LORD is God" (v. 3). In cultic contexts the phrase singles out Yahweh as the only God to be worshiped (Deut 4:35, 39; 1 Kgs 18:39). "Our Maker" in the context alludes not so much to creation as to the formation of Israel as a people (Deut 26:19; 32:6, 15; Isa 54:5). The three following phrases, "to whom we belong," "we are God's people," and "sheep of the flock," of course, allude to the central provision of the covenant, summed up at least in late texts as "You shall be my people and I shall be your God." In the last verse, Yahweh's "merciful love" *(ḥesed)* and "faithfulness" *('emunah)* are both words typically associated with the covenant, of which they are the constant benevolent expression. If the reasons for praise are abstract here, it is because the psalm is not trying to list the loving deeds of Yahweh but to interpret the well-known deeds, summarizing what is behind them all.[48]

---

47. "Enter the gates with thanksgiving," verse 4. The word for "thanks" here sometimes is a technical word for a thanksgiving sacrifice; some scholars think that is the case in this passage.

48. See A. A. Anderson, *The Book of Psalms,* The New Century Bible Commentary (Grand Rapids, Mich.: Eerdmans, 1972) 2:700.

When we pray the psalm, it comes to express all our experience. Fidelity to the historical intention of the psalm does not require us, does not even permit us, to limit our praise and thanksgiving to the works of God that the original author or singer could have listed. For from the beginning the psalm's celebration was meant to acknowledge in each new instance Yahweh's every manifestation of love for his people. It included not only Yahweh's initial creation of Israel but their preservation, their harvests, their deliverance from enemies, the progeny that gave promise of generations to come. Each time Israel gathered in the courts of the Temple, each time they held festival, they were called to remember the fidelity of God's mercy, the manifestations of that love to their very own day.

How can Christians, then, in praying this psalm not include the mercies they have experienced? How can we not shout for joy at the mystery whereby we have been brought into the covenant, at the grafting of the wild Gentile olive branches onto the sturdy tree of Israel (see Rom 11:17-24)? There are, of course, some days when we don't feel up to shouting for joy about anything. No need to lie to ourselves or to God. Our emotions don't simply respond on demand. We may not always be able to do verses 1 and 2 very well, but at least we can do verses 3 and 4, for that is where the will enters in. We can acknowledge that God is indeed God, that we are God's people. And in that acknowledgment is our praise. In choosing again to give ourselves over to our God, we fall down in worship before God; and paradoxically when we lie prostrate in adoration, giving ourselves wholly to God, we are liberated from any person or any thing that could seek to control us.

PSALM 41 EVENING FIRST FRIDAY

(40) 41. Prayer in sickness and betrayal

² Happy those who consider the poor and the weak.
    The LORD will save them in the evil day,
³ will guard them, give them life, make them happy in the land
    and will not give them up to the will of their foes.
⁴ The LORD will give them strength in their pain,
    will bring them back from sickness to health.

⁵ As for me, I said: "LORD, have mercy on me,
    heal my soul for I have sinned against you."
⁶ My foes are speaking evil against me.
    They want me to die and my name to perish.
⁷ They come to visit me and speak empty words,
    their hearts full of malice, they spread it abroad.

⁸   My enemies whisper together against me.
    They all weigh up the evil which is on me.
⁹   They say something deadly is fixed upon me
    and I will not rise from where I lie.
¹⁰ Thus even my friend, in whom I trusted,
    who ate my bread, has turned against me.

¹¹ But you, O LORD, have mercy on me.
    Let me rise once more and I will repay them.
¹² By this I shall know that you are my friend,
    if my foes do not shout in triumph over me.
¹³ If you uphold me I shall be unharmed
    and set in your presence for evermore.

*   *   *   *   *

¹⁴ Blessed be the LORD, the God Israel
    from age to age. Amen. Amen.

Good Jesus, who by word and touch cured all manner of illnesses of body, mind, and soul, heal your servants who cry to you in the pain, debilitation, and disquiet of illness, bringing health and peace. And also heal in us the fever of our sins.

PSALM 46   EVENING FIRST FRIDAY

(45) 46. God is with us

²   God is for us a refuge and strength,
    a helper close at hand, in time for distress,
³   so we shall not fear though the earth should rock,
    though the mountains fall into the depths of the sea;
⁴   even though its waters rage and foam,
    even though the mountains be shaken by its waves.

    The LORD of hosts is with us;
    the God of Jacob is our stronghold.

⁵   The waters of a river give joy to God's city,
    the holy place where the Most High dwells.
⁶   God is within, it cannot be shaken;
    God will help it at the dawning of the day.
⁷   Nations are in tumult, kingdoms are shaken;
    God's voice roars forth, the earth shrinks away.

⁸　The L<small>ORD</small> of hosts is with us;
　　the God of Jacob is our stronghold.

⁹　Come, consider the works of the L<small>ORD</small>,
　　the redoubtable deeds God has done on the earth:
¹⁰　putting an end to wars across the earth;
　　breaking the bow, snapping the spear;
　　[burning the shields with fire.]
¹¹　"Be still and know that I am God,
　　supreme among the nations, supreme on the earth!"

¹²　The L<small>ORD</small> of hosts is with us;
　　the God of Jacob is our stronghold.

When I first came to know Martin Luther's hymn "A Mighty Fortress Is Our God," I was puzzled by his allusions to the "devils" in a hymn that was supposedly based on this psalm. The psalm alludes to enemies aplenty, but nowhere to Satan or his army. But in fact, Luther was doing a valuable hermeneutical service by seeking to recognize what the psalm could mean to sixteenth-century Europeans struggling with the might of the Great Church that for centuries had resisted reform. For as is the case with us as well, the psalms can become prayer only when they address the experience of those who would pray them.

For the Israelite, the powers of chaos were perhaps even more deeply embedded in the structure of reality than the malevolent spiritual beings of Luther's world. Israel's poetry reflects the language of old stories, preserved in Babylonian and Ugaritic texts, of primordial battles between "our" god and the destructive god or monster of the sea. For instance, Baal attacks and cudgels the god Yamm ("Sea") for his arrogance against the gods and especially against Baal himself.[49] Whether or not the Israelites told the old stories, their language itself recognizes the fundamental constant threat of the chaotic forces to break through and subvert the order of God's world, as they do in times of famine, pestilence, and war. But when this language appears in Scripture, it is almost always associated, as it is here, with confession of Yahweh's control over such chaos.

In Christianity the psalm has been a liturgical favorite. At Epiphany the mystery of Christ's baptism was seen as the "waters of a river [that] give joy to God's city" (v. 5), for the baptism of Christ was seen very realistically as giving to the baptismal waters their power. In the feasts of Our Lady, of any

---

49. UT III AB, A 22–29.

virgin, and of martyrs, God's work in these persons was seen as victory over hostile powers: the antiphon for virgins and for Our Lady was "God will help her with his face;[50] God is within, she cannot be shaken." Its use for the feast of the Dedication of a Church reveals the Christian identification of Jerusalem with the mystery of the Church.

In all these cases, the traditional use of the psalm is something more than allegory: a fundamental correspondence between the experiences of the ancients and those of Christians means that the function of the prayer remains closely analogous to its original use, that the old prayer becomes an apt metaphor for our sentiments, our desires, our understandings as we stand two millennia later in the presence of the same God of Israel.

The turbulent situation envisioned by the psalm, the tumult of nations and shaking of kingdoms, alludes to the military and political turmoil of the Middle East, ever perilous in antiquity, as it is today. In this danger Jerusalem stands firm, protected by the presence of Yahweh. The phrase of the refrain, "The Lord of hosts is with us *('immanu),*" recalls the repeated use of the expression "Immanuel (El is with us)" in Isaiah 7–12, where God's presence in his people (in his Temple?) is the strongest protection against the Assyrian military juggernaut.

Remarkably, however, Jews continued to pray the psalm through the Exile and after, even when their God had decisively proved that his presence was not a talisman assuring protection with no reference to Israel's loyalty. The Zion of the psalm became a symbol for the whole Jewish people, whom the divine protection preserved even in the turmoil of defeat, conquest, and persecution. No need to fear the coercive armaments of the conquerors: the One who lifts his voice and causes the earth to shrink away can break the bow, snap the spear, burn the shields with fire. This is the same God in whom Luther trusted in his unequal battle with the satanic forces that he identified behind the Church's centuries-long resistance to any reform inspired by the gospel.

Wherever we see chaos threatening, this prayer can become our expression of confidence. Do you see your community, your church, your nation in the control of the avaricious or the incompetent, of demagogues or fools? Are you given a task that is beyond you? Do you feel yourself overwhelmed by your passions? Is your personal life or your family life falling apart? "Be still," God says to you, "and know that I am God, supreme among the nations, supreme on the earth!" Yes, the Lord of hosts is still with us; the God of Jacob still our stronghold.

50. After the Old Latin, which follows a misreading in the Septuagint manuscript tradition.

PSALM 119:145-152   MORNING FIRST AND THIRD SATURDAY

PSALM 119:105-112   EVE OF SECOND SUNDAY

(118) 119. The law of the Lord

Nun

¹⁰⁵ Your word is a lamp for my steps
and a light for my path.
¹⁰⁶ I have sworn and have made up my mind
to obey your decrees.
¹⁰⁷ LORD, I am deeply afflicted;
by your word give me life.
¹⁰⁸ Accept, LORD, the homage of my lips
and teach me your decrees.
¹⁰⁹ Though I carry my life in my hands,
I remember your law.
¹¹⁰ Though the wicked try to ensnare me,
I do not stray from your precepts.
¹¹¹ Your will is my heritage for ever,
the joy of my heart.
¹¹² I set myself to carry out your statutes
in fullness, for ever.

Koph

¹⁴⁵ I call with all my heart; LORD, hear me,
I will keep your statutes.
¹⁴⁶ I call upon you, save me
and I will do your will.
¹⁴⁷ I rise before dawn and cry for help,
I hope in your word.
¹⁴⁸ My eyes watch through the night
to ponder your promise.
¹⁴⁹ In your love hear my voice, O LORD;
give me life by your decrees.
¹⁵⁰ Those who harm me unjustly draw near;
they are far from your law.
¹⁵¹ But you, O LORD, are close,
your commands are truth.
¹⁵² Long have I known that your will
is established for ever.

Law exists to foster justice, equity, and peace in the human community and between human beings and God. In Deuteronomy Moses speaks of the divine ordinances as wisdom: "Keep them and do them, for that will be your understanding in the sight of the peoples, who, when they hear of all these statutes, will say, 'Surely this great nation is a wise and understanding people.'" Legalism, the clever simulation of law, is what happens when obligation is separated from wisdom, when one loses sight of the purpose of law.

Some years ago, in trying to work out of a depression of many years standing, I found a lot of help in the book *Feeling Good* by David D. Burns, who urges finding more rational substitutes for "should" statements.[51] I learned that I felt much better about it—and also was more likely to do something about it—if instead of telling myself "I ought to clean my room," I thought the reason through and said, "If I clean my room, I will be more likely to invite friends in because I won't be wondering what they think of the chaos." "If I prepare the examples for my lecture well, my students will understand my point better, and I'll get the exhilaration of a lecture clearly presented rather than the frustration of a lot of hesitation and confusion." As long as I was clear about why I might want to do something, I did not experience it as a frustrating burden of responsibility. And of course in the process I sometimes found that I neither wanted nor had good reason to do something.

I have found that my legalism has deep roots. I was appalled recently in reading through the editorials I had written forty-some years ago for my high school newspaper. They were full of pious exhortations but provided no reasons for what I urged, at least none that would make it sound worth doing. At most, I would try to browbeat my readers with guilt: "Is it really asking too much of Christian students to attend a weekly school Mass?"

It would be easy enough to typify Psalm 119 as legalistic. Almost every one of the 176 verses contains one of eight synonyms for "law" or "God's word," namely, "law," "will," "precepts," "statutes," "commands," "decrees," "word," "promise."[52] Yet the psalm hardly breathes the heavy, stultifying spirit of grim duty. Almost every one of the twenty-two eight-verse stanzas contains a profession of delight in God's law or at least of love or passionate longing for it.

Psalm 119 becomes your prayer only when it expresses your experience, your own rejoicing and love of God's will. For it's not the words themselves

---

51. David D. Burns, M.D., *Feeling Good: The New Mood Therapy* (New York: New American Library, 1981) esp. 178–195. Burns urges both clarifying one's understanding of appropriate moral standards and recognizing the reasons (whether rational or irrational!) for the rules one makes for oneself.

52. Only verse 122 contains no synonym at all; verses 3 and 37 (RSV) contain God's "ways" as an equivalent of "law."

but the attitude of your heart that praises God: "Let them so stand for prayer," says Benedict in his Rule, "that their minds are in union with their hearts" (19:7). Can you honestly say, "I take delight in your statutes" (v. 16), or "I open my mouth and sigh as I yearn for your commands" (v. 131)? My own hesitation to say yes demonstrates the reason for preparing for prayer. The prayer becomes yours only if you find ways of examining whether you mean what you say, indeed, if you actually do find ways to mean what you say. Not that you need great palpitations of the heart to be honest. For there is a kind of delight, of longing, of love that is seated not in the emotions but in the will.

I often enough find God's law painful, constraining, and yet I also find that it makes profound sense. I once thought that at the time of Moses, God must have sat down in heaven and made a list of all the things we most like to do and said "Thou shalt not" to test us. And actually this way of thinking about moral obligation has some real correspondence to the medieval "nominalist" understanding of divine law. The difference between Thomists and nominalists was that the latter thought God could choose to make any behavior good or evil by so declaring it, while Thomists maintained that good and evil resided in the very nature of things. Thus, for the Thomist it was not that murder was evil because God declared it so; rather, God declared murder evil because it was evil.

Whatever foolishness we may do in our application of the principle of natural law, the basic insight is surely right. Now, when I can look on God's law without passion, I find it consoling. Jesus tells us to love our enemies and to do good to those who harm us, and I recognize the wisdom of it: if the cycle of violence is ever to end, someone must end it by choosing not to exact blood for blood. It is only when my passions get engaged that I fail to see the beauty of God's law.[53]

Those Jews who originally prayed this psalm, of course, did not think of the Sermon on the Mount. They thought of the Law of Moses, and especially they thought of the traditional wisdom, for this psalm is closer to Sirach and the Wisdom of Solomon than to Exodus and Deuteronomy. But if you are to make this your prayer, you will necessarily go beyond accurate historical reconstruction of what was in the mind of its author. For just as the ancients expressed their joyful adherence to all that they recognized as God's will for

---

53. The revivalist was preaching up a storm: "There's no place in heaven for the folks that guzzle whiskey and beer"; and Amy Sue said, "Amen!" "There's no place for them that go a-dancing," and she said "Amen!" "God's got no place for them that smoke tobacco." "Amen! Give it to 'em," she said. "And the ladies that paint their faces with rouge and lipstick won't come into the Kingdom." "Humpf, now he's stopped preaching and started meddling."

them, the prayer itself challenges you to a joyful acceptance of all you recognize as God's will for you.

More than that, it is impossible for the Christian to think of Law without thinking of the two great commandments in which are summed up all the Law and the prophets, "You shall love the Lord your God with all your heart and all your soul and all your mind" and "You shall love your neighbor as yourself." And even beyond that, the Christian understanding of God's will is inevitably an adherence to the person of Jesus Christ. The same Wisdom of God, the same Word that was proclaimed in Torah and in the wisdom of the sages is the Word which was with God in the beginning and which became flesh in Jesus of Nazareth. In Jesus, in his life, teaching, his rejection and death, we see perfect and free conformity to the will of God. We who are baptized into Christ are called to share in the same free embracing of God's will.

Freedom does not mean doing whatever you feel like doing but rather making one significant choice when you might have made another. Joy is not just the pleasure of getting something you like but the triumph of getting what you value even at the price of great pain. Ask the person who completes a marathon successfully!

Sometimes we pray Psalm 119 in the name of One who forever rejoices in his faithfulness to God's will, a faithfulness that led to his death, but also to his triumph over death. But we pray it in our own name as well, insofar as we, however weakly and fitfully, however painfully, abandon ourselves to the will of the God who wills nothing for us but our good. "I am lost like a sheep; seek your servant for I remember your commands" (v. 176). We also pray the psalm in hope that in the fullness of time God will bring our darkened minds and our rebellious wills into glad embracing of that good, to say without reserve, "Your will is my heritage forever, the joy of my heart" (v. 111).

PSALM 117   MORNING FIRST AND THIRD SATURDAY

(116) 117. In praise to the Lord

¹ Alleluia!

O praise the LORD, all you nations,
acclaim God all you peoples!

² Strong is God's love for us;
the LORD is faithful for ever.

God, let us know your love and faithfulness well enough to want always to praise you through Christ our Lord.

SECOND WEEK

PSALM 119:105-112   EVE OF SECOND SUNDAY

See above, p. 63, Morning First Saturday.

PSALM 16   EVE OF SECOND SUNDAY

(15) 16. True happiness

1   Preserve me, God, I take refuge in you.
2   I say to you LORD: "You are my God.
    My happiness lies in you alone."

3   You have put into my heart a marvelous love
    for the faithful ones who dwell in your land.
4   Those who choose other gods increase their sorrows.
    Never will I offer their offerings of blood.
    Never will I take their name upon my lips.

5   O LORD, it is you who are my portion and cup,
    it is you yourself who are my prize.
6   The lot marked out for me is my delight,
    welcome indeed the heritage that falls to me!

7   I will bless you, LORD, you give me counsel,
    and even at night direct my heart.
8   I keep you, LORD, ever in my sight;
    since you are at my right hand, I shall stand firm.

9   And so my heart rejoices, my soul is glad;
    even my body shall rest in safety.

¹⁰ For you will not leave my soul among the dead,
nor let your beloved know decay.

¹¹ You will show me the path of life,
the fullness of joy in your presence,
at your right hand happiness for ever.

"The text is in shambles," says Erhard Gerstenberger ruefully in his treatment of this psalm; "I will interpret as well as possible the fragments." The disarray of verses 2b-4ab does indeed make it impossible to determine with much confidence how this psalm was in fact used. However, a consideration of the problems facing the restoration of Jewish life in Judea after the Exile may provide a context for a plausible understanding of the purpose of Psalm 16.

Among the Jews returning to Jerusalem after the Exile were certain persons who "could not prove their families or their descent, whether they belonged to Israel" (Ezra 2:59; Neh 7:61). In the next century Ezra, returning to Judea from Babylon, is distressed to encounter a community in which many Jews have married persons whom he identified as not being of Jewish ancestry (Ezra 9). In a document of covenant renewal the Jews describe themselves as "all who have separated themselves from the peoples of the lands to adhere to the law of God" (Neh 10:28).

All these clues suggest that Jews, who as a minority population in Mesopotamia had developed a vivid sense of their national and religious identity, were anxious on return to their homeland to clarify and assert their Jewishness even against their co-nationals in Palestine, who had no need to analyze their Israelite identity simply because they had remained living in the Land of Israel.

Now, the best understanding of this psalm would see it as a profession of exclusive adherence to Yahweh for a situation in which such adherence could not be taken for granted.[1] It could, for instance, have been used as a way of establishing a Jewish identity for persons who could not establish their genealogy, or as a way of integrating spouses of other ethnic backgrounds into

---

1. While the psalm begins like an individual lament with a petition, the lack of complaint or any further development of the petition suggests that the bottom line is not the plea for help. While the psalm contains several expressions of confidence, the emphasis in verses 2b-4 on repudiation of other gods suggests that this is the primary purpose of the poem. (It would seem that the Hebrew terms translated "marvelous" and "faithful" in verse 3 actually were originally allusions to alien gods, but what the psalm originally said about these gods is lost in the wreckage of the badly preserved Hebrew text.) But even if the psalm was in fact an individual lament or the related psalm of trust, and therefore a

the community, or for that matter any persons whose Yahwistic credentials there was reason to suspect.

In the allusions to trouble and danger (the initial petition for help [v. 1] and the expressions of confidence against threats of death [10-11]), the individual through this psalm would commend to Israel's God not only all the pains this mortal flesh is heir to but also those specific trials which postexilic Jews experienced from Gentiles and which are reflected (sometimes quite imaginatively) in such books as Daniel, Nehemiah, Esther, Judith, and 1 and 2 Maccabees.

The references to death in verses 10-11 represent the typical language of individual laments: "You will not abandon my soul to Sheol, nor let your beloved see destruction." Early Christians used this verse to describe the deliverance of Jesus from the realm of death through his resurrection (Acts 2:31; 13:35), understanding it as a prophetic prediction; for since the presumed author, David, had died, they reasoned, he must refer to his descendant, Jesus, who also died but who was not abandoned in Sheol, did not experience destruction[2] but rather rose from death on the third day! While we can hardly argue that the wording of the psalm was meant as a prediction of resurrection, we confess that to Jesus God showed the ultimate loyalty of raising from the dead the Servant whose loyal obedience to God was infinitely greater than that of any other who had ever prayed the words of this psalm.

We likewise can make the words of the psalm our own, as our profession of adherence to the God of Israel and the God of Jesus. Like the ancient Easterner, whose formula of marriage was "You are my wife," whose formula of adoption or legitimation was "You are my child,"[3] when we declare "You are my God," we do not just describe a relationship but deliberately protest our loyalty to God, accept God as our God. For disciples of Jesus that is no easy commitment, since we follow the One whose obedience led him the way of death, even the death of the cross. But if we do in fact accept the God of Israel and the God of Jesus as our God, if we are basically faithful to the pledge we make, all the rest of the prayer follows from this. We may suffer losses

---

prayer for persons in serious danger or trouble, a principal theme specific to this psalm is its insistence on adherence to Yahweh alone of all gods.

2. In the Septuagint, which was known to Greek-speaking Christians, the term was translated "decay," a term all the more significant to Christians, who argued that the three-day rest in the tomb was not long enough to bring decay.

3. Cf. Middle Assyrian Laws A:41 (*ANET* 183) and the Israelite divorce formula "You are not my wife" (Hos 2:4 [2]); Code of Hammurabi 170–171 (*ANET* 173) and Ps 2:7.

from our loyalty to Christ. Christians, for instance, find themselves morally excluded from certain lucrative professions, and certainly from many satisfactions available to those who do not know the Law of Christ. But for all that we lose, we are more than rewarded: it is God who is our portion and our cup, the lot marked out for us and our heritage.

The Israelite expected to be preserved from untimely death (vv. 9-10); we know that God's love goes even beyond that. Whether we die in ripe old age or whether, like Jesus, we die before our time, beyond all human expectation we who have feasted on the body and blood of the risen Lord trust that though we die, God will not abandon us in the grave, will not finally leave us to destruction.

PSALM 118   MORNING SECOND AND FOURTH SUNDAY

(117) 118. A processional song of praise

1   Alleluia!

Give thanks to the LORD who is good,
for God's love endures for ever.

* * * * *

2   Let the family of Israel say:
"God's love endures for ever."
3   Let the family of Aaron say:
"God's love endures for ever."
4   Let those who fear the LORD say:
"God's love endures for ever."

5   I called to the LORD in my distress;
God answered and freed me.
6   The LORD is at my side; I do not fear.
What can mortals do against me?
7   The LORD is at my side as my helper;
I shall look down on my foes.

8   It is better to take refuge in the LORD
than to trust in mortals;
9   it is better to take refuge in the LORD
than to trust in rulers.

10   The nations all encompassed me;
in the LORD's name I crushed them.

¹¹ They compassed me, compassed me about;
in the LORD's name I crushed them.
¹² They compassed me about like bees;
they blazed like a fire among thorns.
In the LORD's name I crushed them.

¹³ I was thrust down, thrust down and falling,
but the LORD was my helper.
¹⁴ The LORD is my strength and my song;
and has been my savior.
¹⁵ There are shouts of joy and victory
in the tents of the just.

The LORD's right hand has triumphed;
¹⁶ God's right hand raised me.
The LORD's right hand has triumphed;
¹⁷ I shall not die, I shall live
and recount God's deeds.
¹⁸ I was punished, I was punished by the LORD,
but not doomed to die.

¹⁹ Open to me the gates of holiness:
I will enter and give thanks.
²⁰ This is the LORD's own gate
where the just may enter.
²¹ I will thank you for you have answered
and you are my savior.

²² The stone which the builders rejected
has become the corner stone.
²³ This is the work of the LORD,
a marvel in our eyes.
²⁴ This day was made by the LORD;
we rejoice and are glad.

²⁵ O LORD, grant us salvation;
O LORD, grant success.
²⁶ Blessed in the name of the LORD
is he who comes.
We bless you from the house of the LORD;
²⁷ the LORD God is our light.

Go forward in procession with branches
even to the altar.

²⁸ You are my God, I thank you.
My God, I praise you.
²⁹ Give thanks to the LORD who is good;
for God's love endures for ever.

King and courtiers solemnly arrayed approach an inner court of the Temple; the priests are there to admit them to the Holy Place. The trumpets sound, the people shout, a great fire blazes on the altar ready for the offerings. King and priest exchange solemn greetings that define the import of the celebration, and the king enters to offer a thanksgiving sacrifice for victory, or at least for survival, in battle. Psalm 118 is a text for some such ceremony. The hypothesis that it is the king who is giving thanks would best explain the mixture of individual concerns (vv. 5-7, 10-14, 16-18, 21) with national or communal matters (vv. 2-4, 10, 15, 23-24). The call to the house of Israel and the house of Aaron is no hyperbole if the matter at hand is the king's victory.

Like the psalms as a whole, this psalm was meant to be used again and again. Perhaps it was used occasionally as a thanksgiving ceremony for victories or escapes of the king that happened from time to time. More likely it was used as part of an autumn New Year's festival, celebrating the cultically symbolized victories of the king, which were seen to assure, even to bring about, his triumph in any contest of the year to come. When the nation no longer had a king, the old psalm was retained, perhaps at first, like other royal psalms, to be ready for the restoration of the monarchy; but then as the restoration was delayed, some began to hear it as a prayer for the Messiah when he was to come, others as a prayer for all the Jewish people or for any Jew.

Without a Davidic king, without the living continuation of thanksgiving sacrifices, Jews as much as Christians simply cannot now pray this psalm as it was originally prayed. How we can pray it sincerely in some kind of continuity with its original use will depend on how we will be able to identify some aspect of our experience in the psalm. And since the experience of Jews and Christians is so different, it is not surprising that we will pray it in very different ways.

For Christians, Psalm 118 has been the Easter psalm par excellence. In Byzantine use the triumphant chanting of several key verses accompanies the lighting of lamps at Orthros. In the Roman Hours it was the cornerstone of the psalmody specific to Sunday Lauds, and even now in the Liturgy of the Hours it is one of the few psalms prayed every week, being used at Morning Prayer and Prayer During the Day on alternating Sundays.

During Easter Week in the Roman Breviary verse 24 replaced chapter, hymn, and versicle at the day Hours, and in the Liturgy of the Hours this verse is still used as an antiphon or response after all the Office readings:

"This day was made by the Lord; let us rejoice and be glad in it."[4] This use was doubtless suggested by the early Christian identification of Jesus with the "stone which the builders rejected [that] has become the corner stone" (vv. 22-23; Matt 21:42; Mark 12:10f.; Luke 20:17; Acts 4:11; 1 Pet 2:4, 7). What in the old use had referred to the king's humiliations in battle now becomes an allusion to the One in whom Christians saw realized beyond expectation all that had ever been hoped of the king.

The chants of "Hosanna" and "Blessed is he who comes in the name of the Lord," proclaimed by those who wave palms before Jesus (Matt 21:9; Mark 11:9; Luke 19:38; John 12:13) come from verses 25-26, as does Jesus' lament over Jerusalem, "You will not see me again until you say, 'Blessed is he who comes in the name of the Lord.'" In Hebrew the term *hoshi'ah-na'* was a wish for the king rather than for the people, so the liturgical translation would do better to read, "Lord, save the king! O Lord, grant success." To see such passages as marvelous predictions of the life of Jesus would be unwarranted, but just as unwarranted would be a refusal to pray the psalm in reference to Christ. Such a refusal misunderstands the canonical nature of the psalms, which were always texts available for prayer rather than purely antiquarian records of formulas once prayed.

When we do so pray, every phrase of the psalm becomes a legitimate expression of the totally new thing on earth that is the paschal mystery of Christ. "Those who fear the Lord" in verse 4 includes us, who are called from the Gentiles to praise God. As Christ's body we make his voice heard, confessing the distress of his passion and glorifying the right hand of the God who delivered him: "I shall not die, I shall live and recount God's deeds" (v. 17). Yes, he does live in us generation on generation. For in praying this psalm we, like the early Church, from the vantage point of Christ's humanity attribute his resurrection to the One whom he called Father: "God raised him up, having loosed the pangs of death" (Acts 2:24).

In the part of the psalm that was always spoken by the bystanders, we confess in our own voice that the stone rejected by the builders, not only in his days but again and again in every generation—yes, all too often even by his Church, indeed by us—has become the corner stone. The image, of course, is drawn from masonry, where a stone whose irregular shape makes it worthless for normal uses may be particularly well suited for a specialized use, such as anchoring a retaining wall or capping an arch or the corner of a wall. Whoever cannot

---

4. Okay, you've got me: the Office of Readings does not use this verse. Furthermore, ironically, in the old Breviary Psalm 118 was suppressed completely from the psalter throughout Eastertide because of a policy of providing shorter psalmody for festivals!

make sense of weakness, suffering, and rejection as access to salvation tells more about his or her failure of imagination than about the nature of God's world!

Our use of the psalm is not limited to such a Christological reading. We can pray it for ourselves, for friends, for our dead, trusting that the God who brought life out of Jesus' death can also bring victory out of our suffering, defeat, rejection, yes, even out of our death.

PSALM 150 MORNING SECOND AND FOURTH SUNDAY

150. Praise the Lord

¹ Alleluia!

Praise God in his holy place,
Sing praise in the mighty heavens.
² Sing praise for God's powerful deeds,
praise God's surpassing greatness.

³ Sing praise with sound of trumpet,
Sing praise with lute and harp.
⁴ Sing praise with timbrel and dance,
Sing praise with strings and pipes.

⁵ Sing praise with resounding cymbals,
Sing praise with clashing of cymbals.
⁶ Let everything that lives and that breathes
give praise to the LORD. Alleluia!

Father Aelred Cody of St. Meinrad's Archabbey once told me that you will never appreciate this psalm till you've seen the exuberance of Ethiopians chanting the last three psalms of Lauds[5] with their drums and sistra, pounding the ground with their prayer sticks. There's nothing imaginary about this song, nothing figurative; it was certainly meant to accompany worship in the Jerusalem Temple. And it was surely accompanied by the frenzied din of the whole orchestra: the blare of horns,[6] the plucking of all kinds of stringed instruments, blowing of pipes, clattering of tambourines, and vigorous clashing of cymbals in the great courtyard of the Temple.

Just how this song was performed is less clear. It is hard to imagine the whole crowd being able to sing it, knowing the full sequence of words (we

---

5. Psalms 148–150.

6. Rather than Liturgy of the Hours' "trumpet," which should be a flared metal tube, the shofar was a ram's horn that could be blown loud enough to gather widely scattered people for battle (Judg 3:27; 2 Sam 20:1).

surely cannot imagine them picking up hymnbooks at the gate!). But if it was chanted simultaneously with the sounding of the instruments, one voice or a chorus would hardly be heard over the clangor—well, perhaps that did not matter. It could be that each instrument sounded after it was invoked, a kind of Young Person's Guide to the Orchestra. My point is not really to try to reconstruct the performance but to recognize that the psalm represents ceremonies that real people actually celebrated in the flesh.

"Praise God in his holy place," cries the psalm; "Sing praise in the mighty heavens." The worship was done in the courtyard of the Temple (only priests entered the actual roofed House of Yahweh), but the earthly Temple was identified with the heavenly court; it was the human access to God's secret dwelling place. "How awesome is this place!" exclaims Jacob regarding Bethel; "This is none other than the house of God, and this is the gate of heaven" (Gen 28:17).

The reason for praise is expressed succinctly and abstractly: "Sing praise for God's powerful deeds, praise God's surpassing greatness"—therefore for what God does and for what God is. In Israel's hymns God's deeds and greatness refer typically to creation and redemption, that is, the Exodus and related themes, God's kingship, and God's loving kindness and fidelity. The psalm does not spell them out, nor can we expect every hymn to contain all good things that might be said.[7] Nevertheless, the psalm represented true worship only insofar as those who joined the festival knew who it was they were worshiping, and why.[8]

No one can pray the psalm today as it was once prayed. Destruction of the Temple in A.D. 70 has made that impossible. Even were Jews to rebuild the Temple, rival Muslim claims would invest the ceremonies with a new political significance. Rabbinic teaching has made the synagogue and especially the home a substitute for the Temple. The Jewish Prayerbook was deliberately designed to replace the daily and festival celebrations. But it is by no means just an imitation of the Temple services. Apposite to this psalm is the traditional rabbinic refusal to admit any musical instrument into prayer except the shofar, and the strict restraints on its use.

While Eastern Christians forbid or stringently limit the use of musical instruments, Western Christians are generally not thus restricted. Still, though the psalm suggests brilliant possibilities for a composer, we don't need an

---

7. A priest of my monastery earlier in the century reputedly began every one of his sermons with the creation and ended with the Second Coming.

8. The psalm does not even contain the proper name "Yahweh" but the title "El," a term which is usually used as a title for Yahweh but which is also the proper name of the chief god of the Canaanite pantheon, father and judge of the gods, with whom the Israelites identified their Yahweh.

orchestra to pray it. Nothing we do will make our celebration commensurate with the God we praise; at best, we only begin in some faltering way to approximate the heavenly liturgy, in which the elders cast their crowns before the throne, singing, "Worthy are you, our Lord and God, to receive glory and honor and power" (Rev 4–5).

Whether we use instruments or not, whether we sing or not, our psalm is only a pale metaphor of the exuberant praise that we owe to God for who God is and for what God has done. Christian piety, in fact, sees our worship as a participation in the liturgy of heaven: it is with the saints and angels that we sing "Holy, holy, holy." Byzantine piety, particularly, sees the liturgy, not as bringing Christ to us, but as introducing the Christian people into the heavenly temple. The Byzantine Church often features an icon of Christ dressed as bishop, celebrating liturgy with angels clad as deacons.

In rendering praise for God's powerful deeds, for God's surpassing greatness, the Christian can hardly by some schizophrenia block out all thought of the distinctive deeds by which we know God or of the greatness God has shown above all in the loving kindness revealed by the gift of God's Son and in the faithfulness demonstrated by Christ's emptying of self for our sake. The mystery of Christ is the matrix in which is cast all our experience of God's love: it is only through Christ that we have come to know God.

By their inclusion in our canon of Scripture, the psalms have become not only the prayers of the Jews. It is no accident that the last word of the psalter is not restricted to the Jews: "Let everything that lives and that breathes give praise to the Lord. Alleluia!"[9]

PSALM 110:1-5, 7

See above, p. 13, Evening First Sunday.

PSALM 115   EVENING SECOND SUNDAY

(113B) 115. God and the idols

> [1]   Not to us, LORD, not to us,
>   but to your name give the glory

---

9. The phrase "everything that lives and that breathes" in the Liturgy of the Hours is a paraphrase of the Hebrew "every *neshamah*." Now, the *neshamah* is the breath of life breathed into the first human being (Gen 2:7). Doubtless those who composed the psalm were thinking of the persons present in the Temple, therefore of Israelites; but they chose to call them, not by an ethnic title like "children of Jacob," but by a name that identifies them simply by their human nature.

for the sake of your love and your truth,
2   lest the heathen say: "Where is their God?"

3   But our God is in the heavens;
    whatever God wills, God does.
4   Their idols are silver and gold,
    the work of human hands.

5   They have mouths but they cannot speak;
    they have eyes but they cannot see;
6   they have ears but they cannot hear;
    they have nostrils but they cannot smell.

7   With their hands they cannot feel;
    with their feet they cannot walk.
    (No sound comes from their throats.)
8   Their makers will come to be like them
    and so will all who trust in them.

9   Israel's family, trust in the LORD;
    he is your help and your shield.
10 Aaron's family, trust in the LORD;
    he is your help and your shield.

11 You who fear the LORD, trust in the LORD;
    he is your help and your shield.
12 The LORD remembers and will bless us;
    will bless the family of Israel.
    (will bless the family of Aaron.)

13 The LORD will bless those who fear him,
    the little no less than the great;
14 to you may the LORD grant increase,
    to you and all your children.

15 May you be blessed by the LORD,
    the maker of heaven and earth.
16 The heavens belong to the LORD
    but to us God has given the earth.

17 The dead shall not praise the LORD,
    nor those who go down into the silence.
18 But we who live bless the LORD
    now and for ever. Amen.

When Israel and Judah collapsed before the overwhelming power of Assyria and later of Babylon and Persia, their faith was critically challenged. Why be loyal to Yahweh, who did not save us? Psalm 115 seems to come out of this quandary, as a kind of liturgy reaffirming loyalty to Yahweh when his enemies seem to be triumphant.[10]

"Not to us, Lord, not to us, but to your name give the glory" (v. 1). The saying is not an abstraction about who deserves praise, God or human beings, but rather a very concrete reason for divine intervention, namely, that Yahweh has more to gain by helping us than we have ourselves. Israel's prayers often called on Yahweh to help in order to save his honor, for example, "O Lord our God, forgive us our sins; rescue us for the sake of your name. Why should the nations say, 'Where is their God?'" (Ps 79:9f). And a salvation oracle in Ezekiel emphasizes Yahweh's self-interest in helping his people: "It is not for your sake, O house of Israel, that I am about to act, but for the sake of my holy name, which you have profaned among the nations to which you came" (Ezek 36:22). Note that in Psalm 79 and Ezekiel, as here, the issue is the protection of God's honor before the Gentiles.

The psalmist then goes on to a remarkable profession of faith in Yahweh's power, despite the fact that for the moment Yahweh is not giving help. The enemies may mock, "Where is their God?" but the psalm boldly responds that "our God is in the heavens; whatever God wills, God does" (v. 3), and it continues with a vituperation of the gods of the enemies that refutes any claim of their present advantage over Israel. Arguing from the lesser to the greater, if the inert gods of the nations cannot even see or move, they can surely claim no victory over Yahweh!

No great loss that the psalm's argument lacks a certain subtlety, for it is a vigorous poetic prayer rather than a philosophical treatise. The Assyrian theologian may very well assert that the statue is not supposed to *be* Asshur but only represents him. No matter. The purpose of the psalm is not to prove but rather to confess that power over us is vested in Yahweh alone, from whom comes all protection (vv. 9-11) and all blessing (vv. 12-14).

Nor is the psalm's confession lost in our world, which does not know the manufacture of idols of silver and gold. They tell of two cattlemen returning from a tent meeting where the preacher excoriated those who violated each of the commandments. The pair walked in somber silence for a distance when the one gulped and said in a remarkable self-justification, "At least I reckon I ain't never made no graven image."

10. Even if the psalm was already used in times of trouble during the preexilic period, the situation is much the same: though the people of Yahweh are in danger of destruction by foreign enemies (vv. 2, 17f.), Yahweh, it would seem, fails to come to their aid.

But the fundamental issue of the psalm is not whether idols or even other gods are in control but whether Yahweh is. Can God act? Can God save? The psalm acknowledges that Yahweh alone can save, that Yahweh has the power to control all the world's *Realpolitik*. The confession goes against appearances. It reinterprets appearances: if Babylon threatens or dominates us, this is Yahweh's free choice: "The heavens belong to the LORD but the earth he has given to men" (v. 16).[11]

If the truth of the psalm is to be vindicated by whether the confidence expressed was fulfilled in the postexilic world, such vindication is at best partial. While Jews were allowed to return to their land from exile, they languished for centuries under Persian, Greek, and Roman domination. If this is God's action, it is at least ambiguous.

The final motive of verses 17-18, which was meant to convince Yahweh to intervene, is the key to understanding the psalm's expressions of confidence. "The dead shall not praise the Lord . . . . But we who live bless the LORD." For the ancients, if God's power and God's faithfulness to Israel are to be accomplished, this must take place here and now, for to them there is no afterlife, no transcendental realm in which their vindication can be accomplished.

Our experience, however, shows us that all too often God's justice, not to mention God's mercy, is not realized in the world of phenomena. It is hard to believe that ten generations and more of black and red Americans have suffered centuries of violence, contempt, and exploitation because they were less righteous than their oppressors! No, any responsible view of the world must acknowledge that God's beloved can live and die unavenged, unrewarded at least in any obvious sense, as did, after all, God's only beloved Son. In our prayer our experience invests the phrase "The dead shall not praise the Lord" with new poetic meaning, unimagined by those who first sang this prayer.

When we pray the psalm, our vision will go beyond that of the ancients. We pray for relief, for vindication; we pray that God's will and God's ways will be manifested. But we know that this manifestation may come in paradoxical ways. God's fidelity may be seen only by those who have eyes to see, in the fidelity of God's martyrs, in the perseverance of God's saints, in the survival of the gospel and the sacraments in God's battered and sinful Church. In all this it is God alone who can claim victory and glory. And we should wish it no other way.

11. The Grail translation, in its attempt at inclusive language, is deceptive: "But to us God has given the earth," a phrase that reflects Genesis 1:28 but misses the context, which acknowledges that Yahweh is free to take from Israel and give to Nebuchadnezzar. One might have tried something like "but the earth he has given to human beings," as the Revised Standard Version does.

PSALMS 42 AND 43   MORNING SECOND MONDAY
AND TUESDAY

(41) 42. The prayer of an exile

2   Like the deer that yearns
for running streams,
so my soul is yearning
for you, my God.

3   My soul is thirsting for God,
the God of my life;
when can I enter and see
the face of God?

4   My tears have become my bread,
by night, by day,
as I hear it said all the day long:
"Where is your God?"

5   These things will I remember
as I pour out my soul:
how I would lead the rejoicing crowd
into the house of God,
amid cries of gladness and thanksgiving,
the throng wild with joy.

6   Why are you cast down, my soul,
why groan within me?
Hope in God; I will praise yet again,
my savior and my God.

7   My soul is cast down within me
as I think of you,
from the country of Jordan and Mount Hermon,
from the Hill of Mizar.

8   Deep is calling on deep,
in the roar of waters;
your torrents and all your waves
swept over me.

9   By day the LORD will send forth
loving kindness;
by night I will sing to the Lord,
praise the God of my life.

¹⁰ I will say to God, my rock:
    "Why have you forgotten me?
    Why do I go mourning
    oppressed by the foe?"

¹¹ With cries that pierce me to the heart,
    my enemies revile me,
    saying to me all the day long:
    "Where is your God?"

⁵ Why are you cast down, my soul,
   why groan within me?
   Hope in God; I will praise yet again,
   my savior and my God.

(42) 43. Longing for God's dwelling place

¹ Defend me, O God, and plead my cause
   against a godless nation.
   From a deceitful and cunning people
   rescue me, O God.

² Since you, O God, are my stronghold,
   why have you rejected me?
   Why do I go mourning
   oppressed by the foe?

³ O send forth your light and your truth;
   let these be my guide.
   Let them bring me to your holy mountain,
   to the place where you dwell.

⁴ And I will come to your altar, O God,
   the God of my joy.
   My redeemer, I will thank you on the harp,
   O God, my God.

⁵ Why are you cast down, my soul,
   why groan within me?
   Hope in God; I will praise yet again,
   my savior and my God.

An Israelite, separated from Jerusalem (42:3, 7; 43:3), oppressed and taunted by enemies (42:4, 10f.; 43:1), longs to return to Zion, and so to God's presence in the sanctuary, vowing on return to sing a thanksgiving song

(43:4). So much we can gather from the psalm. It may have originally been used as a battle prayer in the field, but since there are no military terms, no reference to danger of death (contrast Ps 3:20), this may rather have originated as a prayer used and cherished by Jewish exiles in Babylon.[12]

One need not be cynical to recognize the rhetorical dynamics of the piece. The purpose of the poem is to get God to intervene, specifically to bring me home alive and safe, the householder in peace and prosperity. But if I am trying to convince someone to help me, I would be a fool not to emphasize the interests of the other—what has this person to gain by helping me? And that, of course, is the strategy of this prayer. God's interest is expressed explicitly in 43:4: the vow that if God brings me home, I will sing my thanks at God's altar. Such a vow is a typical motif of biblical petitions (Pss 7:18; 13:7; 22:23ff., etc.).

A song may not be much, but it's all I've got to offer. After all, what do you give to Someone who already has everything? Our psalm does all it can to exploit the motif: the vow of 43:4, "I will *come* to your altar . . . . I will thank you on the harp," is anticipated in the expression of longing in 42:2-3, "When can I *come*[13] and see the face of God?" a phrase that specifies the import of the "yearning" and "thirsting" of verses 2-3.

The expression of thirsting for God, then, as also in Psalm 63, is no mystical meditation but an expression of love intended to persuade Yahweh to bring about my return to Jerusalem and to the Temple, where I can give thanks for my deliverance.

But make no mistake. That the expression of longing is meant to support a call for help does not make it insincere. It is the human condition that the heart is a tumble of hopes, wishes, desires. The ardent desire to return home by no means excludes a nostalgia for worship in the Temple. No more does a recognition of one's poverty before God exclude an honest love of God.

To recognize how the psalm was once prayed gives me help in praying it. This prayer is a protestation of need rather than of how exalted my love of God is. The longing, the thirst, for God is measured not by my purity of devotion but by my poverty. The vow in this psalm takes on greater weight than in other psalms, since it is anticipated from the beginning in the protestations of longing for God and for God's Temple. But my praise is clearly no adequate payment for God's help. I cannot bargain with God as an equal.

---

12. Compare Psalm 137 and also Lamentations with its prayers (1:11-16, 18-22; 2:20-22; 3; etc.), but note that Lamentations was apparently used in Palestine rather than in exile.

13. The Grail version in the Liturgy of the Hours reads "enter," which may fit the context but fails to reflect the correspondence between the language of the beginning of the poem and the end, one of the most common Hebrew rhetorical devices known as *inclusio*.

This prayer, divided into two psalms by biblical tradition, was surely one piece originally. In the Liturgy of the Hours it is also treated as two psalms, one prayed on Monday of the second week and the other on Tuesday. The emphasis, then, is on complaint on one day and on petition on the other.[14]

I have sometimes prayed this psalm when traveling or engaged in a ministry as a prayer of longing for my monastic community, perhaps a piety that is especially appropriate for Benedictines, with their strong experience of encountering God in the place of their brotherhood. One might surely pray the psalm for persons who are separated by imprisonment or illness from the worshiping community. Obviously such prayer is a rereading of the old use, but the very nature of prayer is that the content of the words is bound to change from one person to the next, surely from one age to the next. The key two criteria for responsible prayer are that such changes remain in continuity with the original use and that they correspond to the experience of those who are now attempting to pray.

Our experience of exile is not limited to place, for "we have here no lasting city, but we seek the city which is to come" (Heb 13:14). "Strangers and pilgrims" here (Heb 11:13), we may be rather like Chaucer's Canterbury pilgrims, robustly savoring the journey itself; but the Christian still knows that the ultimate home is that Jerusalem which is on high. We may be more hesitant than those of another age to describe that happy home, whose "gates are richly set with pearl,/ Most glorious to behold;/ Thy walls are all of precious stone,/ Thy streets are paved with gold."[15] God had better come up with something better than a nonstop fish fry or an endless "Te Deum," no matter how stirring. Anything I can imagine, extended to not just a year or a century but to an eternity, would make a good hell. The Christian understanding is that the God whose plan of salvation is deeper than anything that eye has seen or ear has heard or that the human heart has conceived is no less capable of breaking through all expectations, all imaginations, of eternal life.

My soul groans within me, God; I thirst, I know not for what, troubled and restless till I rest in you. Send forth your Light, who has come into the world to lead me to that fountain of life where alone my thirst can be satisfied.

14. In the Easter Vigil, parts of the two psalms are combined as a single response to the seventh reading, Ezekiel 36:16-28: "I shall pour clean water over you . . . I shall give you a new heart and put a new spirit in you."

15. From "Jerusalem My Happy Home"; see John Julian, *Dictionary of Hymnology* (New York: Dover, 1957) 583.

PSALM 19   MORNING SECOND MONDAY

(18) 19. Praise for the Lord, creator of all

² The heavens proclaim the glory of God,
   and the firmament shows forth the work of God's hands.
³ Day unto day takes up the story
   and night unto night makes known the message.

⁴ No speech, no word, no voice is heard
⁵ yet their span extends through all the earth,
   their words to the utmost bounds of the world.

There God has placed a tent for the sun;
⁶ it comes forth like a bridegroom coming from his tent,
   rejoices like a champion to run its course.

⁷ At the end of the sky is the rising of the sun;
   to the furthest end of the sky is its course.
   There is nothing concealed from its burning heat.

                    * * * * *

[⁸ The law of the LORD is perfect,
   it revives the soul.
   The rule of the LORD is to be trusted,
   it gives wisdom to the simple.

⁹ The precepts of the LORD are right,
   they gladden the heart.
   The command of the LORD is clear,
   it gives light to the eyes.

¹⁰ The fear of the LORD is holy,
   abiding for ever.
   The decrees of the LORD are truth
   and all of them just.

¹¹ They are more to be desired than gold,
   than the purest of gold
   and sweeter are they than honey,
   than honey from the comb.

¹² So in them your servant finds instruction;
   great reward is in their keeping.
¹³ But can we discern all our errors?
   From hidden faults acquit us.

¹⁴ From presumption restrain your servant
and let it not rule me.
Then shall I be blameless,
clean from grave sin.

¹⁵ May the spoken words of my mouth,
the thoughts of my heart,
win favor in your sight, O LORD,
my rescuer, my rock!]

I am frankly dismayed by what the Liturgy of the Hours has done to this psalm in omitting the last eight verses. It is true that these final verses may once have been an independent poem, but never could the poor truncated fragment verses 2-7 have stood alone without some kind of conclusion. The combining of the two parts in the canonical text was surely deliberate, taking an exuberant old poem that confesses how the heavens by their very being praise God and using it at the service of a poem that joyfully lauds the Law of the Lord. If the editors really had to omit the treatment of the Law to make the psalm better correspond to the more general character of the hymns of praise with which the psalmody of Morning Prayer always ends, one might wish that they had at least given the psalm a real conclusion by repeating the first verse or two of the psalm at the end.

The sun and moon, the stars and all the heavens, praise you, God, without speech and serve you without knowing it. Warm our hearts to marvel at the wonders of your creation, enlighten our minds to know your will, and move our dull wills to love and serve you aright.

PSALM 45   EVENING SECOND MONDAY

(44) 45. Royal wedding song

² My heart overflows with noble words.
To the king I must speak the song I have made,
my tongue as nimble as the pen of a scribe.

³ You are the fairest of the men on earth
and graciousness is poured upon your lips,
because God has blessed you for evermore.

⁴ O mighty one, gird your sword upon your thigh;
in splendor and state, ⁵ ride on in triumph
for the cause of truth and goodness and right.

Take aim with your bow in your dread right hand.
⁶ Your arrows are sharp, peoples fall beneath you.
The foes of the king fall down and lose heart.

⁷ Your throne, O God, shall endure for ever.
A scepter of justice is the scepter of your kingdom.
⁸ Your love is for justice, your hatred for evil.

Therefore God, your God, has anointed you
with the oil of gladness above other kings;
⁹ your robes are fragrant with aloes and myrrh.

From the ivory palace you are greeted with music.
¹⁰ The daughters of kings are among your loved ones.
On your right stands the queen in gold of Ophir.

* * * * *

¹¹ Listen, O daughter, give ear to my words:
forget your own people and your father's house.
¹² So will the king desire your beauty;
he is your lord, pay homage to him.

¹³ And the people of Tyre shall come with gifts,
the richest of the people shall seek your favor.
¹⁴ The daughter of the king is clothed with splendor,
her robes embroidered with pearls set in gold.

¹⁵ She is led to the king with her maiden companions.
¹⁶ They are escorted amid gladness and joy;
they pass within the palace of the king.

* * * * *

¹⁷ Children shall be yours in place of your forebears;
you will make them rulers over all the earth.
¹⁸ May this song make your name for ever remembered.
May the peoples praise you from age to age.

The royal court had hymns and songs for many purposes. Already the story of David as Saul's musical therapist suggests that a singer would not be out of place in the royal court, and 1 Kings 10:12 alludes to the king's singers, as do many passages of Chronicles' later reconstruction of the court. Such singers would perform for entertainment at banquets and for religious ceremonies in the king's sanctuary. Successful songs were preserved and adapted for generations. Such a successful song is this wedding hymn.

Though this song may have been composed originally for the wedding of a king of Israel or Judah with a Phoenician princess,[16] the very fact that it was preserved suggests that it was used repeatedly, presumably at other royal weddings.

The singer begins and ends the poem with a commendation of his work unprecedented elsewhere in the Old Testament (vv. 2, 18),[17] addresses both groom (vv. 3-10, 17-18) and bride (vv. 11-13), and lauds the ceremony (vv. 14-16).

The themes of the praise, exhortations, and promises are appropriate to the royal status of the parties. The king (even at his wedding) is seen as the ideal warrior establishing justice (vv. 6, 7b-8) and continuing the royal line (vv. 7a, 17). The queen transfers allegiance from her family to the king, and in return is assured of royal prestige (vv. 11-13).

Where are they now, the king and queen for whom this song was first composed? The subsequent royalty at whose weddings the work was later sung? "May this song make your name for ever remembered" (v. 18a), the ancient singer hoped; "May the peoples praise you from age to age" (v. 18b). But they've all been gone for twenty-five centuries and more. As for names, despite the poet's hope, no one remembers for whom such a poem was first sung or those whose wedding feast it later graced.

But the song has remained, evoking for generation upon generation images of those nuptials, images of the ideal of Israel's king as the glorious and powerful guarantor of justice, peace, and stability. When the land succumbed to the Assyrians and Babylonians, when there was no king to fete with wedding songs, the song, like other royal psalms, was preserved for the days of restoration. And as the restoration was delayed, the song came ever more vividly to express the people's hopes for that restoration, when the Lord's anointed would truly establish justice, peace, and prosperity in a stability that this time would never again succumb to external enemies or internal corruption.

The author of Hebrews 1:8 came honestly by his messianic reading, though going a bit too far in seeing it as a prediction of the Messiah's superiority to the angels: "Your throne, O God, is forever and ever; the scepter of righteousness is the scepter of your kingdom."[18]

---

16. See the problematic verse 13. Such diplomatic alliances are recorded of Solomon (1 Kgs 11:1) and Ahab (1 Kgs 16:31).

17. But somewhat similar in deuterocanonical literature is Jesus Ben Sira's commendation of his own book (Sir 24:30-34) and the introduction and conclusion of the prose 2 Maccabees (2:19-32 and 15:37-39).

18. Nevertheless, the author, like all of us a child of the times, even comes honestly by the typical first-century methodology of polemically interpreting biblical texts as predictions of contemporary events and personages. We find a similar understanding in the biblical interpretation of the Qumran community as well.

If we're going to pray the psalm, it is hardly sufficient to use it to try to understand Iron Age marriage customs and court usages! Honest prayer exists only when the old words spark to life, expressing our experience in some kind of continuity with their origin.

A "democratization" of the psalm is not unreasonable, applying the psalm to every marriage of Christians or Jews, for it is we, formed by the Word of God, who carry on the attempt to realize the stable justice and peace that was the ideal of the kings of Israel and Judah. Indeed, there are some scholars who would see the psalm as democratic in its origins, intended for any Israelite/Jewish couple at their marriage, endowing the bride and groom with royal honors. Though I consider such a reading historically inaccurate, it does correspond to later Jewish and Christian marriage practice and thought.

Even more appropriate for constant use is a Christocentric praying of the psalm. That is something quite different from a Christological *interpretation,* which would see the king of the psalm as predicting Christ, the queen as meaning the Church or the Christian soul, the children who will be princes as the apostles. Rather, as the ancients used the text now for one king, later for another, Christians would claim that all the more the song can be sung for Jesus, in whom are fulfilled and are to be fulfilled paradoxically and beyond any expectation all the hopes once invested in the anointed king. The power of those old kings was used as often for exploitation as for justice. Their descendants have long since lost the kingdom; none of their names are remembered with the passion evoked by the name of Jesus.

And the bride? Like all other biblical themes, we find that this one becomes ours only as we find an appropriate analogy. Paul, developing an ancient theme of Israel as God's spouse (Hos 1–3; Jer 3:1), sees the Church as Christ's bride (Eph 5:23-32; 2 Cor 11:2). The grounds of the analogy are clear enough: lifelong union, mutual and complementary love and support, the call to fidelity, the fruitfulness of the union, all of which are themes that we celebrate explicitly or implicitly in this song. Most other ways of praying the psalm will be dependent on this basic analogy. The antiphon for feasts of apostles, "You will make them rulers over all the earth: they will forever remember your name," sees the apostles as the children of the king, through whom he establishes his reign. In feasts of holy women the nuptials with the Church are seen as specifically realized in the saint of the day. A strong theme of Christian spirituality and mysticism has seen the individual Christian and the Christian soul as bride of Christ.

Christ, of course, is no polygamist, nor does the physical eros that is proper to marriage define the mystery of Christ and his Church. But such limitations are of the nature of analogy and do not contradict the deep affinity in the very being of the corresponding realities.

Because the psalm celebrates not just marriage but a wedding, the psalm is prayed at Christmas, as the commemoration of the incarnation, when the Word was joined to human nature as the seminal beginning of the union of Christ and Church.

Christ, Bridegroom and King, hear my voice as I join in the chanting of this song to you and your bride, which still makes your name remembered from generation to generation.

PSALM 65   MORNING SECOND TUESDAY

(64) 65. A song of springtime

2 To you our praise is due
in Zion, O God.
To you we pay our vows,
3 you who hear our prayer.

To you all flesh will come
4 with its burden of sin.
Too heavy for us, our offences,
but you wipe them away.

5 Blessed those whom you choose and call
to dwell in your courts.
We are filled with the blessings of your house,
of your holy temple.

6 You keep your pledge with wonders,
O God our savior,
the hope of all the earth
and of far distant isles.

7 You uphold the mountains with your strength,
you are girded with power.
8 You still the roaring of the seas,
(the roaring of their waves,)
and the tumult of the peoples.

9 The ends of the earth stand in awe
at the sight of your wonders.
The lands of sunrise and sunset
you fill with your joy.

10 You care for the earth, give it water;
you fill it with riches.

Your river in heaven brims over
to provide its grain.

And thus you provide for the earth;
[11] you drench its furrows;
you level it, soften it with showers;
you bless its growth.

[12] You crown the year with your goodness.
Abundance flows in your steps;
[13] in the pastures of the wilderness it flows.

The hills are girded with joy,
[14] the meadows covered with flocks,
the valleys are decked with wheat.
They shout for joy, yes, they sing.

Vows were a typical part of Jewish piety. Persons in trouble, persons with a great need, would promise something to God, often a sacrifice, if God would see to their need (Gen 28:20; Judg 11:30-31; 1 Sam 1:11; 2 Sam 15:7-8); then when the prayer was answered, they would fulfill their promise. This explains how Psalm 65 was used. In years of drought or years when drought threatened, pious Israelites made such vows in their prayers for rain. Then, when they came to offer their thanksgiving sacrifices, they would pray this psalm. Verse 2 defines the offerings as a fulfillment of vows,[19] and the "blessings of your house" with which "we are filled" (v. 5) seems to allude to the festive banquet of the thanksgiving sacrifice thus offered (cf. Ps 22:26-27 and Deut 12:11-12, 17-18).

That the rain is the present issue is shown by verses 10-14, the conclusion of the poem, which also makes up a good third of its verses. Rain in the land of Israel is notably unreliable. While the average annual rainfall of Jerusalem is the same as that of London, Berlin, or Collegeville, Minnesota, it varies dramatically from year to year. Even in a year with an adequate total, an imbalance in the times of the rain can bring disaster. With inadequate storage and transportation,[20] not to speak of problems of exploitation and hoarding by persons of greater privilege, there was little to protect the mass

19. Note, though, that the words "To you we pay our vows" in the Grail translation represent a form that is passive in Hebrew: "To you vows are paid."

20. A large part of a shipment of grain from Egypt to Palestine would be consumed by the animals, their drivers and guards. Remember that in a long famine Joseph moved his family rather than the food (Gen 45:17ff.).

of society from famine in times of drought. There was, then, good cause for gratitude when the rains finally came.

But how to make a whole prayer out of "Thank you"? What's left to say after saying "Thank you"? Actually, there was no way in the biblical world to stop at "Thank you." Claus Westermann has shown that there is no Hebrew equivalent for our verb "thank," that the expression which we translate as "to thank" actually means "to praise" and always includes an external and public acknowledgment of the kindness done by the other.[21]

There is certainly nothing small-minded about this prayer of thanksgiving for rain. From this gift of rain the vision of the poem leaps in time to the primordial foundation of the earth (vv. 7-8), in space to the fear and hope of all the earth standing before God (vv. 6, 9), beyond the world to the source of the rain in the heavenly river (v. 10).[22] The gift and its effects are described in vivid and concrete language (vv. 10-14).

Neither the vow in distress nor the thanksgiving sacrifice is characteristic of our world. When we pray the psalm, at least these elements will become metaphors of what is found in our experience, of our recognition in distress that we are not self-sufficient, of our expression of gratitude in deliverance through songs of thanksgiving, and even through the mystic realization of Christ's sacrifice, whose name, *Eucharistia,* means "thanksgiving."

But there is more that is alien to us. There is disparity in the very perception of how the rain is God's gift. We know a lot about where the rain comes from, about water vapor in the air from vegetation and the seas, about its condensation in clouds and rain at lower temperatures, about cold fronts and low pressure systems. We can see satellite pictures of cloud patterns on television, and radar images of approaching rain. The ancients, of course, knew none of this. They only knew that the rain and the drought were unimaginably greater than any human work. It was, then, the god who formed the clouds for this day's rain and sent them, or the god who was angry and sent the east wind with its drought. Even when we thank God for the

---

21. *Praise and Lament in the Psalms,* trans. Keith R. Crim and Richard Soulen (Atlanta: John Knox, 1981) 25ff. Normally in a situation where we would thank another person, the Hebrew will wish a blessing on that person either with (1 Sam 23:21; 25:33) or without (1 Sam 26:25) mention of the benefit performed.

22. The Egyptian psalmist likewise sees the Syro-Palestinian rains as coming from a heavenly river in a hymn to Aton, the sun disk:

All distant foreign countries, thou makest their life (also),

For thou hast set a Nile in heaven,

That it may descend for them and make waves upon the mountains

. . . To water their fields in their towns (*ANET* 370).

rain, then, it is really for something quite different that we are thanking this God.

It was at least the genius of Israel to recognize that it was the same God who sent them the rain and the drought, that moreover this was the God who alone could give victory and peace to his people, and finally this was the God who oversaw justice and vindicated the rights of the defenseless in society. For Israel at least, there was only one God; you could not play one god against another, hoping that one god would protect you when another was angry; nor could you blame one god for your troubles when another was pleased with you. Israel's God was reliable, not capricious.

Still, when we moderns thank God for the weather, we see God much further behind the chain of causality. Even if we believe that God sometimes intervenes to send the rain,[23] our God does so only through the low pressure systems.

We may want to pray this psalm in thanksgiving for gifts beyond that of the rain, taking the rain as a metaphor for all God's gifts, much as we use the "daily bread" of the Lord's Prayer to express all our daily needs. After all, we will search the psalter in vain for a prayer of thanksgiving, say, for relief from months of aridity in prayer or for the just settlement of a hospital strike. And the Bible itself, after all, shows evidence of such reappropriation of old psalms for new purposes on the basis of analogy (see Ps 30).

Nevertheless, I should not want consistently to spiritualize the praying of this psalm. I am, after all, no pure spirit, and like all flesh my very life depends on the food nourished by the rain. Still, when I consider how deeply rooted in the created world I find God's gift of the rain, it is helpful to my prayer to find that the psalm sees the granting of rain not just as today's decree in the heavenly court but also places it in the context of the Creator, whose primordial battle with the unruly sea wrests order from chaos.

PSALM 49 EVENING SECOND TUESDAY

(48) 49. The problem of justice and death

² Hear this, all you peoples,
   give heed, all who dwell in the world,
³ people high and low,
   rich and poor alike!

_____

23. A student of mine remarked about his bishop's call for prayers to end a drought: "For four thousand years all of creation has been pleading with God to get rid of humanity, but God hasn't answered their prayer. Why should we suppose God will be more anxious to answer us?"

⁴ My lips will speak words of wisdom.
   My heart is full of insight.
⁵ I will turn my mind to a parable,
   with the harp I will solve my problem.

                    * * * * *

⁶ Why should I fear in evil days
   the malice of the foes who surround me,
⁷ people who trust in their wealth,
   and boast of the vastness of their riches?

⁸ For the rich cannot buy their own ransom,
   nor pay a price to God for their lives.
⁹ The ransom of their souls is beyond them.
¹⁰ They cannot buy endless life,
   nor avoid coming to the grave.

¹¹ They know that both wise and foolish perish
   and must leave their wealth to others.
¹² Their graves are their homes for ever,
   their dwelling place from age to age,
   though their names spread wide through the land.

¹³ In their riches, people lack wisdom;
   they are like the beasts that are destroyed.

                    * * * * *

¹⁴ This is the lot of those who trust in themselves,
   who have others at their beck and call.
¹⁵ Like sheep they are driven to the grave,
   where death shall be their shepherd
   and the just shall become their rulers.

   With the morning their outward show vanishes
   and the grave becomes their home.
¹⁶ But God will ransom my soul,
   from the power of death will snatch me.

¹⁷ Then do not fear when others grow rich,
   when the glory of their house increases.
¹⁸ They take nothing with them when they die,
   their glory does not follow them below.

¹⁹ Though they flatter themselves while they lived:
   "They will praise me for doing well for myself,"

²⁰ yet they will go to join their forebears,
and will never see the light any more.

²¹ In their riches, people lack wisdom;
they are like the beasts that are destroyed.

Not all the psalms are, in fact, Iron Age poetry. Psalm 49 seems to come from the Persian or even the Hellenistic period, so some time in the last five hundred years before Christ, when long experience under foreign domination had forced a greater international awareness on Israel. In genre this psalm is closely related to the Wisdom of Solomon (first century B.C.E.?). While formally addressed to the "rulers of the earth," the Wisdom of Solomon was, as its themes would suggest, actually meant for the ears of young Jews who were tempted by Hellenistic culture and philosophy, attempting to show them that the true wisdom resided in their Jewish tradition. Similarly, Psalm 49 is formally addressed to "All you peoples . . . all who dwell in the world" but most likely was heard only by Jews and perhaps prospective converts. No longer composed for the Temple, this psalm would seem to have been used in early Jewish community gatherings, in the origins of what came to be the synagogue, as a kind of confession of faith, somewhat as certain Christian Churches use the Beatitudes liturgically.

The issue is an old one, a perennial one in the story of humanity: How are the poor to make sense of life in the face of the arrogance of the rich (vv. 6-7)? The Hebrews asked this in Egypt, as did the victims of Israel's prosperous landholders in their turn (Amos 2:6-16; Isa 1:17, 21-23; 3:14-15; 5:8). The original inhabitants of our continent asked this when their land was taken from them by Europeans, who arrogantly claimed the right of discovery, and such was the question of Africans taken into slavery. It is still asked wherever human beings sense themselves to be exploited or neglected by those whom the rapine of history has enriched. Fairly or unfairly, it is asked wherever poverty or impotence confronts wealth and power.

The response is remarkably realistic, with the realism taught by generations of injustice. No expectation here of a revolutionary change of fortunes, no assurance that good will beat evil at its own game. The psalm does not advise, "Wait a bit, and things will get better." Rather, the psalm says that the game of power is, in the end, not worth winning; indeed, that if you follow through to the very end, the game cannot be won. In the end death takes the wise and the foolish, the rich and the poor, the powerless and the powerful alike. You can bribe neither God nor death; the grave will take no ransom (v. 8).

In a couple of ambiguous phrases the psalm affirms that when the rich die, the now powerless righteous will be better off: "The just shall become their rulers" (v. 15); and in clear contrast to verse 8, verse 16 says: "God will ransom my soul, from the power of death will snatch me." But the psalm does not develop the point, neither clearly maintaining that the righteous will outlive the wicked (contrast Ps 37:35-38) nor describing a world beyond, where the righteous will be vindicated and rewarded (contrast Dan 12:2f.; 2 Macc 7, esp. vv. 30-38.)

Surely the psalm dates to a period before the middle of the second century B.C.E., when a doctrine of a real afterlife was coming to acceptance among Jews, especially fostered by an attempt to defend God's justice during the persecution of Antiochus IV Epiphanes, when only the most faithful Jews were killed, while those who compromised or apostatized got on just fine, thank you. In a psalm that was meant to be an affirmation of the community's faith rather than a treatise in speculative theology, the reticence would reflect uncertainty in the community about just how God would vindicate the righteous, while confidently affirming such a vindication.

When we read this psalm, we are not addressing God; rather, we address one another and hear ourselves addressed. We are bringing the old exhortation back to life month by month. It is an exhortation that renews its power each time it is spoken. In the Rule of Benedict, one of the instruments of good works is to keep death daily before one's eyes. Such awareness of our fragility need not be paralyzing; rather, it can renew our energy by showing us how precious each day is. And it certainly can help to bring things into perspective. All our possessions and all our power will do us no good on the day when we return naked to the mother of all. And if we have abused or neglected others in our pursuit of such wealth and power, these will finally rise up to our shame in witness against us.

Far from relieving us of the task of laboring toward a just society, this awareness of our mortality calls us all the more insistently. If the bread given to the hungry will testify for us in the judgment, how much more our share in the attempt to establish an order to eliminate the causes of hunger. Not that such works will last forever or that cumulatively they will bring about the reign of God on earth. Something always goes wrong, or the new order itself becomes oppressive. But what marvels were done at the time, say by the credit union movement of the 1930s and 1940s, to promote the dignity of persons who otherwise felt themselves neglected or exploited by the system!

The monastic, the religious, the full-time volunteer, can hear this as both confirmation and challenge. Though not always living up to their ideals, they do so enough to be oddities, all of them. They say by the way they live that there is more to life than being free to choose your own job, having someone to go to bed with, having control of your money, having children in your image, having security. But the psalm is also confrontation, presenting demanding questions about where one's heart and one's treasure really are. Not that the ancients were recommending the ascetic life. Far from it. They took it for granted that one married, that one sought security for one's descendants, that one defended one's honor against one's enemies. But once they have challenged us about the final meaning of life, once they have reminded us of our death, they are no longer in control of the insights to which their questioning may provoke a new generation.

Still, every Christian stands challenged in a similar way. A friend has kept his retail store closed on Sundays for thirty years, against the policy of the mall where it is located, not just out of respect for the Lord's Day, but to allow his employees to spend the day with their families. In recent negotiations for the renewal of the lease, he was ready to relocate the shop rather than sign a contract to keep the store open. That, I should think, was a decision worth making in the face of the kind of question raised by Psalm 49. The wisdom of this poem was meant to challenge the assumptions of its society. It still fulfills its goal as it challenges us.

PSALM 77   MORNING SECOND WEDNESDAY

(76) 77. God and God's people:
    the lessons of past history

2   I cry aloud to God,
      cry aloud to God to hear me.
3   In the day of my distress I sought the Lord.
      My hands were raised at night without ceasing;
      my soul refused to be consoled.
4   I remembered my God and I groaned.
      I pondered and my spirit fainted.

5   You withheld sleep from my eyes.
      I was troubled, I could not speak.
6   I thought of the days of long ago
      and remembered the years long past.
7   At night I mused within my heart.
      I pondered and my spirit questioned.

8   "Will the Lord reject us for ever
      and no longer show favor to us?
9   Has God's love vanished for ever?
      Has God's promise come to an end?
10 Does God forget to be gracious,
      or in anger withhold compassion?"

¹¹ I said: "This is what causes my grief,
  that the way of the Most High has changed."
¹² I remember the deeds of the L ORD,
  I remember your wonders of old,
¹³ I muse on all your works
  and ponder your mighty deeds.

¹⁴ Your ways, O God, are holy.
  What god is great as our God?
¹⁵ You are the God who works wonders.
  You showed your power among the peoples.
¹⁶ Your strong arm redeemed your people,
  the children of Jacob and Joseph.

¹⁷ The waters saw you, O God,
  the waters saw you and trembled;
  the depths were moved with terror.
¹⁸ The clouds poured down rain,
  the skies sent forth their voice;
  your arrows flashed to and fro.

¹⁹ Your thunder rolled round the sky,
  your flashes lighted up the world.
  The earth was moved and trembled
²⁰ when your way led through the sea,
  your path through the mighty waters
  and no one saw your footprints.

²¹ You guided your people like a flock
  by the hand of Moses and Aaron.

Unlike other lament psalms, Psalm 77 never gets around to making a request. It contains bitter complaint (vv. 2-11) and a remarkably long confession of God's past saving acts (vv. 12-21; cf. Pss 22:4-6; 80:9-12; 89:20-38). But like Psalm 88 and the prayer of Samson in Judges 15:18, this psalm never explicitly asks for God's help. The unrelieved gloom of Psalm 88 suggests that it lacks a petition because it is considered useless: God will never respond. In the Samson prayer, on the other hand, it seems there is no request because it is considered unnecessary: if only God hears the complaint, God will surely intervene.

Only complaint and confession here. What is God supposed to make of it? The confession of past help is related to the complaint through verse 11. After bitter and almost accusatory complaint, "Will the Lord reject for ever? Will he show his favor no more? . . . Has God's promise come to an end?" it is the complaint of verse 11 that introduces the confession of past saving deeds: "I said, 'This is what causes my grief, that the way of the Most High has changed.'" This complaint is followed by the description of the former "way of the Most High," Yahweh's deliverance of Israel from Egypt (vv. 12-21), told with language that reflects old myths about the battle of creation (vv. 17, 21).

It would at first seem, then, that the whole description of past benefits has the same function as it does in Psalms 22:4-6; 80:9-12; 89:20-38, where it is introduced to complain that Yahweh no longer acts as he once did. Still, it is significant that the poem does not follow the description with a call asking God to intervene after all as in the days of old, or else with a continuation of the complaint. With the poem thus ending with a vivid description of the deliverance of the people and their protection in the wilderness, this confession of God's mighty deeds might rather be seen as a kind of expression of confidence, or at least as a muted appeal to Yahweh to save again as in the past.

When we pray the psalm today, the very ambiguities of the psalm make it more flexible for our use. For instance, it is not clear whether the psalm was meant to articulate the troubles of an individual or of the community.[24] Perhaps it was deliberately left ambiguous to allow for use in either kind of situation or as it was adapted from one type of use to another. At any rate, the unclarity of the psalm makes it easy for us to use it for ourselves, in intercession for another, or in pleading for community needs.

The problem of the function of the confession of God's past deeds makes the prayer more responsive to our own attitude of the moment: if we are confident of God's help, it can become an expression of our trust; if we are not, it only gently urges us to confidence through reflection on the story of salvation, or it can even express our bitterness at God's silence.

There is nothing sweet about the psalm. Its complaint is reminiscent of Job: "My soul refused to be consoled" (v. 3). The psalm gives us permission to accuse God, to express our anger and sorrow and fear without having at once to assure God that we only halfway mean it. God is big enough to take our anger. In fact, in the Book of Job it is the friends, who have naively defended God's justice, who are condemned; and it is Job, who has railed against God, expressing his anger and pain and confusion, who is praised: "You have not spoken of me what is right as my servant Job has," says the Lord to the friends (Job 42:7).

---

24. The Grail translation is too specific in adding "us" to the questions of verse 8: "Will the Lord reject *us* forever?" If anything, verse 3, "In the day of *my* distress," would suggest individual concerns, though the psalm could, like the poems of Lamentations, be used as the response of an individual to the calamities of the people.

For all Job's frustration, he keeps coming back to God, keeps addressing God, even if in anger and disappointment. Where else can he turn? As Peter replies when Jesus asks the Twelve if they, too, will leave him, "Lord, to whom else shall we go? You have the words of everlasting life" (John 6:68). If even within an unequivocal expression of distress we can acknowledge God as the only source of deliverance, our confession is vindicated of sentimentality, tested as it is against reality.[25]

Psalm 77 was traditionally used on Holy Thursday with the antiphon "In the day of my distress I sought the Lord," thus becoming a meditation on Jesus' prayer in the garden. As such, it becomes a powerful reminder that our prayer in trouble and our intercession for others in distress is always a sharing in the prayer of the One who has borne our griefs and carried all our sorrows.

PSALM 97   MORNING SECOND WEDNESDAY

(96) 97. Earth rejoices in its king

1. The LORD is king, let earth rejoice,
   let all the coastlands be glad.
2. Surrounded by cloud and darkness;
   justice and right, God's throne.

3. A fire prepares the way;
   it burns up foes on every side.
4. God's lightnings light up the world,
   the earth trembles at the sight.

5. The mountains melt like wax
   before the LORD of all the earth.
6. The skies proclaim God's justice;
   all peoples see God's glory.

7. Let those who serve idols be ashamed,
   those who boast of their worthless gods.
   All you spirits, worship the Lord.

8. Zion hears and is glad;
   the people of Judah rejoice
   because of your judgements, O LORD.

25. See Walter Brueggemann, *Israel's Praise: Doxology Against Idolatry and Ideology* (Philadelphia, Fortress, 1988) 139: "The praise has power to transform the pain. But conversely the present pain also keeps the act of praise honest."

⁹　For you indeed are the LORD
　　most high above all the earth,
　　exalted far above all spirits.

¹⁰　The LORD loves those who hate evil,
　　guards the souls of the saints,
　　and sets them free from the wicked.

¹¹　Light shines forth for the just
　　and joy for the upright of heart.
¹²　Rejoice, you just, in the LORD;
　　give glory to God's holy name.

Ruler and Judge of the world, make our hearts faithful to you. Keep us from setting anything before the love of you. Arouse in us zeal to bring justice to the oppressed, so that we may have no cause to fear but may rejoice with all creation when you come in glory to judge the earth.

PSALM 62　EVENING SECOND WEDNESDAY

(61) 62. God, the rock of strength

²　In God alone is my soul at rest;
　　from God comes my help.
³　God alone is my rock, my stronghold,
　　my fortress; I stand firm.

⁴　How long will you attack me
　　to break me down,
　　as though I were a tottering wall,
　　or a tumbling fence?

⁵　Their plan is only to destroy;
　　they take pleasure in lies.
　　With their mouth they utter blessing
　　but in their heart they curse.

⁶　In God alone be at rest, my soul;
　　from God comes my hope.
⁷　God alone is my rock, my stronghold,
　　my fortress; I stand firm.

⁸　In God is my safety and glory,
　　the rock of my strength.
　　Take refuge in God, ⁹ all you people,

trusting always.
Pour out your hearts to the Lord
for God is our refuge.

10 Common folk are only a breath,
the great are an illusion.
Placed in the scales, they rise;
they weigh less than a breath.

11 Do not put your trust in oppression
nor vain hopes on plunder.
Do not set your heart on riches
even when they increase.

12 For God has said only one thing;
only two do I know:
that to God alone belongs power
13 and to you, Lord, love;
and that you repay us all
according to our deeds.

Ah, my poor soul, stop running; you'll not find rest but in your God. No
need for resentment, no need for fear. And you, God? In you, power and love
are but one.

PSALM 67   EVENING SECOND WEDNESDAY AND MORNING THIRD TUESDAY

(66) 67. A harvest song

2 O God, be gracious and bless us
and let your face shed its light upon us.
3 So will your ways be known upon earth
and all nations learn your saving help.

4 Let the peoples praise you, O God;
let all the peoples praise you.

5 Let the nations be glad and exult
for you rule the world with justice.
With fairness you rule the peoples,
you guide the nations on earth.

6 Let the peoples praise you, O God;
let all the peoples praise you.

⁷ The earth has yielded its fruit
for God, our God, has blessed us.
⁸ May God still give us blessing
till the ends of the earth stand in awe.

Let the peoples praise you, O God;
let all the peoples praise you.

"May the Lord bless you and keep you; may the Lord make his face shine on you and be gracious to you; may the Lord lift up his countenance on you and give you peace." Thus, according to Numbers 6:24-26, the priest was to bless the Israelite people. Since the words of the blessing are addressed to the people, the blessing was presumably done at major feasts, when the whole people was present. Psalm 67 comes out of much the same tradition, using three of the same expressions: "bless," "be gracious," and "let his face shine," spoken (in the Hebrew) as a wish in the third person rather than addressed directly to Yahweh.[26]

What's different about a blessing, compared with other types of intercessory prayer, is that the blessing does not depend on a situation of trouble. When Yahweh is angry with his people, Moses prays to avert God's punishment, or David prays for his son's life when he is ill. But a blessing will be given at a turning point in life, a wedding (Gen 24:60), to one's children before one's death (Gen 27), or in connection with a religious ceremony (Lev 9:22; 2 Chr 30:27). Without reference to any danger or crisis, then, the blessing means to promote the overall well-being of the recipient through fertility, prosperity, health, and peace.

Psalm 67 begins, as we have seen, and also ends with a normal blessing, wishing in the third person for Yahweh's blessing—except that while a typical blessing is addressed to the recipient in the second person ("May God bless you," or like Num 6:24f.; Gen 27), in this psalm the recipient is in the first person plural ("May God bless us"). But in a curious dissonance, the psalm shifts to direct address of God in verse 2: "So will *your* ways be known upon earth . . . ." Accompanying that shift are other things that are not characteristic of blessings, a motive why Yahweh should bless, and interest in the nations of the earth. It is as if in the crucial task of trying to convince God to bestow the blessing, those who used the psalm could not trust the efficacy

26. The translation in the Liturgy of the Hours is somewhat deceptive in trying to smooth out the first verses by changing the Hebrew "May God be gracious and bless us . . ." to second-person forms to correspond to the "you" in verses 3-6, "O God, be gracious and bless us."

of the traditional third-person form of the blessing but had to address God directly and personally as "you."

The first task of verses 3-6 is to convince God to come through with the blessing. And as is regularly the case in the rhetoric of petition, if you're going to convince God to act, you want to stress how it is in God's interest to intervene. The argument in this case goes thus: If you bless us, the nations will recognize your power and graciousness. How similar this is to the repeated assertion in Ezekiel that after punishing his people for their sin, God will restore them "that the nations may know" that Yahweh has the power to act (Ezek 36:23, 36; 37:28 . . .)! But it is not just that the Gentiles will envy Israel; rather, seeing God's power, they will submit themselves to Yahweh in praise (vv. 4-6) and in fear and reverence (v. 8), recognizing God's just governance of the earth (v. 5). How we pray this psalm depends on whom we identify ourselves with in the psalm, Israel or the Gentiles.

We may overhear Israel praying this psalm, asking for God's blessing that we, the Gentiles, may marvel at God's power and generosity. And hearing this prayer, we recognize that it is fulfilled as we praise God's faithfulness and love toward Israel, and submit ourselves to that God in reverence and awe. For our faith as Gentile Christians has its origin in Israel. The blessings of Abraham and Moses, of David and the prophets, the blessing of the survival of Israel through exile and defeat—all this is part of our story. It is true that we will recognize Jesus as central to the answer to this ancient prayer of Israel. Not that the ancients were praying for the coming of Jesus! They were asking for health and peace, prosperity and fertility. But the very nature of asking for a blessing is that God may send you good things that you never dreamed of, and perhaps even things that you never would want to pray for!

We may also pray this psalm as heirs[27] of Israel—only through our incorporation in Christ, son of Mary, descendant of Abraham and Sarah, of Jacob and Leah. As such, we pray the psalm for God's gifts to us, for fertility and prosperity and peace. But the prayer can be a dangerous one if we are honest when we try to convince God that it is to God's advantage to bless us, that by seeing these blessings the nations will recognize God's work and submit themselves to God in praise and awe. For fertility and prosperity will not do that: our GNP may provoke envy or admiration but hardly conversion.

The great blessing of Israel that has most clearly led to any conversion of the Gentiles is the mystery of victory through defeat, of life through death, the mystery of God's participation in our human weakness and misery in

---

27. To recognize ourselves as heirs does not necessarily make us the only heirs of Israel to the exclusion of the Jewish people!

Jesus. It may be that what blessing God will give us in response to our prayer will be a participation in that mystery. If this is our blessing, we may at first resist it, we may endure our agony in the garden, but in the end we will embrace it and find in it our profoundest joy, our victory, our fullness of life.

PSALM 80   MORNING SECOND THURSDAY

(79) 80. The ravaged vine

2   O shepherd of Israel, hear us,
    you who lead Joseph's flock,
    shine forth from your cherubim throne
3   upon Ephraim, Benjamin, Manasseh.
    O Lord, rouse up your might,
    O Lord, come to our help.

4   God of hosts, bring us back;
    let your face shine on us and we shall be saved.

5   LORD God of hosts, how long
    will your frown on your people's plea?
6   You have fed them with tears for their bread,
    an abundance of tears for their drink.
7   You have made us the taunt of our neighbors,
    our enemies laugh us to scorn.

8   God of hosts, bring us back;
    let your face shine on us and we shall be saved.

9   You brought a vine out of Egypt;
    to plant it you drove out the nations.
10 Before it you cleared the ground;
    it took root and spread through the land.

11 The mountains were covered with its shadow,
    the cedars of God with its boughs.
12 It stretched out its branches to the sea,
    to the Great River it stretched out its shoots.

13 Then why have you broken down its walls?
    It is plucked by all who pass by.
14 It is ravaged by the boar of the forest,
    devoured by the beasts of the field.

15 God of hosts, turn again, we implore,
    look down from heaven and see.

> Visit this vine [16] and protect it,
> the vine your right hand has planted.
> [17] They have burnt it with fire and destroyed it.
> May they perish at the frown of your face.
>
> [18] May your hand be on the one you have chosen,
> that one you have given your strength.
> [19] And we shall never forsake you again;
> give us life that we may call upon your name.
>
> [20] God of hosts, bring us back;
> let your face shine on us and we shall be saved.

In 721 B.C.E., after a long siege, Samaria fell to the brutal Assyrian army. The northern Hebrew kingdom was no more. But throughout its history the land had undergone foreign invasions. Already within a decade of the death of Solomon and the North's separation from Jerusalem, it had suffered a disastrous raid for plunder by Pharaoh Sheshonk, and throughout the ninth century Syrian armies had repeatedly conquered the Galilean and trans-Jordanian territories.

Psalm 80 doubtless represents a lament prayed often during that long history of pillage and atrocities, and for years after in hopes of restoration. Through refugees, no doubt, who flooded to the south it entered the repertoire of the southern kingdom of Judah. The Judahites apparently used it to lament not only the plight of their northern neighbor, their buffer against the Mesopotamian powers, but also the growing depredations on the south by Assyria and later Babylon. For as the only remnant of the Israel of premonarchic and early monarchic times, they increasingly applied the title "Israel" to themselves, and terms like "Joseph," "Ephraim," and "Manasseh," which indicated only northern tribes, became metaphors for Judah.

The prayer consists of invocation (vv. 2-3), complaint (vv. 5-7 and 9-14), and petition (the repeated refrain vv. 5, 8, 20, and its expansion in vv. 15-19). After an initial cry for help (vv. 2-4), the argument runs as follows:

> Lord, our continuing troubles are your work (vv. 5-7).
> But in our origins you went to great lengths to establish and prosper us in
>   our land—expressed in the image of planting a vine (vv. 9-12).
> Then why have you devastated us? Again under image of a vine (vv. 13-14).
> Deliver us and restore us (vv. 15-18).
> Then we will be loyal to you (v. 19).

"Why have you broken down its walls?" asks the bewildered complainant rhetorically, implying that God's behavior is incomprehensible if not reprehensible

(v. 13). Now, the prophets in fact would have had no trouble answering that question. Isaiah, for instance, in applying the same imagery to Judah, says that it is because the vine brought forth bad grapes; and lest the point be lost in the imagery, he explains the bad fruits as bloodshed and violence in place of justice and right (Isa 5:1-7). Now, in fact, the communal laments of the psalter seldom contain any acknowledgment of sin (Ps 79:8-9); our troubles are the effect of our wicked opponents, God's enemies (Ps 75:3-8, 18f.; cf. Ps 73:9), not of our own sin and folly. It was no Jeremiah, no Hosea, who composed these psalms! Psalm 80, while complaining of the enemies' conquest of the land, looks back with longing to the good old days when we were the ones who conquered the land from the Canaanites—through God's help, of course.

Faulty though these psalms be, still they were preserved and were taken up into Scripture. Each text of the Bible is true and good, but not necessarily perfect and complete. The psalms, and especially these laments of the community, are apt to engage in the strategy of blaming, seeking the source of one's troubles outside oneself. Now, often enough there is something external that contributes to our troubles. It's only that a more mature spirit will recognize more complexity, will recognize one's own responsibility as well.

How many of the persecutions experienced by the Church are explained in part by the economic stranglehold exerted by vast Church landholdings, whether in Henry VIII's England, Maria Theresa's Austria, or early twentieth-century Hungary! Often, though, these economic grievances are also accompanied by a resentment of the moral restraints the Church would impose on self-indulgent and ambitious human nature.

A greater awareness of the ambiguities behind human conflict need not render us incapable of praying for relief. Even though we bear part of the fault, God remains engaged in our struggles with compassion and love. Just as the people of Judah learned to pray the psalm of their old rival Israel as a metaphor for their own needs, you likewise pray the psalm anew for all who suffer violence. Thus, you pray for those you perceive as victims of persecution, aggression, discrimination, who as long as humanity survives will suffer somewhere, but to whose prayers God will always attend. You may be speaking out of your own pain and anger, as will many women in our world, for instance; you may be interceding for others who cannot articulate their prayer, who perhaps cannot recognize God as the one who might hear their prayer.

You will also surely plead with God over the devastation you see within the Church, as the figures who represent the virtues in Dante's *Purgatorio* pray the communal lament Psalm 79 against Boniface VIII's arrogation of temporal power.[28] Not that strange things won't happen when we do such prayer. I may be praying in distress at the hierarchy's blind acceptance of a policy that puts a higher priority on the ability of candidates for ministry to remain bachelors than on the power to preach the gospel with fire. Meanwhile, the monk on my right may be lamenting the know-it-all theologians who are undermining the Church's authority by questioning the decisions of the Pope!

But we have absolutely no need to fear praying against the subversion of the gospel in Rome, against the apathy and bungling in the provincial house, against the "bums" in Washington. For the prayers we pray are quite different from the other means we use—and sometimes must use—to try to bring about what we perceive as God's will. When we act and when we speak, we have the responsibility to carefully think through our goals and our means, lest we make things worse than we found them. Not so in prayer, because the accomplishments of prayer are wrought by God. What we leave in God's hands is safe, for God knows when we are wrong or how we are wrong. And God loves us enough to give us bread, even though we may be humbly and persistently pleading for a stone.

PSALM 81   MORNING SECOND THURSDAY

(80) 81. A festal song for harvest time

> 2 Ring out your joy to God our strength,
>   shout in triumph to the God of Jacob.
>
> 3 Raise a song and sound the timbrel,
>   the sweet-sounding harp and the lute;
> 4 blow the trumpet at the new moon,
>   when the moon is full, on our feast.
>
> 5 For this is Israel's law,
>   a command of the God of Jacob,
> 6 imposed as a law on Joseph's people,
>   when they went out against the land of Egypt.
>
>   A voice I did not know said to me:
> 7 "I freed your shoulder from the burden;
>   your hands were freed from the load.
> 8 You called in distress and I saved you.

28. Canto 33, vv. 1ff.

I answered, concealed in the storm cloud;
at the waters of Meribah I tested you.
⁹ Listen, my people, to my warning.
O Israel, if only you would heed!

¹⁰ Let there be no foreign god among you,
no worship of an alien god.
¹¹ I am the LORD your God,
who brought you from the land of Egypt.
Open wide your mouth and I will fill it.

¹² But my people did not heed my voice
and Israel would not obey,
¹³ so I left them in their stubbornness of heart
to follow their own designs.

¹⁴ O that my people would heed me,
that Israel would walk in my ways!
¹⁵ At once I would subdue their foes,
turn my hand against their enemies.

¹⁶ The LORD's enemies would cringe at their feet
and their subjection would last for ever.
But Israel I would feed with finest wheat
and fill them with honey from the rock."

God of our ancestors, we confess that you brought Israel out of Egypt and formed them into your people, and that through Jesus Christ you have given us a share in their covenant. Open our hearts to hear and obey you readily, lest we find ourselves choosing to place something else ahead of you.

PSALM 72   EVENING SECOND THURSDAY

(71) 72. The kingdom of peace

¹ O God, give your judgement to the king,
to a king's son your justice,
² that he may judge your people in justice
and your poor in right judgement.

³ May the mountains bring forth peace for the people
and the hills, justice.
⁴ May he defend the poor of the people
and save the children of the needy
(and crush the oppressor).

⁵ He shall endure like the sun and the moon
    from age to age.
⁶ He shall descend like rain on the meadow,
    like raindrops on the earth.

⁷ In his days justice shall flourish
    and peace till the moon fails.
⁸ He shall rule from sea to sea,
    from the Great River to earth's bounds.

⁹ Before him his enemies shall fall,
    his foes lick the dust.
¹⁰ the kings of Tarshish and the seacoasts
    shall pay him tribute.

The kings of Sheba and Seba
    shall bring him gifts.
¹¹ Before him all rulers shall fall prostrate,
    all nations shall serve him.

¹² For he shall save the poor when they cry
    and the needy who are helpless.
¹³ He will have pity on the weak
    and save the lives of the poor.

¹⁴ From oppression he will rescue their lives,
    to him their blood is dear.
¹⁵ (Long may he live,
    may the gold of Sheba be given him.)
They shall pray for him without ceasing
    and bless him all the day.

¹⁶ May corn be abundant in the land
    to the peaks of the mountains.
May its fruit rustle like Lebanon;
    may people flourish in the cities
    like grass on the earth.

¹⁷ May his name be blessed for ever
    and endure like the sun.
Every tribe shall be blessed in him,
    all nations bless his name.

¹⁸ Blessed be the LORD, the God of Israel,
    who alone works wonders,

¹⁹ ever blessed God's glorious name.
Let his glory fill the earth.

Amen! Amen!

Year after year while there was a king in Jerusalem, this prayer was sung for the king, likely at such an annual feast as the New Year. It was sung for a hero like Hezekiah or Josiah, for a scoundrel like Manasseh or Jehoiakim, for a well-meaning but weak ruler like Ahaz or Zedekiah.

We are perhaps so used to hearing this psalm appropriated as an Epiphany text that it sounds to Christians like a prediction of Christ: "The kings of Tarshish and the seacoasts shall pay him tribute. The kings of Sheba and Seba shall bring him gifts. . . . may the gold of Sheba be given him." "He shall endure like the sun and the moon from age to age." (vv. 10, 15, 5). But in fact, granted the Semitic tendency to exaggeration, everything in the psalm makes perfect sense as a prayer for the reigning king. The concerns are just typical concerns for the monarch, long life, justice, victory, and prosperity.

"Long may he live," they prayed (v. 15). There were always, of course, those who would rather the king be gathered soon to his ancestors, but it was not such persons who were asked to prepare the royal liturgies. And generally a long reign was good for the people as a whole, as kings' deaths often brought instability, and whenever the mighty are fighting for power, little people get crushed under their feet.

"Give judgment to the king . . . that he may judge your people in justice and your poor in right judgment" (v. 1). The king was not thought of as making new laws but as applying the traditional law, and seeing to the adjudication of disputes. Both of these tasks gave ample opportunity either to promote peace and stability through impartiality or to enrich oneself, one's family and supporters through graft and inappropriate judgments from which there could be no appeal. The concern is especially for the poor and weak (vv. 4, 12-14), for as Benedict says in his Rule (concerning guests), the rich can shift for themselves. This special responsibility of the king for the defenseless was not invented by Israel; already in ancient Mesopotamia Hammurabi claimed, "In order that the strong might not oppress the weak, that justice might be dealt the orphan (and) the widow [I proclaimed my code]" ("Code of Hammurabi," reverse xxiv:60ff., *ANET* 178).

The prayer asks for victory. Kings who get sizable payments of tribute (vv. 10, 11) can afford to make lighter demands on their own people. Besides, David's expansion of the kingdom to a respectable empire over surrounding nations was ever afterward considered normative: when the Philistines or Moab had returned to their original independence, in Israel this was considered rebellion (Psalm 2), and reconquest would be blessed by Yahweh. The reestablishment of an empire will inspire even distant wealthy nations such as Tarshish, Sheba, and Seba to participate in the exchange of gifts characteristic of friendly nations.[29]

Prosperity will follow on the fertility of the land (v. 16). Related to this seems to be the odd language of verse 6: "He shall descend like rain on the meadow, like raindrops on the earth," which expresses an understanding of the king as source of the nation's fertility. In a world of irregular rainfall[30] and primitive transportation, a shortfall of rain always brought hunger and often starvation. It also could drive small landowners to debt and eventually to the loss of their land.

All these wishes are found within prayer addressed to Yahweh. For the kind of kingship described here is not found in the course of things; if a reign is to be prosperous and benign, this is God's gift.

Well, we don't have kings, and in countries that do have kings, they no longer have the role of the ancient king. If sovereignty rests with the people, as democratic theory would have it, then whether a nation has an option for the poor depends on whom we elect to the legislature, to congress, to parliament.

But actually, long before this psalm was canonized as part of the Bible, Israel had been without a king. Almost six hundred years before Christ the last king of David's line was sent into exile. Doubtless at first the Jews preserved the hymn in order to have the right prayers to perform when the monarchy would be restored. But when there still was no king centuries later, they began to read the old hymns differently. They became prophecies of the King to come, who would make things right between Israel and God. The Jews realized that no king had brought the blessings predicted by the old songs. Even if for a while there was victory, prosperity, justice for the poor, it had certainly not lasted "like the sun and moon from age to age." They began to look to the future.

That is where the Christians got the idea of praying the psalm in terms of the Messiah. It was already a Jewish idea before them. The title "Christ" is an allusion to this Jewish hope for a king who would finally make things right between Israel and God. In some ways it is unfortunate that for Christians "Christ" became the principal title of Jesus. For Jesus and the Gospels used many other traditions to help them make sense of Jesus: the suffering servant of Deutero-Isaiah, the innocent sufferer of the psalms, the sacrificial lamb, the Word of God and the Wisdom of God, the new Adam.

29. See the visit of the Queen of Sheba in 1 Kings 10:1-10.

30. While Jerusalem has the same average rainfall as London or Collegeville, Minnesota, one year differs greatly from another.

Even so, this psalm truly expresses some of what Christ does insofar as his kingdom is already present, albeit imperfectly, wherever people find that the call of the gospel makes sense and strive to build a society according to its vision. And it anticipates what Christ will bring about in that eschatological kingdom for which we pray daily in the Lord's Prayer.

Insofar as the praying of Psalm 72 is a prayer for the coming of Christ's kingdom, it becomes a prayer for all who have any responsibility to bring about the reign of peace and justice. It becomes a prayer for leaders of nations, and indeed for those who elect them. It becomes a prayer also for those who lead us in the Church or even in a religious community. Not that they are in any way kings. But the prayer is for the realization of Christ's kingdom; and the teaching and decisions of pope and bishops, of abbots and superiors, yes, of editors and teachers, have much to do with whether the gospel has any chance at all.

PSALM 51   MORNING SECOND FRIDAY

See above, p. 53, Morning First Friday.

PSALM 147:12-20   MORNING SECOND AND FOURTH FRIDAY

PSALM 147:1-11   MORNING FOURTH THURSDAY

It's not entirely arbitrary that the Liturgy of the Hours divides Psalm 147 into two sections, to be prayed on different days. In this it follows the ancient Septuagint and Vulgate translations, which followed a tradition that considered this psalm to be two prayers. Each half of the psalm does have its own structure and could stand alone as a prayer, though the two parts also share similar themes, and both seem to date from after the Exile (vv. 2, 13f.).

The prayers are both hymns, consisting, therefore, of invitation to praise and reasons for praise. Among the reasons given by both are political-military protection (vv. 2, 10f.; 13a, 14a) and fertility (vv. 8; 13b, 14). We will look first separately at each section of the psalm as it was prayed in antiquity, and then will consider how we can make it our prayer.

PSALM 147A (VV. 1-11)

(146) 147. A song of thanksgiving

¹   Alleluia!

> Sing praise to the LORD who is good;
> sing to our God who is loving:
> to God our praise is due.

2   The LORD builds up Jerusalem
    and brings back Israel's exiles,
3   God heals the broken-hearted,
    and binds up all their wounds.
4   God fixes the number of the stars;
    and calls each one by its name.

5   Our Lord is great and almighty;
    God's wisdom can never be measured.
6   The LORD raises the lowly;
    and humbles the wicked to the dust.
7   O sing to the LORD, giving thanks;
    sing psalms to our God with the harp.

8   God covers the heavens with clouds,
    and prepares the rain for the earth;
    making mountains sprout with grass
    and with plants to serve our needs.
9   God provides the beasts with their food
    and the young ravens when they cry.

10 God takes no delight in horses' power
    nor pleasure in warriors' strength.
11 The LORD delights in those who revere him,
    in those who wait for his love.

"Praise the Lord for he is good . . . for he is loving." Lest the praise become self-congratulatory, the goodness and love of Yahweh are immediately defined by God's care for the helpless: bringing back Israel's exiles, binding up wounds, raising the lowly. It is true that the prayer glories in some kind of political restoration (the rebuilding—and refortifying—of Jerusalem, the return of the exiles). But verses 10-11, which were originally meant to express contempt for the self-assurance of the great powers that have subdued God's people, serve also to warn against any supposition that the way to true recovery is in emulating the military prowess of the great nations. If Israel is to know peace, it is by the blessing that Yahweh gives to those who put their trust in him rather than in their armaments, their horses, and the strength of their soldiers. For Yahweh is powerful to help. If God has power over the stars and has the wisdom to know each of those myriads by name, beside all that it is but a little thing to bind up the wounds of the brokenhearted, to raise the lowly, and to humble the wicked.

Even in praising God's gifts of fertility, the psalm avoids any spirit of self-congratulation, for the rain that God pours on the mountains is not destined specifically for Israel, not even just for human beings, but for the beasts of the field and the ravens of the air.[31]

Yet none of this is expressed by way of a lesson. The psalm is an exhortation to praise God, not to think about God and self in certain ways. The psalm affects the attitudes of those who use it only insofar as it determines what they will pray about and what will remain unmentioned. In the long run this is perhaps a more effective way of forming attitudes, for issues are never presented directly to the worshiper to accept or to refute. The psalm does not confront you by asking, for instance, "What makes you think the whole world is meant to serve you?" To do so would invite a reasoned response that would surely be informed by prejudice and arrogant passion. On the other hand, to thank God in the same breath for the plants that serve human needs and for the food of the beasts and young ravens suggests gently and playfully that we are all creatures together.[32]

PSALM 147B (VV. 12-20)

(147) 147B. In praise of God the Almighty

12 O praise the LORD, Jerusalem!
    Zion, praise your God!

13 God has strengthened the bars of your gates,
    and has blessed the children within you;
14 has established peace on your borders,
    and feeds you with finest wheat.

15 God sends out word to the earth
    and swiftly runs the command.
16 God showers down snow white as wool,
    and scatters hoarfrost like ashes.

17 God hurls down hailstones like crumbs,
    and causes the waters to freeze.
18 God sends forth a word and it melts them:
    at the breath of God's mouth the waters flow.

---

31. In fact, in the Hebrew there is no relationship at all between the rain and humanity. The phrase in verse 8 of the Grail translation, "and with plants to serve man's/our needs," is supplied from the Septuagint, which may, however, have retained a phrase that has accidentally fallen out of the Hebrew manuscript tradition.

32. The whole theme of Walter Brueggemann's *Israel's Praise: Doxology Against Idolatry and Ideology* (Philadelphia: Fortress, 1988) is that by interpreting ambiguous experience, liturgy creates the world we live in.

¹⁹ God makes his word known to Jacob,
to Israel his laws and decrees.
²⁰ God has not dealt thus with other nations;
has not taught them divine decrees.

Alleluia!

The address to Jerusalem with which this prayer starts is even more dramatic in Hebrew, for the verbs and pronouns are all feminine singular,[33] since in Hebrew the word for "city" is feminine, as are the names of most cities, just as the names of tribes are masculine. It is true that in addressing the city one might still have used a plural verb to indicate an address to all the inhabitants, but the personification of the city suggests that the city is thought of as having a reality that is not just the sum of all the individuals who inhabit it.

Much like Psalm 147A, this prayer gives thanks, but very briefly, for political and military protection ("God has strengthened the bars of your gates . . . has established peace on your borders"—vv. 13a, 14a) and fertility ("[God] has blessed the children within you . . . and feeds you with finest wheat"—vv. 13b, 14b).

What follows in verses 15-18 sounds at first as if it is developing only the theme of fertility: as in verses 8-9 of Psalm 147A, the rain nourishes the crops that feed us. The psalm delightfully uses almost all the available vocabulary for the freezing water of the impressive and infrequent winter storm, the snow and hail, the frost and ice; but the emphasis is on how they all obediently hearken to the summons of God's word (in both the first and last verses of the section). It thus turns out that the language about the weather has served as an introduction to the final motive given for praise. The effective word that controls the weather is also the word that Yahweh has given to his people in Torah. While the earlier motives for praise have mentioned the kind of thing for which all the national gods of the Middle East were responsible, Torah is God's gift uniquely to Israel.

And Torah is indeed a gift. It is better to know God's will than not to know it. And of all the nations, it is only to Israel that God has given this gift.

A key to how we might pray this psalm is found in the Roman liturgy, which, following old tradition, prays Psalm 147 for the Dedication of a Church, a feast that looks beyond the church building to the mystery of the congregation that gathers there. This liturgy picks up imagery of the Book of Revelation, identifying the Church as the *Urbs Ierusalem beata,* the "blessed

---

33. Yes, in Hebrew second-person forms are differentiated by gender as well as number.

city Jerusalem." To claim Jerusalem as our mother is not to deny Jerusalem to the Jews; on the contrary, it is to acknowledge that our knowledge of God comes from the Jewish people.

As for Jews, even they cannot pray this psalm simply as it was prayed in ancient times, for even if they pray it in Israel, addressing their people in the city of Jerusalem, in view of the claims of Arab Muslims and Christians on the Holy City, the prayer will take on a polemical character that it did not have for those who first proclaimed it. How rightly Heraclitus said, you cannot step into the same river twice.[34]

We pray, then, in praise of the God from whom every good gift comes, the God who reaches down to us in our frailty, from whom all that we receive is grace, the God whose love is poured out abundantly on all, on the beasts of the field, on the young ravens, and on us. If at times your heart stretches beyond the gifts of security and fertility that can be seen—well, all these other things are God's gifts as well. In fact, you are only doing what the psalm itself does in 147B, where the fertility motif of the rain suggests the transcendent gift of Torah!

And when you pray 147B (more frequently than 147A, be it noted, if you pray the Liturgy of the Hours), you thank God above all for the word that God has revealed to Israel. Now, when you do so, you are already thanking God for Christ, for as Christians we believe that the Word made flesh is not another word than the word already spoken through the prophets' vision, the word of wisdom, the word announced in Torah. In Jesus that ancient vision and wisdom and will of God in its full richness has become incarnate. It is only the feebleness of our own sight that fails to see in him the fullness of God's revelation.

And for us it is above all in Jesus rather than in the prescriptions of Torah that we recognize God's will for us; more than following a set of rules, we are called to follow Christ, who is both gentler and more demanding than the first laws and decrees when he summarizes all the Law and the Prophets in personal terms, in love of God without limits and love of neighbor like love of self. And the One whom we strive to follow has himself reached glory only through paths of obedience that led through rejection and shame, suffering and death. When we give thanks for God's word, we praise God for that Word who in compassion has come to lead the way before us.

---

34. I know that he said this more subtly (or obscurely), but it wouldn't be as dramatic if I quoted it exactly.

PSALM 121 EVENING SECOND FRIDAY

(120) 121. The Lord, our protector: a pilgrimage song

¹ I lift up my eyes to the mountains;
  from where shall come my help?
² My help shall come from the LORD
  who made heaven and earth.

³ May God never allow you to stumble!
  Let your guard not sleep.
⁴ Behold, neither sleeping nor slumbering,
  Israel's guard.

⁵ The LORD is your guard and your shade;
  and stands at your right.
⁶ By day the sun shall not smite you
  nor the moon in the night.

⁷ The LORD will guard you from evil,
  and will guard your soul.
⁸ The LORD will guard your going and coming
  both now and for ever.

From Friday evening of the second week of the psalm-cycle in the Liturgy of the Hours to the end of the third week, except for the weekend, most of the psalms for Evening Prayer are taken from Psalms 120 to 134. These are known as the "gradual psalms" or "songs of ascent," after a term in the title of each which means "a song of the steps," or the like. As is the case with many of these ancient titles, the phrase comes without a context and so is obscure to us. The explanations that some commentators give with considerable confidence I find more ingenious than convincing.

Whatever the title means, these psalms do have some common characteristics. Generally they like to repeat words in successive lines: "my help," vv. 1b, 2a; "sleep not," vv. 3b, 4a; "guard," vv. 4b, 5a, 7ab, 8a; in Psalm 122: "Jerusalem," vv. 2b, 3a; "tribes," v. 4ab; "peace," vv. 6ab, 7ab; etc. These psalms somehow have a compelling attractiveness. I find, curiously enough, that when I allow my students freely to choose which psalm they will treat in exegesis, a disproportionate number will make their choice from these psalms.

It is also characteristic of these psalms that they don't fit the typical psalm categories of laments, hymns, and thanksgiving psalms. As a consequence, it is hard, sometimes, to imagine how they were performed. A rabbinic tradition seems to have associated them with a series of steps between the Court of the Women and the Court of the Gentiles in the Jerusalem Temple (Middot 2:5), and Origen is said to have claimed that they were customarily sung by pilgrims going to Jerusalem.[35]

Psalm 121 is apparently spoken in two voices: the "I" of verses 1-2 would seem to be the same person who is addressed as "you" (singular) in verses 3-8.

"I lift my eyes to the mountains" (v. 1a), presumably of Judea, where Yahweh dwells on Mount Zion; "from where shall come my help?" (v. 1b). As a rhetorical question, this can express frustration and distress, corrected by the following line; or it can be simply an introduction to the expression of confidence, "Where else but from Yahweh?" This identification of God as the great maker of heaven and earth confesses his power to save. In response to this, another voice pronounces a blessing (May your guard protect you and not sleep, v. 3), which is then followed by a confession or an oracle that God will indeed provide protection.

Who is the speaker of verses 1-2—an individual or one who speaks in the name of Israel? Who pronounces the blessing of verse 3 and the assurances of verses 4ff.—simply the chanter? or a priest? or a prophet? Some of these ambiguities surely come about because a psalm that was once used in one way was later reused by different persons for different purposes.

In fact, the very uncertainties in some ways help you to keep the prayer fresh. You can pray it now in one way, now in another. You can identify with the first voice and hear the blessing wished upon you, or you can respond to the first voice as that of an individual or of a whole community, of the whole Church, even in verse 1 as the desperate cry "From where shall come my help?" of those who do not know how to answer "My help shall come from the LORD."

The assurance of divine care has always been expressed in suggestive imagery that largely defies straightforward explanation. What are the dangers from sun and moon? Are they sunstroke and madness? Or the powers of hostile gods? Or is this simply assurance that though all the universe be against you, the Guard of Israel will protect you?

We know, of course, from experience that God's protection is no sweet and gentle thing. God's protection of Jesus and of the martyrs came only through the grave. There is always the danger—but also the hope—that God's deliverance will come to us in the same way. After all, the psalm was traditionally prayed in the Office for the Dead.

---

35. Cited without any further reference in John Mason Neale and R. F. Littledale, *A Commentary on the Psalms from Primitive and Medieval Writers,* vol. 4 (London: Joseph Masters, 1883²; reprinted New York: AMS Press, 1976).

PSALM 116:1-9   EVENING SECOND FRIDAY

PSALM 116:10-19   EVE OF THIRD SUNDAY

(114) 116. Prayer of one saved from death

¹   Alleluia!

I love the LORD, for the LORD has heard
the cry of my appeal.
²   The Lord was attentive to me
in the day when I called.

³   They surrounded me, the snares of death,
with the anguish of the tomb;
they caught me, sorrow and distress.
⁴   I called on the LORD's name.

O LORD, my God, deliver me!

⁵   How gracious is the LORD, and just;
our God has compassion.
⁶   The LORD protects the simple hearts;
I was helpless so God saved me.

⁷   Turn back, my soul, to your rest
for the LORD has been good,
⁸   and has kept my soul from death,
(my eyes from tears,)
my feet from stumbling.

⁹   I will walk in the presence of the LORD
in the land of the living.

(115) A promise in gratitude to God

¹⁰   I trusted, even when I said:
"I am sorely afflicted,"
¹¹   and when I said in my alarm:
"There is no one I can trust."

¹²   How can I repay the LORD
for his goodness to me?
¹³   The cup of salvation I will raise;
I will call on the LORD's name.

¹⁴   My vows to the LORD I will fulfill
before all the people.

¹⁵　O precious in the eyes of the LORD
is the death of the faithful.

¹⁶　Your servant, LORD, your servant am I;
you have loosened my bonds.

¹⁷　A thanksgiving sacrifice I make;
I will call on the LORD's name.

¹⁸　My vows to the LORD I will fulfill
before all the people,

¹⁹　in the courts of the house of the LORD,
in your midst, O Jerusalem.

The Israelite who was in trouble from sickness, in battle, in disputes with neighbors, or from false accusations was likely to make a vow to offer a sacrifice to Yahweh if she or he got through unharmed.[36] Psalm 116 is a prayer to be used at the time of such a sacrifice in order to identify the purpose of the offering. Given the variety of things for which one might offer thanks, it is not surprising that the psalm does not indicate very specific circumstances of the deliverance (verses 3, 6), for it was meant to be used by anyone who had a sacrificial vow to fulfill.

The whole section verses 12-19 is simply an elaborate way of declaring, "What I am doing, I do to fulfill a vow by offering a sacrifice in thanksgiving to Yahweh for saving my life." Two rites of the ceremony are mentioned: the drink-offering (Num 15:1-10) and the sacrifice proper:

The cup of salvation I will raise;	A thanksgiving sacrifice I make;
I will call on the Lord's name.	I will call on the Lord's name.
My vows to the Lord I will fulfill . . .	My vows to the Lord I will fulfill
before all his people (vv. 13-14).	before all his people (vv. 17-18).

Verses 15-16, set off as in a frame by these two descriptions of the rite, are the confession of the reason for the sacrifice, deliverance from death:

O precious in the eyes of the Lord
is the death of his faithful.
Your servant, Lord, your servant am I;
you have loosened my bonds.[37]

36. That such vows were sometimes made by women is indicated by the legislation of Numbers 30:3ff.

37. These lines have the same structure as the confession of verses 5-6: (a) an affirmation about Yahweh's care for certain persons; (b) an affirmation about self that corresponds to the objects of Yahweh's care; (c) confession that God rescued the psalmist:

They begin with a description of God's love of his servants, and only then tell how this merciful God has helped the servant who now prays. The expression "precious . . . is the death of his faithful" does not mean what the liturgical use implies, that God is pleased with the heroism or fidelity shown by the death of the martyrs but rather that the faithful are too precious to Yahweh to let them die! Compare the equivalent passage in Psalm 72:14: "From oppression [the King] will rescue their lives, / to him their blood is *dear*" (Hebrew *"precious,"* as in Psalm 116:15).

Not even Jews have been paying vows with animal sacrifice in Jerusalem for a couple of millennia, much less Christians.[38] Still, the use of the psalm in the Office for the Dead, on feasts of the Lord (Holy Thursday, Good Friday, Corpus Christi), and on feasts of saints (apostles and martyrs) shows that Christians have thought they had reason to pray it, in most cases because the deliverance from death was seen to be realized in the resurrection of Christ or the grace-filled afterlife of the deceased Christian or of the saint.

This kind of reading begins with Christian experience rather than with the text. While God had not prevented the Christian, the saint, even Jesus, from dying, the experience of the disciples with the risen Christ and the faith of Christians told them that God had brought victory out of defeat, glorious life out of death. For this gracious gift Christians wanted to give thanks. They did so first of all in the *Eucharistia,* which, as its name indicates, was the great "thanksgiving" for salvation in the mystery of Jesus' passion and resurrection. But, like the Israelite before them searching for words to give thanks for recovery from sickness or acquittal from false accusations, they also searched the old sacred songs for words to express their gratitude. And when they found this psalm, the words sprang to new life on their lips, yet in profound continuity with their old use.

How gracious is the Lord, and just;	(a)
our God has compassion.	
The Lord protects simple hearts;	
I was helpless	(b)
so he saved me.	(c)

Note that "simple hearts" describes not good but needy persons: the "simple" in Proverbs are the immature who are in need of instruction, encouragement, even rebuke, but are not yet "fools," that is, not yet hardened in folly and so beyond hope.

38. Well, actually, near Jerusalem in the town of Tayibeh, Christians do vow a sheep to St. George when they are in trouble. If all goes well they take the sheep to the ruins of the old Church of Saint George, kill it, and smear the blood on the doorpost in the shape of a cross. The flesh they give to a poor person. The rite clearly goes back to Israelite and even Canaanite practices. But the way they explain it differs: the gift is given to St. George, and the action culminates in a charitable gift to the poor rather than a sacred meal.

We likewise seek to find words for our gratitude for our experiences of deliverance from death. Whatever represents death for me can become the theme of the song—a brush with serious sickness, the life-devouring tedium of a meaningless job, the darkness of depression, the self-destructiveness of a life yielded over to greed, self-indulgence, lust, hatred, hypocrisy. If I have been rescued from any of these things, I truly need words to express my marvel and my gratitude. It would be hard to find better than these, for from the beginning the distress and the deliverance were described in images that allowed the poem to be used by anyone who had been saved from death.

But I need not limit my gratitude to the events of my personal story. The story of Christ's resurrection is also mine; it is, in fact, Christ's resurrection that is realized in all these stories of my salvation. Moreover, to us who have been given the gift of knowing the power of Christ's resurrection belongs the privilege of finding words of gratitude on behalf of those who know not whence their deliverance came.[39]

PSALM 92   MORNING SECOND SATURDAY

This psalm will be treated under Morning Fourth Saturday.

PSALM 8   MORNING SECOND AND FOURTH SATURDAY

8. *Divine glory and human dignity*

²   How great is your name, O LORD our God,
    through all the earth!

   Your majesty is praised above the heavens;
³ on the lips of children and of babes
   you have found praise to foil your enemy,
   to silence the foe and the rebel.

⁴ When I see the heavens, the work of your hands,
   the moon and the stars which you arranged,
⁵ what are we that you should keep us in mind,
   mere mortals that you care for us?

---

39. In the Septuagint the psalm is divided into two separate prayers, verses 1-9 and verses 10-19, and in the Liturgy of the Hours these two prayers are assigned to different days. But even those of us who are bound to the Liturgy of the Hours would probably not risk damnation by praying the whole psalm on the Friday of Week 2, and saying Psalm 121 the next evening instead of Friday.

⁶ Yet you have made us little less than gods;
    and crowned us with glory and honor,
⁷ you gave us power over the work of your hands,
    put all things under our feet.

⁸ All of them, sheep and cattle,
    yes, even the savage beasts,
⁹ birds of the air, and fish
    that make their way through the waters.

¹⁰ How great is your name, O LORD our God,
    through all the earth!

Surely one of the all-time favorites among the psalms,[40] Psalm 8 was in its origins perhaps not as "nice" as it now sounds to us. For the phrase of verse 3, which sounds quite out of place to us, "to foil your enemy, to silence the foe and the rebel," may well be the key to an understanding of the original use of the psalm. The text of the end of verse 2 and verse 3 is too obscure in Hebrew to really reconstruct how the psalm originally read; the translation of the Liturgy of the Hours, which essentially follows the reading of the Septuagint, is not very convincing. But these verses contain a fair amount of creation language (cf. vv. 4-9), which may reflect a much earlier use. Thus allusions to "heaven and earth," "founding,"[41] and to the enemies may be an allusion to the cosmic struggle of creation, common throughout the ancient Middle East and often alluded to in Scripture (see the allusions to Leviathan, Rahab, the serpents, found in various combinations in Job 9:13; 26:12; Pss 74:13; 80:11; Isa 51:9).

We cannot with any confidence reconstruct the whole ancient use of the psalm. Erhard Gerstenberger may be right in attributing it to small Jewish congregations in the postexilic era striving to affirm their human worth in the face of Gentile domination and even persecution. In any case, in its present

---

40. It was even printed among the poetic selections of my eighth-grade literature anthology some decades ago, though you may be sure that at Central Junior High our teacher did not breach the high wall between Church and State by letting us read it. Of course in those days it would have been the Catholic priests who would have protested our being subjected to a reading from a Protestant Bible.

41. The translation of the Liturgy of the Hours badly errs in translating "On the lips of children and of babes / you have *found* praise. . . ." The Hebrew reads, literally, "you have *founded* [established, set firm] praise." Thus, while the Hebrew makes it clear that the praise is God's accomplishment, the Liturgy of the Hours suggests that it is only God's happy discovery of what already inheres in the innocent children. But there's not a hint of such Pelagianism in the Hebrew!

form of the psalm expresses an understanding that simply by praising God for the creation of humanity, the prayer itself constitutes a kind of counterattack on God's enemies.

And even now the psalm still does that, whether we realize it reflexively or not. For to pray the psalm is to affirm a view of humanity that is, in fact, deeply subversive to every way of looking at human persons that would undermine their dignity, a challenge to every materialism that would reduce human beings to consuming units or producing units or fighting units. I remember my puzzlement at news reports of battles when I was a child during the Second World War.[42] They would report the "casualty" figures, which lumped together dead and wounded—whoever would not be able to continue to fight. But I innocently thought that there was a considerable difference between being wounded or being dead, and thought the numbers should distinguish.

To pray this psalm is a subversion also of every legalism or formalism, every exploitation of Christians that would forget that the gospel is meant for human beings. An overriding principle of canon law is "*Suprema lex salus hominum*—The highest law is the salvation of human beings." Yet how often we have failed to observe this in fact!

This psalm illustrates some of the problematic of translating Scripture in gender-inclusive language. Whatever may be the pastoral necessity at this point of using such language, in liturgy for instance,[43] the exclusive use of such translations cannot help but impoverish our understanding of the old texts. Let us look at an example. The Inclusive Language Version, based on the Grail translation (that of the Liturgy of the Hours) and published by GIA Publications, uses first-person plural forms in verses 5 and 7: "What are we that you should keep us in mind?" "[You have] put all things under our feet." Sentiments that are fair enough and true enough. But we have lost the concreteness of the Grail's "What is man that you should keep him in mind?" "[You have] put all things under his feet." With the Grail translation, which closely corresponds to the Hebrew, the mind is constantly moving from the

---

42. About the time we skipped over Psalm 8 in our anthology.

43. You will note that I generally use inclusive language, even in reference to God, except when describing the thought of the ancients, where such language would distort their categories of thought. But one may hope that the issue will eventually lose its urgency (perhaps from the day when a future pope ordains a woman as bishop?). We do well to remember a similar problem in the early Church. The central role of the Jews in the ancient Scriptures was generally not a stumbling block to Gentiles (the Marcionites are a notable exception) insofar as they learned to hear the old words as the story of their origins and to identify the old words as being addressed to themselves as metaphors of their own experience.

image of the first human being to that of human beings as a whole, to that of each individual or of any individual person. Such concrete ambiguity is precisely characteristic of poetry and is behind the rich variety of ways in which the psalm has been prayed and is prayed. One could go a long way by translating it something like "What is man that you keep him in mind, woman that you care for her?" Such a rendering explicitly reflects the Genesis creation account that stands behind the poem: "God created man in his image; in the image of God he created him; male and female he created them" (Gen 1:27)[44] and continues with God's instruction: "Have dominion over the fish of the sea and the birds of the air, and the living creatures that crawl on the ground." But it misses a specific character of this poem, that unlike the Genesis writer, who switches back and forth between singular and plural, the poet here consistently uses the singular. The ambiguity between the general and the particular is clearly deliberate and is part of the charm for those who can abandon themselves to the poet's vision.

And, in fact, those who have gone before us in faith were not deceived by terms like "man" and "him" into thinking that the psalm was only about males, for they used the psalm regularly in the Offices of the Mother of God and of any holy woman! They also used the psalm on numerous feasts of the Lord—Ascension, Trinity, Transfiguration, Finding of the Cross—doubtless in part because of New Testament writers, who saw the psalm as a prediction of Christ (Heb 2:6-8; 1 Cor 15:27; Eph 2:22). But even if we take seriously the meaning of the psalm itself, there is justification in praying it specifically in reference to Christ. For if you can legitimately pray the psalm marveling at God's graciousness to you, or in reference to a new baby, in reference to a woman you admire, in awe at a human achievement in technology, can you not pray it in reference to the One in whom humanity reaches perfection with no distortion of sin and folly?

---

44. In Hebrew this word "man," *'adam,* is, like the German word *Mensch,* not gender-specific; it is used to refer to both men and women, and there is no corresponding feminine noun as there is for other words for human beings: *'ish* and *'ishah, gever* and *geveret.* But the pronouns in this verse for both "him" and "them" are, in the Hebrew, pronouns of the "common" gender. This means that they are used in circumstances in which they can refer simultaneously to both men and women or potentially to either males for females. However, exactly the same pronouns can also be used in specific contexts to distinguish men from women. In that sense they are just like the traditional English pronouns of the common gender, "he/him/his."

THIRD WEEK

PSALM 113   EVE OF THIRD SUNDAY

(112) 113. In praise of God's goodness

¹ Alleluia!

Praise, O servants of the LORD,
praise the name of the LORD!
² May the name of the LORD be blessed
both now and for evermore!
³ From the rising of the sun to its setting
praised be the name of the LORD!

⁴ High above all nations is the LORD,
above the heavens God's glory.
⁵ Who is like the LORD, our God,
the one enthroned on high,
⁶ who stoops from the heights to look down,
to look down upon heaven and earth?

⁷ From the dust God lifts up the lowly,
from the dungheap God raises the poor
⁸ to set them in the company of rulers,
yes, with the rulers of the people.
⁹ To the childless wife God gives a home
and gladdens her heart with children.

Out of the depths of destitution and contempt, voices cry in distress. And from afar you hear and come to their aid. Oh, for this we praise you, our God!

PSALM 116:10-19   EVE OF THIRD SUNDAY

This psalm was treated above for Evening Second Friday (p. 119).

PSALM 93   MORNING THIRD SUNDAY

(92) 93. God, king of the world

> ¹ The LORD is king, with majesty enrobed;
> the LORD is robed with might,
> and girded round with power.
>
> The world you made firm, not to be moved;
> ² your throne has stood firm from of old.
> From all eternity, O Lord, you are.
>
> ³ The waters have lifted up, O LORD,
> the waters have lifted up their voice,
> the waters have lifted up their thunder.
>
> ⁴ Greater than the roar of mighty waters,
> more glorious than the surgings of the sea,
> the LORD is glorious on high.
>
> ⁵ Truly your decrees are to be trusted.
> Holiness is fitting to your house,
> O LORD, until the end of time.

At the Babylonian New Year festival the priests recited the dramatic ancient story of how their god Marduk saved the lives of the gods in a savage battle with the great sea monster Tiamat, and then, splitting her body in two, made from it the earth below and the sky above. In recognition of this exploit, the gods built him a sanctuary, set up his throne, and solemnly acknowledged him as king.

> Let us make humble obeisance at the mention of his name; . . .
> Most exalted be the Son, our avenger;
> let his sovereignty be surpassing, having no rival.[1]

A somewhat similar story was told in Ugarit of their principal god, Baal, who had defeated and dismembered the god of the sea, Yamm, and apparently for that was proclaimed king by the other gods.

---

1. "Enuma Elish" 6:102ff. *ANET* 514, 69.

Many allusions in the Bible suggest that Israel had known some such story about Yahweh. Not that the story is actually told, but that in the language of praise and threat, imagery is applied to Yahweh that seems to reflect a battle with the sea monster of chaos. Thus Psalm 74:13: "It was you who divided the sea by your might, you who shattered the heads of the monsters in the sea"; Job 26:12: "By his power he stilled the sea; by his understanding he smote Rahab"; and Isaiah 51:10f. playing with this same imagery to allude to the Exodus: "Was it not you that cut Rahab in pieces, that pierced the dragon? Was it not you that dried up the sea, the waters of the great deep; that made the depths of the sea a way for the redeemed to pass over?" See also Job 9:13; Pss 74:13f.; 89:9f.; Isa 27:1.

Such memories seem to be reflected in Psalm 93, a hymn exulting in Yahweh's kingship. For a third of the poem is devoted to the turbulent waters,[2] which, however, leave Yahweh and the earth he founded quite unmoved.

The poem begins with the joyous proclamation "Yahweh is king." Expressed in the third person, the phrase may reflect a formula solemnly spoken at the anointing of a new human king, "So-and-so is king!" (cf. 2 Sam 15:10 and 2 Kgs 9:13). But from the second verse the psalm addresses Yahweh mostly in the second person, dwelling on the stability of the world order that Yahweh has established.

That stability is a great gift of Yahweh, for the forces of chaos are constantly threatening to erupt. We in our day have the study of meteorology to give us at least some understanding of what causes droughts; through biology and epidemiology we know a little bit about what causes diseases and how they are spread; even war can be understood to some extent through the social sciences. And we have the impression that our knowledge gives us some kind of control, some ways of averting these disasters or at least of mitigating their effects. The ancients had no such illusions. Nevertheless, with Yahweh as Creator, with Yahweh in control, the earth would never sink into total chaos.

As in Psalms 19 and 147, the psalm goes beyond praise of Yahweh's governance of nature to reflect on God's revelation to Israel. "Truly your decrees are to be trusted.[3] Just as God's conquest of the waters assures the stability of the world, the revelation of God's will to Israel has the power to preserve his people from chaos.

---

2. In Hebrew the "rivers." Note that in the Ugaritic story an epithet of the sea god Yamm is "Judge River."

3. The Hebrew term translated as "decrees" means something like "testimonies" and could conceivably refer to the whole story of God's dealings with Israel. Still, as it is actually used, the word almost always refers to things that are to be done, hence the usual translation "decrees."

Yahweh as king is not a chess player moving inanimate pieces. The king makes things happen by command, by persuasion, by threat, but always through the will of others. Fortresses will be built, wars fought, taxes paid, justice done only if citizens can be convinced to build, fight, pay, and do. If peace and justice, good order and compassion, are to be found in Israel, it can only be through the wise and just laws that Yahweh has given his people and through the story of God's graciousness to them, which inspires their loyalty and obedience.

For us, to pray this psalm is simply to expand the petition "Thy kingdom come" of the Lord's Prayer. And we can pray the psalm honestly, like that petition, only in conjunction with the following petition, "Thy will be done," and only if we commit ourselves to the doing of that will. For not everyone who says "Lord, Lord" shall enter the kingdom of heaven, but the one who does the will of the Father who is in heaven (Matt 7:21).

Far from destroying my freedom, the revelation of God's will enhances it. For freedom is the opportunity to make significant choices. And what choice could be more significant than choosing to reject or to accept the will of the Creator and Master of the universe? Moreover, paradoxically I am never so free as when I lie prostrate in abandonment to God, for when I am wholly given to God, I am free from the coercive power of every human being. And God's will is wholly for my welfare; in God's will is our peace.

True, sometimes it is not clear precisely what God wants of you or me just now. Even so, you know its outline in the command to love the Lord your God with all your heart and all your soul and all your mind, and to love your neighbor as yourself. And you are more likely to find it if you abandon yourself to God's will beforehand, if you search for it in Scripture and in the community of the faithful, than if you just follow your caprice.

The search for God's will, the struggle to do it, is not just a private drama within your heart but is your participation in the great cosmic conflict in which the creative voice of God stills the roaring of the waters of chaos. In this psalm we find words to articulate our desire to stand on God's side in that struggle.

PSALM 148   MORNING THIRD SUNDAY

148. Cosmic praise

1   Alleluia!

> Praise the LORD from the heavens,
> praise God in the heights.

² Praise God, all you angels,
  praise him, all you host.

³ Praise God, sun and moon,
  praise him, shining stars.
⁴ Praise God, highest heavens
  and the waters above the heavens.

⁵ Let them praise the name of the LORD.
  The Lord commanded: they were made.
⁶ God fixed them forever,
  gave a law which shall not pass away.

⁷ Praise the LORD from the earth,
  sea creatures and all oceans,
⁸ fire and hail, snow and mist,
  stormy winds that obey God's word;

⁹ all mountains and hills,
  all fruit trees and cedars,
¹⁰ beasts, wild and tame,
  reptiles and birds on the wing;

¹¹ all earth's nations and peoples,
  earth's leaders and rulers;
¹² young men and maidens,
  the old together with children.

¹³ Let them praise the name of the LORD
  who alone is exalted.
  The splendor of God's name
  reaches beyond heaven and earth.

¹⁴ God exalts the strength of the people,
  is the praise of all the saints,
  of the sons and daughters of Israel,
  of the people to whom he comes close.

Alleluia!

The vast heavens, the unmeasured sea, all feathered birds, all furry beasts and bald, animals with scales or shell inarticulately proclaim the wisdom and power of their Creator. God, fill our hearts with awe and wonder, that with the heavenly choirs we may add our voices to creation's hymn of praise. This we ask in Jesus' name.

ANOTHER PRAYER

Our human voices alone are not equal, God, to the praise that is your due, but we recognize your glory bespoken in the roaring of the sea, the majesty of the mountains, the wisdom of the ants, and the wonder of the newborn child. And so we wish to join with all humanity, with all the off-spring of Abraham, and with all whom you have redeemed, in singing your majesty and your tender love, which you have manifested especially in coming close to us in Torah and in your Word made flesh.

PSALM 110:1-5, 7   EVENING THIRD SUNDAY

This psalm was treated above, p. 13, under Evening First Sunday.

PSALM 111   EVENING THIRD SUNDAY

(110) 111. The great deeds of God

1   Alleluia!

I will thank the LORD with all my heart
in the meeting of the just and their assembly,
2   Great are the works of the LORD,
to be pondered by all who love them.

3   Majestic and glorious God's work,
whose justice stands firm for ever.
4   God makes us remember these wonders.
The LORD is compassion and love.

5   God gives food to those who fear him;
keeps his covenant ever in mind;
6   shows mighty works to his people
by giving them the land of the nations.

7   God's works are justice and truth,
God's precepts are all of them sure,
8   standing firm for ever and ever;
they are made in uprightness and truth.

9   God has sent deliverance to his people
and established his covenant for ever.
Holy is God's name, to be feared.

10   To fear the LORD is the first stage of wisdom;
all who do so prove themselves wise.
God's praise shall last for ever!

The hymns of any period are bound to pick up much of the spirit of the age. Thus, the eighteenth-century hymn "The King of Love My Shepherd Is" is much more personal (some would say sentimental) in its language than the old version of the same psalm in the Scottish Rhymed Psalter, "The Lord's my shepherd, I'll not want." Similarly, Psalm 111 looks for all the world like some of the writings we know from the last centuries before Christ. Like the Wisdom of Jesus ben Sirach and the Wisdom of Solomon,[4] it shows the desire to reflect on the story of Israel's history out of the perspective of wisdom thought. The use of an acrostic as well, with each line beginning with a successive letter of the Hebrew alphabet, is particularly characteristic of late biblical poetry.[5]

The dating of the psalm is perhaps not crucial to an understanding of how it views God and God's people. To wonder about dating, however, does help us to remember that the psalm has its origins within the limitations of a particular moment in Israel's life.

The psalm was proclaimed in temple or synagogue. A singer, on behalf of the congregation or by way of testimony to them, praises their God. The reasons given are for the most part fairly abstract, Yahweh's "works" (vv. 2, 3, 6 [the term was omitted in the version used in the official Liturgy of the Hours, but is restored in the present inclusive language version], 7); "wonders" (v. 4); "justice" (vv. 3, 7); "compassion and love" (v. 4); "covenant" (vv. 5, 9). The most concrete historical allusion is in verse 6, where God has given his people the land of the nations, surely an allusion to the conquest of the land of Canaan. Much less clearly, the wording in Hebrew, "He gives [or 'gave'] *prey* [not just 'food'] to those who fear him," suggests that verse 5 refers not to Israel's daily bread but to the gift of quails in the desert (Exod 16:1-13; Num 11).

Though the thanksgiving expressed here for the mercy and love manifested in God's mighty works is truly humble, when it comes to naming those works concretely the psalm gives thanks first of all for helping us steal our land from the Canaanites! We can, of course, tell ourselves that the whole earth belongs to God, that God can, therefore, take from the Canaanites and give to the Israelites because it all belongs to God anyway. However, even believers, if they read the tale historically, will not be too quick to attribute directly to God what was typically attributed in the ancient Middle East to the gods of each nation. And in fact, among Israel's neighbors conquerors regularly saw their conquests as the gift of their gods, often even reporting the

---

4. Early second and first centuries before Christ, respectively.

5. But note that the acrostic poems of Lamentations date to the sixth century B.C.E. and that Deuteronomy, at about the same period, for all its intense interest in the story of Israel's origins can also use wisdom categories to promote obedience to its law (Deut 4:6; 16:19; 34:9; and the older song of Moses, 32:6, 29).

prior exhortation of the god to go and subjugate the land.[6] The story, then, of Israel's occupation of Canaan is the story of any other desperate landless people seeking a homeland and seizing whatever they are able to secure. That from the beginning they thought this was the command and the gift of their God is the most natural thing in the world.[7]

What is perhaps most remarkable is that Israel's story of desperate land-grabbing was told and retold in a way that became ever more a call to moral responsibility: the God who gave the land to Israel became a God who demanded justice and compassion even toward the slave and the alien, for the children of Israel knew what it was to be slaves and aliens. Psalm 111 cites explicitly that covenant which was not only Yahweh's promise of protection for his people but also his demand of them for justice and compassion (note that verse 7 names his "sure precepts").

When we pray this psalm, we still give thanks for the old story of God's love for Israel, for that story is ours as well. Without Israel there could be no Christ; without Israel we would not know how to begin to name God. Whatever injustice may be bound up in that story is part of our story as well. But God has known how to bring good out of evil.

The psalm dwells not on the specific gifts but on the compassion and love, the justice and fidelity, that inspired God's mighty works. The problem with such abstraction is that by failing to express the gifts as experience knows them, it can fail to engage the heart of the one who prays. The advantage, though, of the abstract is that it can come to express whatever it appropriately describes. When the Jew today prays the psalm, it becomes a thanksgiving not only for the origins of the people but for the incredible tale of their survival in God's covenant. When you say the psalm, it becomes prayer only as your gratitude comes to life through your experience. Christians can hardly help but think of their covenant in the blood of Christ and the gospel's inheritance of the lands of the nations, imperfect as its realization may be.

6. Thus Ka Mose attacked the Hyksos "through the command of Ammon" (*ANET* 232). And, "at the command of my Lord Ashur I (Tiglath-Pileser I) was a conqueror . . . from beyond the lower Zab River to the Upper Sea which (lies toward) the West" (*ANET* 275, cf. *ANET* 268: "Naran Sin in the Cedar Mountain").

7. Now, many historians actually suspect that the origins of Israel came through a much more gradual and peaceful settlement than the Book of Joshua suggests, that small Hebrew agricultural villages grew up between the great Canaanite cities, and that through marriages and strategic alliances many Canaanite settlements came to identify themselves with the worshipers of Yahweh. But this is not the story as it was known to those who prayed this psalm, nor was it for such an irenic process that they intended to give thanks.

Our Christian story, too, has its share of violence, fraud, prejudice, deception, and ignorance, whether we think of the way in which conquest and conversion were linked in Latin America, of repeated persecutions of Jews, or of mission efforts that have sometimes been a problematic mixture of generosity and bribery. But if the work of God is entrusted to human hands, it is bound to be compromised. The marvel is that, despite this, God does bring his gospel to be heard, does bring about conversion of heart and zeal for justice and compassion. And for this we give thanks with all our heart.

PSALM 84   MORNING THIRD MONDAY

(83) 84. Longing for God's temple

² How lovely is your dwelling place,
  LORD, God of hosts.

³ My soul is longing and yearning,
  is yearning for the courts of the LORD.
  My heart and my soul ring out their joy
  to God, the living God.

⁴ The sparrow herself finds a home
  and the swallow a nest for her brood;
  she lays her young by your altars,
  LORD of hosts, my king and my God.

⁵ They are happy, who dwell in your house,
  for ever singing your praise.
⁶ They are happy, whose strength is in you,
  in whose hearts are the roads to Zion.

⁷ As they go through the Bitter Valley
  they make it a place of springs,
  (the autumn rain covers it with blessings).
⁸ They walk with ever growing strength,
  they will see the God of gods in Zion.

⁹ O LORD God of hosts, hear my prayer,
  give ear, O God of Jacob.
¹⁰ Turn your eyes, O God, our shield,
  look on the face of your anointed.

¹¹ One day within your courts
  is better than a thousand elsewhere.

The threshold of the house of God
I prefer to the dwelling of the wicked.

12 For the LORD God is a rampart, a shield.
The LORD will give us favor and glory.
The LORD will not refuse any good
to those who walk without blame.

13 LORD, God of hosts,
happy are those who trust in you!

Let our restless hearts, God, find rest in you. And let those who seek find you in the temple of the Body of Christ, where angels stand in awe and the elders cast themselves down in worship.

PSALM 96   MORNING THIRD MONDAY

(95) 96. God, king and judge of the world

1 O sing a new song to the LORD,
sing to the LORD all the earth.
2 O sing to the LORD, bless his name.

Proclaim God's help day by day,
3 tell among the nations his glory
and his wonders among all the peoples.

4 The LORD is great and worthy of praise,
to be feared above all gods;
5 the gods of the heathens are naught.

It was the LORD who made the heavens.
6 his are majesty and honor and power
and splendor in the holy place.

7 Give the LORD, you families of peoples,
give the LORD glory and power;
8 give the LORD the glory of his name.

Bring an offering and enter God's courts,
9 worship the LORD in the temple.
O earth, stand in fear of the LORD.

10 Proclaim to the nations: "God is king."
The world was made firm in its place;
God will judge the people in fairness.

11 Let the heavens rejoice and earth be glad,
     let the sea and all within it thunder praise,
12 let the land and all it bears rejoice,
     all the trees of the wood shout for joy

13   at the presence of the LORD who comes,
      who comes to rule the earth,
      comes with justice to rule the world,
      and to judge the peoples with truth.

Formally this psalm addresses not Israel but the world: "Sing to the Lord, all the earth" (v. 1); "Give the LORD, you families of peoples . . ." (v. 7). Nonetheless, like the address to the gods in Deutero-Isaiah, "Tell us what is to come hereafter, that we may know that you are gods" (Isa 41:21-24), this hymn was doubtless meant for the sake of Israel and performed in the temple or in early synagogue assemblies. Even in today's rhetoric we will sometimes address persons who are not present. Thus, in the first day of the war against Iraq, January 17, 1991, a speaker in the U.S. House of Representatives addressed the Iraqi president: "Give it up, Saddam. You have no more SCUDs left. Give it up, Saddam. You have virtually no Air Force. Give it up, Saddam. You have had over 50 of your tanks give up and run up the white flag, and the numbers are increasing as the hours go by."[8] The speech was not really meant for transmission to Iraq but to influence votes in the House on a resolution of support for the president and the armed forces in the war. Similarly, it was Israel's vision of God and the world that this psalm was meant to form.

The world that we know is not somehow the raw world in itself but the world as it is interpreted by those with whom we live. The fellow, for instance, who knows only red, yellow, blue, green, purple, and orange will experience colors in a quite different way from the woman who has been socialized to observe and esteem the differences between chartreuse, kelly green, forest green, and aquamarine.[9] Muslim Arabs whom I have known learn since their childhood never to speak about the future without adding "*inshalla* [God willing]" or saying "I want to" rather than "I shall"; they instinctively have a different sense of human fragility and accomplishment from mine. Ideas that are taught by careful argument are probably less effective in forming one's world than are those that are simply presupposed in speech and behavior, for the latter never have to be examined, are literally

8. Michael G. Oxley, *Congressional Record* (January 17, 1991) H535.

9. The example, of course, whether for good or bad, presents a gender-based difference of socialization that is common, though not universal, in our society.

never questioned; but if a question is never raised, there is no chance that a "wrong" answer will be given. Liturgy has a central role in the way communities create the world their members live in.[10]

Whether the address is to the whole predominantly pagan world (vv. 1, 7, 9b) or to those who know and can announce the good news (vv. 2b-3, 10), the message is that Yahweh governs all the earth as king, that before Yahweh the gods of the nations are powerless, that Yahweh will bring about justice by judging all the world. Quite likely the psalm was used liturgically in a feast that celebrated Yahweh's primordial triumph over chaos, whereby he became cosmic King.[11]

Like our feast of Easter, the Israelite feast, by telling the story and perhaps reenacting it symbolically, was not just commemorating an anniversary but was renewing the very primordial events. In that renewal Yahweh triumphed over chaos, was acknowledged as King, and entered upon his reign. Similarly, at Easter we are not just saying, "On this date long ago Jesus rose from the dead," but "Jesus Christ is risen today!"

Israel knows that the praise they offer here and now is not adequate to the triumph they are celebrating. As in Psalm 148 they will call on the heavenly court, the sun and moon, the heavens and earth and seas, to praise their God, so now they call upon the nations. Nor is such praise without a motive. For by conquering chaos Yahweh has vindicated his kingship over all the earth and over whatever gods there may be. The king of Babylon, triumphing in his conquest of Syria, Palestine, and Egypt, may have the delusion that Marduk is king. But in our assembly we have heard again that the king is Yahweh, and we are ready to proclaim it to all the world.

Just how subversive our claim is depends on what we say of Yahweh's kingship. If our claim is that Yahweh makes our armies invincible, Babylon can deal with that; they need only send their brutal soldiers to show us. But if we tell of the God who delivers slaves from Egypt, that is dangerous. In the Philippines under Ferdinand Marcos, in Eastern Europe in 1990, whole populations came to realize that they could just stop obeying their repressive governments, that governments cannot govern if the citizens will not obey. Now, that is subversion! Kings and conquerors are afraid of ideas like that. In the 1980s the government of one Latin American nation is supposed to have forbidden the singing of the *Magnificat* when they realized that their people had

10. A very suggestive study of the world-making character of the liturgy of psalms is Walter Brueggemann's *Israel's Praise: Doxology Against Idolatry and Ideology* (Philadelphia: Fortress, 1988). I am heavily indebted to him for his contribution to the world that I perceive.

11. See Psalm 93, Morning Third Sunday, p. 128.

discovered how dangerous were words like "He has put down the mighty from their thrones and has lifted up the lowly; the hungry he has filled with good things, but the rich he has sent away empty."[12]

The *kings* of the nations will not want to hear of a King who will judge them, but the nations themselves—that is another matter. The conquests of Assyria or Babylon may have enriched their kings and nobles, but not the peasants who tilled their fields, who raised the barley for the beer of the king's soldiers and tax collectors. The peasants will have reason to rejoice if they can believe that a just judge is coming to pass judgment on the arrogance and exploitation that their own gods have sanctioned.

But if the psalm is sung on behalf of the oppressor, to bolster the court of our king, to reassure us that Yahweh will judge the rebellions of Moab and Ammon and the Philistines, reducing them again to servitude and restoring our empire—then the song has lost its newness and power and has become a part of the tiresome old story of human oppression.

But the real news has gotten out. The Gentiles have been told that the God who brought the Hebrew slaves out of Egypt is King. And some at least have believed it. The evidence is this, that the coming of the kingdom was not with the weapons of the exploiting kings, but through the failure and death of Jesus, which gave to the powerless, to slaves and to thinkers, the power to grasp their lives out of the power of kings.

As long as the Church knows this kind of God, yes, whenever Christians rediscover this kind of God, the announcement that God is King again becomes good news, and the song that proclaims it, even though it be twenty-five hundred years old, is a brand new song.[13]

And for a world that has seen God's just judgments themselves repeatedly subverted, where cynics or bunglers have co-opted revolutions of liberation and justice even in Christ's Church, yes, for a world that honestly knows that things will get worse again, the message has got to have an eschatological dimension. Chaos is fundamentally conquered but still struggles. Even if only beyond space and time, God is in sovereign control; God will indeed judge the nations, will judge the living and the dead, and God's kingdom will have no end.

12. I and my acquaintances have heard the report repeatedly, but none has been able to document it. Is this a contemporary example of a legend whose trueness to reality is patent even if the historicity cannot be established?

13. In the Christian manuscript tradition, an addition was made to verse 10, so that the Septuagint reading, "God has reigned," became, "God has reigned from the Tree." It was a sure Christian instinct that recognized that God's kingship became idolatry unless bound up in the confession of deliverance through defeat and death as well as from them.

PSALM 123   EVENING THIRD MONDAY

(122) 123. A prayer for mercy: a pilgrimage song

1   To you have I lifted up my eyes,
    you who dwell in the heavens;
2   my eyes, like the eyes of slaves
    on the hand of their lords.

    Like the eyes of a servant
    on the hand of her mistress,
3   so our eyes are on the LORD our God
    till we are shown mercy.

4   Have mercy on us, LORD, have mercy.
    We are filled with contempt.
5   Indeed all too full is our soul
    with the scorn of the rich,
    (the disdain of the proud).

We pray, God, especially for our brothers and sisters whose voices are contemptuously ignored by state and Church, by all who ought to hear them—even perhaps by ourselves, turning them over to you to bring them now some sort of equity, and complete justice when your kingdom fully comes.

PSALM 124   EVENING THIRD MONDAY

(123) 124. Thanksgiving for protection:
            a pilgrimage song

1   "If the LORD had not been on our side,"
    this is Israel's song.
2   "If the LORD had not been on our side
    when they rose up against us,
3   then would they have swallowed us alive
    when their anger was kindled.

4   Then would the waters have engulfed us,
    the torrent gone over us;
5   over our head would have swept
    the raging waters."

6   Blessed be the LORD who did not give us
    a prey to their teeth!
7   Our life, like a bird, has escaped
    from the snare of the fowler.

Indeed the snare has been broken
and we have escaped.
8 Our help is in the name of the LORD,
who made heaven and earth.

The "gradual psalms," Psalms 120–134, all seem to be formally a bit odd; they don't seem to quite fit the typical patterns of lament, hymn, or thanksgiving as found in other psalms. That is why it is somewhat harder to imagine just how they were actually used in ancient times. They may have first been used in some early form of the synagogue, where Jews, cut off from temple worship but wanting to worship their God, developed new rites and formulas. Eventually they were used in connection with pilgrimages to Jerusalem for the major feasts.

Psalm 124 is rather like a thanksgiving song, apparently giving thanks for one act of deliverance. However, it is expressed in the first person plural rather than singular; it contains no direct second person address to Yahweh; it lacks the typical formula of a thanksgiving song, "I will thank you" or "I will thank the Lord";[14] and finally the narrative describing the deliverance is expressed completely in metaphor.

Over half the psalm, verses 1-5, consists of an elaborate conditional sentence that imagines what if Yahweh had not helped us. "If the Lord had not been on our side . . . , If the Lord had not been on our side . . . , then . . . , then . . . , then . . . ." This is followed by a marveling and grateful description of our deliverance.

Since almost everything is expressed through metaphor, we cannot determine just *what* the danger is from which the worshipers have been delivered. Verse 2 refers to the people who "rose up against us." But verse 3 has already shifted to metaphor, for human beings could hardly in fact swallow us alive; we are thinking either of wild beasts or of mythical monsters. Verses 4 and 5 see the peril as the surging waters of a flood (cf. Ps 69:2-3, 15-16). Deliverance is described as rescue from the beasts or monsters, and then as the escape of a bird from a hunter's snare (vv. 6-7).

Precisely because the story is told only in images of ravenous teeth, violent waters, and the rescue of a pitiful bird, the song survived, for the images could articulate many an experience of the postexilic community, the despair of Israel in exile, and threats to the people like the dangers described in the books of Daniel, Judith, and Esther. After all, however imaginatively these stories are told, they certainly reflect hostility and suspicion against Jews and

---

14. Using a specific Hebrew verb, *hodah,* customarily translated "thank" but actually meaning something more like "praise."

actual incidents of threat and violence. If the psalm originally referred to Israel's survival of the Exile, each new threat that they survived was added to the tale of deliverance. And it is the imagery of threat and deliverance that makes the psalm so easy for us to pray.

The story of Israel's survival of exile is part of our story as well. Had the survivors of Assyrian and Babylonian aggression simply collapsed, had they allowed defeat to undermine their faith in Yahweh, had they simply acknowledged Yahweh as another manifestation of Ashur or Marduk, there would be neither Judaism nor Christianity today. The miracle of the Exile is that through defeat and suffering, Jews were able to deepen and purify the old naive confidence in their God, were able finally to hear the message of the prophets that Yahweh's reign over the nations meant that he could use the nations to punish his people's crimes, but also that Yahweh's love always pursued them, even in shame and suffering.

But the psalm on our lips comes to express all our experience. It expresses first of all that one event which is the primary metaphor of every Christian experience of salvation: the deliverance of Jesus from the belly of the grave. The resurrection of Christ is the matrix of the Christian life; every time I am delivered from any kind of evil, this is a participation in the paschal mystery.

The Church has survived enemies from without, from the persecutions of the first Christians to totalitarian regimes of our own day. Perhaps even more miraculously the Church survives its own sins, the tepidity and the intolerance, the exploitation, greed, lust, self-righteousness, hypocrisy, and plain stupidity with which we are so generously endowed. We go on proclaiming the gospel, and then out of weakness or cynicism we undermine that gospel in what we do. But age upon age that gospel is still heard; again and again persons are startled by the news and strive, however imperfectly, to walk in the way that is there described.

Men and women rescued from any kind of danger, including those spiritual perils of addiction, self-deception, and every species of selfishness and ignorance and folly, know the kind of deliverance for which this prayer gives thanks. We find here words that begin to express our gratitude. Half the psalm is spent in reflection on what might have been; rather than blotting it out of our mind, gratitude is willing to face openly just what we have done and where it could have led us. The image of the hopeless bird in the snare is a perfect picture of grace:[15] whatever heroic choices and actions we have been called to make, ultimately all is grace; even our willingness to surrender to that grace is at the deepest level God's work, and we would have it no other way.

---

15. In Hebrew the "has/have escaped" of verse 7 is passive, "has/have been rescued": nothing Pelagian about that!

PSALM 85   MORNING THIRD TUESDAY

(84) 85. The coming age of peace and justice

2 O LORD, you once favored your land
and revived the fortunes of Jacob,
3 you forgave the guilt of your people
and covered all their sins.
4 You averted all your rage,
you calmed the heat of your anger.

5 Revive us now, God, our helper!
Put an end to your grievance against us.
6 Will you be angry with us for ever,
will your anger never cease?

7 Will you not restore again our life
that your people may rejoice in you?
8 Let us see, O LORD, your mercy
and give us your saving help.

* * * * *

9 I will hear what the LORD has to say,
a voice that speaks of peace,
peace for his people and friends
and those who turn to God in their hearts.
10 Salvation is near for the God-fearing,
and his glory will dwell in our land.

11 Mercy and faithfulness have met;
justice and peace have embraced.
12 Faithfulness shall spring from the earth
and justice look down from heaven.

13 The LORD will make us prosper
and our earth shall yield its fruit.
14 Justice shall march in the forefront,
and peace shall follow the way.

When you or I try to get someone to change his or her attitude or behavior, we instinctively use a rhetorical device called the *captatio benevolen-
tiae,* the attempt to gain the other's good will, especially by praising the
person's past behavior or attitudes. "You were so generous to us four years ago
when I was laid off for three months; I do hope you'll be able to wait for the

rent for another month while I'm looking for a job." Such a reminder of past benefits is typical of communal laments, much more so than of laments of the individual. We find it in Psalms 44:2-9; 74:2, 12-15; 80:9-12; 83:10-12; 89:3-5, 10f., 20-38, 50; only Psalm 79 has no such reminder. And we find the same device in prayers of Moses (Exod 32:11; Num 14:19; Deut 9:26-27, 29).

That is how Psalm 85 begins, exactly as does Psalm 44, with a reminder of Yahweh's past merciful deliverance of his people (vv. 2-4). Unlike other psalms, which usually refer to the conquest of the land, this psalm does not indicate a specific historical event; if it refers to the return from exile, it does so in a way that suggests that this is just the greatest example of God's repeated forgiveness and deliverance of Israel.

Then comes a petition for help (vv. 5-8) and some sort of an elaborate expression of confidence (vv. 9-12).

In describing the past help, all the emphasis had been on the calming of God's anger and the forgiveness of Israel's sin. While the people's sin, then, is not clearly mentioned in the petition, it is implied in the wish for Yahweh to call off his anger (vv. 5b-6).

The whole second half of the psalm expresses confidence that Yahweh will indeed help his people. Many scholars see this as an oracle reported by a prophet, an interpretation that is perhaps supported by the introduction of a new voice, the "I" of verse 9, by the change of language from second person address to third person discourse about Yahweh, and the ascription of the promise to "what the Lord God has to say." While it may seem to us rather odd to preserve a ready-made oracle to be "heard" by the Temple prophet whenever the psalm must be used, it is not impossible, since the Temple did have prophets whose job apparently was to experience oracles of salvation in accord with God's covenant promises (Jeremiah 6:14; 8:11 criticizes abuses of the institution). Or perhaps a psalm with the response of a specific prophet was preserved in prophetic circles, rather like Hosea's negative response in Hosea 6:4-6 to a prayer of distress in 6:1-3 or the oracle of Jeremiah 14:10 rejecting the communal lament of 14:7-9.

The psalm, then, with its prophetic response, was later incorporated into the psalter along with a preponderance of other prayers that were originally meant for repeated use. But it is also quite possible that the phrase "I will hear what the Lord God has to say" refers, not to pursuit of a prophetic oracle, but to reflection on the covenant promises already spoken repeatedly by Yahweh to Israel, summarized in verses 9-10 and developed poetically in verses 11-14. Doubtless the phrases "peace for his friends" and "help . . . for those who fear him" were heard, not as conditions that must be met before Yahweh will help, but simply as apt identifications of Israel, Yahweh's people.

When we pray a psalm like this, our prayer is bound to be influenced by three things. First, the prophetic movement has profoundly shaped our sense of sin. The psalm, after all, does not forthrightly acknowledge sin but only suggests it halfheartedly as it centers on God's anger with the people (vv. 5-6) rather than on the sin that must have provoked it (note that in their ancestors' case they more forthrightly acknowledge that God's anger was provoked by their sin [vv. 3-4]). The expectation of help, then, looks not for forgiveness but for the prosperity that God assures to those who fear him and are faithful to the covenant (implied in Hebrew of "his friends").[16] We are likely to pray with a far more explicit awareness of sin.

Secondly, the model of "punishment" is less pronounced in our understanding of the disasters that befall us. To speak of "punishment" means that we think of God out there seeing our sin, getting angry, and showing displeasure by hurting us (whether to teach us not to do it again or to get even with us). We, on the other hand, are more likely to see the disaster as a causal effect of the sin itself: our nation is hated abroad because of a history of arrogance and hypocrisy in pursuit of our selfish goals; my marriage is on the rocks because (at least in part) my perfectionistic demands made my partner feel frustrated and inadequate, and ready to look somewhere else for relief and self-esteem.

Finally, we look for deliverance, not as a miracle from the outside, but from within the world we have corrupted. If the Church is to recover its dissipated prestige, it will not be because God tricks the world into a change of mind, but by the recovery among Christians of a spirit of compassion, thirst for justice, and fervor. Nor will the deliverance always be what we would have wanted. A friend of mine who destroyed her marriage by trying to make her husband as good as she thought she was, who went through years of bitterness, has come to peace. Without having to judge him, she wishes her husband whatever happiness he can find in his new marriage. And she recognizes God's saving grace in the insight and tranquility she has found by giving up and abandoning herself to God, yes, recognizes even her surrender to God as God's work.

The psalm's expression of confidence, then, bespeaks God's will for us rather than a simple prediction of the future. We can frustrate it only by resisting the transformation that God seeks to work in us beginning with our prayer, or by failure to recognize God's saving work because God chooses to deliver us in a way that is quite different from that which we had decided that God must do.

16. Verse 9d, "those who turn to God in their hearts," is too obscure in Hebrew for translation; the Liturgy of the Hours' guess at its meaning benefits from the prophetic tradition of conversion.

PSALM 67   MORNING THIRD TUESDAY

This psalm was treated above, p. 101, under Evening Second Wednesday.

PSALM 125   EVENING THIRD TUESDAY

(124) 125. Unshakable trust: a pilgrimage song

¹ Those who put their trust in the LORD
  are like Mount Zion, that cannot be shaken,
  that stands for ever.

² Jerusalem! The mountains surround her,
  so the LORD surrounds his people
  both now and for ever.

³ For the scepter of the wicked shall not rest
  over the land of the just
  for fear that the hands of the just
  should turn to evil.

⁴ Do good, LORD, to those who are good,
  to the upright of heart;
⁵ but the crooked and those who do evil,
  drive them away!

On Israel, peace!

Grant true liberty, God, to all who languish under alien rule and to all whose freedom is forfeited in bondage to the world, the flesh, and the devil; and protect the oppressed from emulating their oppressors.

PSALM 131   EVENING THIRD TUESDAY

(130) 131. The peaceful heart: a pilgrimage song

¹ O LORD, my heart is not proud
  nor haughty my eyes.
  I have not gone after things too great
  nor marvels beyond me.

² Truly I have set my soul
  in silence and peace.
  A weaned child on its mother's breast,
  even so is my soul.

³ O Israel, hope in the LORD
both now and for ever.

The weekday psalms at Evening Prayer this week, as we have seen, are all taken from the "gradual psalms" and are all a bit odd. So also is this captivating little prayer. Generally described as a psalm of confidence, it might better be identified as a protestation of innocence (cf. Pss 7:4-6, 9; 26:4-5, 11; 101), for it is essentially a denial (vv. 1-2) of that haughtiness which is often seen as offensive to Yahweh (Pss 10:4; 18:28; 101:5). Since the protestation of innocence is typically part of an individual lament, this prayer was likely used as a part of a ceremony calling for Yahweh's help in times of trouble.

After the psalm's claim to have avoided pride, it is only in the last verse that the theme of trust appears explicitly. This verse, a wish on behalf of Israel, is probably a secondary addition, transforming a prayer of the individual into a prayer for (or exhortation to) the community.

As in every society, not all the characters of the Earlier Testament recognized their limits. The king of Assyria, sent (as Isaiah sees it) by Yahweh to punish sinful Israel, attributes his success to his own might:

My hand has found
the wealth of peoples like a nest;
and as abandoned eggs are gathered,
so I have gathered all the earth;
and none there was to move a wing,
or open the mouth, or chirp (Isa 10:14).

The prophet then adds Yahweh's rebuke:

Shall the ax boast over the one who hews with it,
or the saw magnify itself against one who wields it? (Isa 10:15).

Or the Northern Israelites, not recognizing their devastation as Yahweh's punishment, boast that the war damage provides a perfect opportunity for urban renewal:

The bricks have fallen,
but we will build with dressed stones;
the sycamore has been shattered,
but we will substitute cedar (Isa 9:9).

This is what the psalm denies, the arrogance that would not recognize one's limits: "I have not gone after things too great or marvels beyond me."

Psalm 8 marvels rightly at the power God has given to human beings in the world. Psalm 131 rightly claims not to have gone beyond such power.

No Israelite, no Jew, ever had a better claim to this psalm than the Jew Jesus of Nazareth, whom we acknowledge to be the very Wisdom of God revealed to us in our flesh, but who grew up in the least of villages in the Galilean hills, who spent most of his life as an unknown craftsman, who attempted to change the world with nothing but God's truth—a sure formula for the failure he experienced, though such failure, of course, turns out to reveal God's glory and to transform the world. We who are incorporated into Christ in baptism can speak this psalm simply in the name of him whose heart was not proud, whose eyes were not haughty, who in the garden struggled through to silence and peace. And ultimately we call on God's people—yes, as God's people we hear the call—to place such trust in the Lord.

If you attempt the psalm in your own name, it surely cannot become a boast about your humility! Rather, try to make it an honest admission that whatever good there is in you is God's work. Make no great production of it, as if you were renouncing something great. And for God's sake, don't get depressed about it. Michelangelo's statue *David* does not have to find some way of asserting its autonomy from the artist: its glory is in expressing the artist's fire, though in fact no other piece of marble could have expressed that fire in quite the same way, especially since the design was constrained by the shape of the stone, which had already been partially carved for a different statue by a previous artist. Whatever glory is yours, you have it as God's work. Characteristic of this work, however, is the principle that God acts only through the freedom of each person, striving to develop the holiness of each person precisely through the specific character of that person and out of that person's unique story.

The less you strive to achieve the perfection of humility, and the more you try to discover what God wants of you day by day and to hand yourself over in simple obedience to God's will, the better chance you have of achieving some beginning of humility.

PSALM 86   MORNING THIRD WEDNESDAY

(85) 86. Loyalty in God's service

1   Turn your ear, O LORD, and give answer
    for I am poor and needy.
2   Preserve my life, for I am faithful;
    save the servant who trusts in you.

3   You are my God, have mercy on me, Lord,
    for I cry to you all the day long.

⁴ Give joy to your servant, O Lord,
   for to you I lift up my soul.

⁵ O Lord, you are good and forgiving,
   full of love to all who call.
⁶ Give heed, O LORD, to my prayer
   and attend to the sound of my voice.

⁷ In the day of distress I will call
   and surely you will reply.
⁸ Among the gods there is none like you, O Lord,
   nor work to compare with yours.

⁹ All the nations shall come to adore you
   and glorify your name, O Lord,
¹⁰ for you are great and do marvelous deeds,
   you who alone are God.

¹¹ Show me, LORD, your way
   so that I may walk in your truth.
   Guide my heart to fear your name.

¹² I will praise you, Lord my God, with all my heart
   and glorify your name for ever;
¹³ for your love to me has been great,
   you have saved me from the depths of the grave.

¹⁴ The proud have risen against me;
   ruthless enemies seek my life;
   to you they pay no heed.

¹⁵ But you, God of mercy and compassion,
   slow to anger, O Lord,
   abounding in love and truth,
¹⁶ turn and take pity on me.

   O give your strength to your servant
   and save your handmaid's child.
¹⁷ Show me a sign of your favor
   that my foes may see to their shame
   that you console me and give me your help.

Here is another psalm that was used to pray for one's life. The ancients simply faced more dangers to life than we do in the developed West. Whatever we must say about our unhealthy diet, pollution, and violence, the ancient Israelites, like underdeveloped peoples everywhere, did have a much lower life expectancy. Even though the lucky survivors—without tobacco, fossil fuel emissions, and artificial dyes, with more grains in their diet and less meat—were perhaps healthier, still any one person was less likely to survive. There was little useful therapy for illnesses like pneumonia and cancer, and poor understanding of how contagious diseases were spread; they rectified personal grievances through revenge rather than through publicly accountable police and courts. In such a world the average person's life was frequently in peril. None of the monarchs of Judah after Solomon seems to have lived to the age of seventy. Of the first fourteen, six died before age fifty.[17] No wonder there are so many prayers for deliverance from death!

Often a prayer for help will describe the suppliant's distress in vivid and pathetic images. Not so this psalm. There is only verse 1, "I am poor and needy," and verse 14, "The proud have risen against me; / ruthless enemies seek my life; / to you they pay no heed." Rather, this psalm uses another strategy to seek divine intervention. It consists of repeated calls for help and fulsome praise of God's mercy.

Like the poor widow in the Gospel badgering the unjust judge (Luke 18:2-5), the psalm is not timid in asking for help. The first six verses contain eight imperative verbs, the last two verses, three (four in the Grail translation). But even these imperatives are, for the most part, various and very general ways of saying "hear" and "save my life."

Verse 11, the most developed petition of the lot, may seem a bit odd to us: Why, we ask, is the psalmist praying for moral enlightenment while fleeing potential murderers? But the same motif is found in other such laments, e.g., Pss 27:11; 25:4f.; 143:8, 10. The idea seems to be that if I become God's truly obedient servant, then God will certainly save my life. Otherwise, in speaking of self the emphasis of this psalm is not that one is righteous but that one is in need and belongs to God. To say "I am faithful . . . your ser-

17. According to the regnal formulas of the 1 and 2 Kings, the oldest possible age of the first fourteen kings was as follows (when insufficient data is provided, I give the length of the reign; because of possible ways of counting first and last years of age and reign, the ages given are maximum): Rehoboam died at fifty-eight years or less (1 Kgs 14:21). Abijam, his son, reigned only three years (1 Kgs 15:2); therefore, unless he was born when his father was eleven years old, he was under fifty years. Asa, who reigned forty-one years (1 Kgs 15:10), was probably over fifty. Jehoshaphat died by age sixty (1 Kgs 22:42), Jehoram by age forty (2 Kgs 8:16f.), Ahaziah by age twenty-two (2 Kgs 8:26), and since Ahaziah's mother, the usurping Queen Athaliah reigned up to seven years, she may well have been about fifty at death (2 Kgs 11:4ff.). Jehoash died by age forty-seven (2 Kgs 12:1-2 [RSV 11:21—12:1]). Amaziah died by age fifty-four (2 Kgs 14:2), Azariah by age sixty-eight (2 Kgs 15:2), Jotham by age forty-one (2 Kgs 15:33), Ahaz by age thirty-six (2 Kgs 16:2), Hezekiah by age fifty-four (2 Kgs 18:2), and Manasseh by age sixty-seven (2 Kgs 21:1).

vant, the child of your handmaid" is not so much to claim piety as it is a reminder to God that one belongs to God's household.

The psalm's greatest effort goes into praising Yahweh for his generous love and power to save (vv. 5, 7, 8-10, 13), culminating in the great traditional formula of praise in verse 15 (cf. Exod 34:6; Num 14:18; Neh 9:17; Joel 2:13; Jonah 4:2; Pss 103:8; 111:4; 145:8). Rather than looking inward at one's trouble, the psalm looks outward at God. Rather than depicting one's misery, the psalm tries to engage Yahweh's attention by praise of God's generosity. You'll catch more flies with honey than with vinegar, they say.

The psalm still furnishes us with a good model and even a good text for our prayer. The richness of the praise still strikes us as right: "God of mercy and compassion, slow to anger . . . abounding in love and truth" (v. 15). "Among the gods there is none like you, O Lord, nor work to compare with yours" (v. 8). God is both well-disposed and capable of helping, though we may see God's help less anthropomorphically than did the ancients, more deeply embedded in God's creation, in the skill and good will God gives to our fellow humans, and in the word of God that inspires others and ourselves, no matter how secular a manner in which it is communicated.[18] And for us God's help will have an eschatological character unknown to those who first prayed the psalm. God may not make everything all right now as we would want it, but in the ultimate world that transcends here and now, God will definitively deliver from all death, in that realm where there will be no more mourning or weeping or pain (Rev 21:4).

The fact that neither complaint nor petition specifies the need very distinctly makes the prayer broadly adaptable. From the beginning it was meant to be used by anyone whose life was in danger. Then surely we can pray it in intercession for those who need it but may not have the words to pray, may not even know where to turn. Reading the morning papers or watching the evening news can in that sense be a good preparation for prayer.

Aware that the prayer was meant for situations of life and death, we may find it uncomfortable to try to pray the psalms for our petty needs. That is just as well—it becomes a stimulus to look beyond the world of our little irritations. Still, we do have issues that are big enough for this prayer. We do all face death, you know. And even though it may not be imminent, at least we who have allowed ourselves to reach middle age know that the prospect of eventual death can be deeply disturbing. And there are other events and situations in life that so wrench our souls as to threaten the life of the spirit. A friend wrote me months after being betrayed by the woman he deeply loved, "I know there are those who have it so much worse. But my pain is

---

18. For instance, one of the less offensive Marxist principles, "From each according to his ability, to each according to his need," seems to have its origin in Acts 2:44f.

mine. Who's going to take it?" Such pain could find its expression in a psalm like this. Or surely our betrayal of God by serious sin, even by spiritual apathy, is threatening to the life of the spirit. No matter that this was not the idea of those who gave us the psalm: this is a desperation which we do face, for which we must find words to cry for help. And the old words fit us precisely because they were meant for anyone in desperate need.

Further, when we do pray this psalm out of our varied experience, in America, in Australia, in Japan, in Africa, the pledge of the psalmist is on its way to being fulfilled. "All the nations shall come to adore you and glorify your name, O Lord" (v. 9).

PSALM 98   MORNING THIRD WEDNESDAY

(97) 98. Praise to God, ruler of the world

1 Sing a new song to the LORD
    who has worked wonders;
    whose right hand and holy arm
    have brought salvation.

2 The LORD has made known salvation;
    has shown justice to the nations;
3 has remembered truth and love
    for the house of Israel.

    All the ends of the earth have seen
    the salvation of our God.
4 Shout to the LORD, all the earth,
    ring out your joy.

5 Sing psalms to the LORD with the harp
    with the sound of music.
6 With trumpets and the sound of the horn
    acclaim the King, the LORD.

                    * * * * *

7 Let the sea and all within it, thunder;
    the world, and all its peoples.
8 Let the rivers clap their hands
    and the hills ring out their joy

9 at the presence of the LORD, who comes,
    who comes to rule the earth.
    God will rule the world with justice
    and the peoples with fairness.

God, renew in us vividly the remembrance of your mercies to Israel and the blessings that through them you have extended to the nations in Jesus, your Son and our Brother, so that the ancient psalms may become brand new songs on our lips and in our hearts.

PSALM 126   EVENING THIRD WEDNESDAY

(125) 126. Song of the returned exiles:
a pilgrimage song

¹   When the LORD delivered Zion from bondage,
it seemed like a dream.
²   Then was our mouth filled with laughter,
on our lips there were songs.

The heathens themselves said: "What marvels
the LORD worked for them!"
³   What marvels the LORD worked for us!
Indeed we were glad.

⁴   Deliver us, O LORD, from our bondage
as streams in dry land.
⁵   Those who are sowing in tears
will sing when they reap.

⁶   They go out, they go out, full of tears,
carrying seed for the sowing;
they come back, they come back, full of song,
carrying their sheaves.

You have delivered us, prays this psalm, so deliver us. God's work is never finished. The human condition is that we must again and again ask for the same things. Life is like a soap opera—no sooner are you out of one fix (or even before you're out of it) than you're in another one. That, after all, is where the soap operas got the idea.

This psalm, like Psalm 85, begins by marveling at deliverance already brought about for the people, but what deliverance? While some translations (beginning before Christ with the Greek Septuagint) understand this as the end of the Babylonian Exile[19] (NAB: "When the Lord brought back the captives of Zion"), the Hebrew seems originally to have meant simply "When

---

19. Including, it would seem, the Grail psalter used in the Liturgy of the Hours, which translates, "When the Lord delivered Sion from bondage."

the Lord reversed the fortunes of Zion." So it would seem that this was meant to refer to any or every past dramatic deliverance or recovery, such as the restoration of the Davidic dynasty with the coup against Athaliah (2 Kgs 11) or the withdrawal of Sennacherib from the siege of Jerusalem (2 Kgs 18:13–9:37). As generations passed, each time the city was rescued from a new danger the phrase took on new meaning.

After a little reflection on how even the Gentiles marveled at Yahweh's help for his city and on "our" joy, the joy of the citizens, at their deliverance, the psalm goes on to ask, in almost the same words as the first line, for help again. Yahweh has shown his power and his mercy to save us in the past; we are in trouble, so we ask him to save us again.

Rather than a straightforward expression of confidence as in Psalm 60:14 ("With God we shall do bravely and he will trample down our foes"), this poem expresses its confidence in a metaphor: "Those who are sowing in tears will sing when they reap." This image apparently reflects the agricultural practice of Canaanites, who saw the burial of the fertility god in the planting of seed, and his resurrection in the growth of the new crop. However, those who used the psalm may well have attached a more secular thought to the practice—one weeps at the risk taken in the lean winter by burying the precious grain in the ground in the uncertain hope of a future harvest. We may be in distress now, but God will save us, and we will have the last laugh (vv. 2, 6).

In the twenty-five hundred years or so since this psalm was first prayed, God has repeatedly saved his people. After the recovery of Jerusalem from the Syrian Greeks at the time of the Maccabees, for instance, that deliverance surely became part of the story remembered in these verses. It is impossible to expect Christians to pray this psalm without calling to mind what we see as the central act of salvation by which every other salvation is defined, namely, the incarnation, passion, death, and resurrection of Jesus Christ, of which Luke says, "They still disbelieved for joy, and wondered" (24:41). Now, Jesus uses the imagery of this psalm in John's Gospel in allusion to his resurrection: "The hour has come for the Son of Man to be glorified. Truly, truly, I say to you, unless a grain of wheat falls into the earth and dies, it remains alone; but if it dies, it bears much fruit" (12:23-24).

But then, the whole story of how the gospel has survived to our own day becomes for us part of the history of God's restoration of the fortunes of Zion. This is suggested by the antiphon for Psalm 126 in the traditional Office of Apostles: "Going they went, and wept, casting their seeds." The preaching of the gospel may have brought the death of the apostles, but out of this God has brought them to share in Christ's resurrection and has brought his gospel to all nations.

All the stories of our communities, yes, the very story of your life, your deliverance from despair or cynicism, from indifference or arrogance, is part of this history of salvation. And still now, in each new crisis of the whole Church, in every plight of our communities, and in all the perils of your life, this story is the foundation of confidence that our God is still able to save and willing so to do.

PSALM 127   EVENING THIRD WEDNESDAY

(126) 127. Praise of God's goodness:
      a pilgrimage song

1 If the LORD does not build the house,
    in vain do its builders labor;
    if the LORD does not watch over the city,
    in vain do the watchers keep vigil.

2 In vain is your earlier rising,
    your going later to rest,
    you who toil for the bread you eat,
    when God pours gifts on the beloved while they slumber.

3 Yes, children are a gift from the LORD,
    a blessing, the fruit of the womb.
4 The sons and daughters of youth
    are like arrows in the hand of a warrior.

5 O the happiness of those
    who have filled their quiver with these arrows!
    They will have no cause for shame
    when they dispute with their foes in the gateways.

This psalm consists completely of affirmations rather than wishes or petitions. These affirmations are vaguely related to the affirmations about God in hymns, in that they describe the beneficence of Yahweh in terms that should lead to praise. Compare Psalm 147:12ff.:

O praise the LORD, Jerusalem! . . .
God has strengthened the bars of your gates,
and has blessed the children within you.

Still, with the rebuke (or warning) of verse 2 ("In vain is your earlier rising . . .") and the blessing of verse 5, the psalm looks more like an instruction than a hymn, or better, a kind of confession of beliefs held in common, for the intention is not so much to convince as to remind. It was likely pronounced in some kind of small assembly like the early synagogue, perhaps in connection with the birth of a child.

The object of the confession is divine grace: what the Israelite most wants, progeny and security, is ultimately God's work rather than the result of human planning and striving. It doesn't deny that human beings build the building or guard the city ("builders" and "watchers" it names them—v. 1), but their efforts will fail if Yahweh doesn't build and guard. With the affirmation that children are God's gift (v. 3), we recognize that the first line refers to the founding of a family as well as the construction of a house. In Ruth 4:11 Boaz is blessed with the wish that his wife be "like Rachel and like Leah, who both built the house of Israel," and in Deuteronomy 25:9 one "builds" one's deceased brother's house by levirate marriage. It is Yahweh who builds David's house in 2 Samuel 7:27 (cf. 1 Sam 2:35, etc.).

And the theme of protection in verse 1b corresponds to the martial imagery of the sons as arrows and their role of protection in verse 5b.

Despite the valiant attempt of the inclusive Grail translation to give equal time to daughters, the psalm reflects patriarchal concerns. It's the grown-up sons who will back up the father in the gate. It is *our* confession, not that of those who gave us the psalm, that daughters can fulfill the same function as sons.

When we take up this psalm in prayer, the confession of grace becomes renewed in our midst. The Christian cannot help but hear reverberations of the Pauline doctrine of grace in the psalm. Building the house, guarding the city, begetting—and conceiving—children are still recognized as God's work, God's gift; but they also perforce become metaphors of all our profoundest desires. The building of a just and compassionate national spirit, the development of a vibrant and effective parish or religious community, the establishment of a life of service to God—these too are recognized as God's work if they are ever to come into existence.

This does not malign human achievement or deny human dignity. To acknowledge that God's grace must precede and support any good thought, any laudable desire, any generous act, is no more degrading than it is for an athlete to acknowledge an absolute need for air to breathe. God's grace is the very stuff of human virtue; God's grace presupposes and enhances human freedom.

As for the gift of children, one would hope that we would find more to them than the psalmist's expectation of support and protection, though the comfort and help one may get from one's adult children is surely a great gift. But the very survival of your genes is a marvelous gift to every generation. I would not so much as exist but for my great grandmother Muller and for every one of my ancestors. For my genetic makeup or yours is absolutely essential to our very existence. Any other constellation of genes might indeed have produced a beautiful, talented person, but it wouldn't have been you or me.

But human beings have evolved genetically to the point where much of our identity, much of who we are, does not come from our genes. With the complexity of our brains and the immaturity of human young at birth,[20] our relations with parents, teachers, mentors, and peers have much to do with what makes me who I am today and what makes you to be you. My adopted grandnephew and grandniece enrich the family with other genes. But play with them a while and you will recognize from the way they think and behave that they do indeed belong to their families.

In the days when we prayed the gradual psalms daily in the monastic Office, while studying in Rome I used to regale myself by wishing the blessing of Psalm 128 on a dour, traditionalist priest who sat opposite me in choir: "May you see your children's children. Peace upon Israel." But in time, as I came to know him better, I recognized that there was more than cynicism to the wish. As a pious, learned, and effective teacher with a strong streak of no-nonsense compassion, he had for forty years influenced pastors, who in turn through their ministry would affect generations to come, sometimes for ill but mostly for good. It was the genes of his personality, as it were, that were being passed on. "Better is childlessness with virtue," says the Book of Wisdom, "for there is immortality in the memory of virtue, known as it is to God and to human beings alike" (Wisdom of Solomon 4:1). Similarly, celibate religious communities, maiden aunts, even in some mysterious way the truly hidden hermit, need not be without heirs.

PSALM 87   MORNING THIRD THURSDAY

(86) 87. God's city, mother of all nations

1 On the holy mountain is the city
2 cherished by the LORD.
  The LORD prefers the gates of Zion
  to all Jacob's dwellings.
3 Of you are told glorious things,
  O city of God!

4 "Babylon and Egypt I will count
  among those who know me;

---

20. Baby chicks are up and launched on their lifetime career of pecking for food within minutes after birth. Amoebae are already adults from the moment they divide.

> Philistia, Tyre, Ethiopia,
> these will be her children
> ⁵ and Zion shall be called 'Mother'
> for all shall be her children."
>
> It is God the Lord Most High,
> who gives each a place.
> ⁶ In the register of peoples God writes:
> "These are her children,"
> ⁷ and while they dance they will sing:
> "In you all find their home."

What do you do with a psalm in which more than half the verses provide major exegetical problems? You make do with what is clear and with those elements that will remain regardless of how you resolve the obscurities.

Some of the most striking lines in the translation used in the Liturgy of the Hours are not at all what the Hebrew says. Thus, verse 5, "Zion shall be called 'Mother' for all shall be her children," and, "It is he, the Lord Most High, who gives each his place," in fact read, "To Zion it shall be said, man and man is born in her," and, "It is he who establishes it, the Most High." And verse 7, "And while they dance they will sing: 'In you all find their home,'" actually reads more like, "And singers and dancers alike, all my springs are in you." Well, for the most part these Hebrew sentences don't make much sense, so the translators figure that the ancient scribes miscopied the text and that perhaps other scribes, as they sometimes did, made things even worse by trying to correct the errors. The translators, therefore, have tried their best to imagine how the lines might have originally read and at least to provide a guess that corresponds to the general thrust of the whole poem.

The poem as a whole is clearly saying that God has a unique love for Jerusalem (or its Temple) and that in time to come persons of many nations will be recognized as native citizens of Jerusalem. The poem is related to exilic and postexilic texts like Isaiah 19:19-25; 45:22-23; 56:3, 6-8; Zechariah 8:20-23; Malachi 1:11. Such passages accept Gentiles, or perhaps in some cases Jews dispersed in foreign nations, as faithful worshipers of Yahweh.

The Babylonians had singled out Judah's elite (2 Kgs 24:12-16) for deportation in the 590s and 580s, while others fled to Egypt. Thus the best minds of the people had encountered the two great powers of the day in exile. Later they would benefit from the tolerant policies of the Persians, who promoted the restoration of Israelite worship in Jerusalem. Doubtless on a personal level they sometimes also experienced many a compassionate gesture from Gentile neighbors or even royal officials, as people in distress always have and always will.

The perspective this provided—the vivid awareness of the political insignificance of Israel and the possibilities of nobility among the Gentiles—provoked Jews to explore more deeply the relationship of the Gentiles to Israel's God. It was no longer enough to see them only as enemies of God or (as the great prophets had recognized) instruments of Yahweh's anger to punish his rebellious people. Prophets began to recognize a coming day when the Gentiles, or at least proselytes to Judaism from the Gentiles, would come streaming to worship Yahweh in Jerusalem.

Not all Jews welcomed this openness to the Gentiles. When the Temple was being rebuilt in the late 500s, the Samaritans offered to help, but their aid was indignantly rejected (Ezra 4:1-3), and in the following century a basic strategy for the restoration of Judah was to forbid marriage to Gentiles or even to require the divorce of non-Jewish wives (Ezra 9–10; Neh 13:23-30). So along with outward-looking oracles and books with sympathetic Gentile characters (Ruth and Jonah), the Bible has preserved the voices of those who feared that openness to non-Jews risked the dilution and loss of Jewish identity. Often enough the Bible will present in different places opposing points of view on the same subject, with each side having important values to defend.

Psalm 87, at any rate, looks forward to a day when Gentiles, whether the many or only the few converts, will be true worshipers of Yahweh and will be accepted as full citizens of God's holy city, Zion.

Praying this psalm as Christians, we recognize with wonder and awe that we, who have been gathered from the Gentiles, have in Jesus Christ been granted full citizenship in God's people: "You have come to Mount Zion and to the city of the living God, the heavenly Jerusalem, and to innumerable angels in festal gathering." Such awareness does not depend on a theology of replacement, a theology that would deny any legitimacy to Judaism, maintaining that all Judaism's claims have passed over to the Church. At the very least, we can leave that question in the hands of God. What we Christians do know from experience is that in Jesus Christ the Hebrew Scriptures have become our story, that the God of Abraham has become our God, that we recognize the demands of Moses and the vision of the prophets as addressing us with their full power, and that the songs of Zion fit our hearts and lips as our own prayers.

After all, neither Rabbinic Jews nor Christians can claim to be simply identifiable with the undifferentiated Jews of the immediate postexilic period, who once sang this psalm in their synagogues or temple. From them, through differing experiences and consequently with differing ways of reading Scripture, came Rabbinic Jews, Sadducees, Essenes, Hellenistic Jews, Christians, various kinds of Gnostics, and the Prophet of Islam.

Now, since it is in fact through the Christian community that we have discovered the God of Israel, since it is only through the story of Jesus, through the convincing power of his words and his demonstration of God's love in sharing our limits and our pain, we can never forget that whatever share we have in Zion is ours through the strange—and thoroughly Jewish—Rabbi from Nazareth. In him, we confess, all God's wisdom has shone forth in hidden splendor.

PSALM 99   MORNING THIRD THURSDAY

(98) 99. The power and holiness of God

¹ The LORD is king; the peoples tremble.
He is throned on the cherubim; the earth quakes.
² The LORD is great in Zion;

You are supreme over all the peoples.
³ Let them praise your name, so terrible and great,
so holy, ⁴ full of power.

You are a king who loves what is right;
you have established equity, justice and right;
you have established them in Jacob.

⁵ Exalt the LORD our God;
bow down before God's footstool.
The LORD our God is holy.

⁶ Among the priests were Aaron and Moses,
among those who invoked the Lord's name was Samuel.
They invoked the LORD who answered.

⁷ The Lord spoke to them in the pillar of cloud.
They did God's will; they kept the law,
which the Lord our God had given.

⁸ O LORD our God, you answered them.
For them you were a God who forgives;
Yet you punished all their offenses.

⁹ Exalt the LORD our God;
bow down before God's holy mountain
for the LORD our God is holy.

Move our hearts, Holy God, to cast ourselves in awe before you and to find freedom in ready obedience to your holy will.

PSALM 132   EVENING THIRD THURSDAY

(131) 132. God's promise to David: pilgrimage song

¹ O LORD, remember David
and all the many hardships he endured,
² the oath he swore to the LORD,
his vow to the Strong One of Jacob.

³ "I will not enter the house where I live
nor go to the bed where I rest.
⁴ I will give no sleep to my eyes,
to my eyelids I will give no slumber
⁵ till I find a place for the LORD,
a dwelling for the Strong One of Jacob."

⁶ At Ephrata we heard of the ark;
we found it in the plains of Yearim.
⁷ "Let us go to the place of God's dwelling;
let us go to kneel at God's footstool."

⁸ Go up, LORD, to the place of your rest,
you and the ark of your strength.
⁹ Your priests shall be clothed with holiness;
your faithful shall ring out their joy.
¹⁰ For the sake of David your servant
do not reject your anointed.

¹¹ The LORD swore an oath to David,
and will not revoke that word:
"A son, the fruit of your body,
will I set upon your throne.

¹² If your sons keep my covenant in truth
and my laws that I have taught them,
their sons too shall rule
on your throne from age to age."

¹³ For the LORD has chosen Zion;
has desired it for a dwelling:
¹⁴ "This is my resting-place for ever,
here have I chosen to live.

¹⁵ I will greatly bless her produce,
I will fill her poor with bread.

¹⁶ I will clothe her priests with salvation
and her faithful shall ring out their joy.

¹⁷ There David's stock will flower;
I will prepare a lamp for my anointed.
¹⁸ I will cover his enemies with shame
but on him my crown shall shine."

In 2 Samuel 7 David resolves to build a "house" (or temple) for Yahweh in Jerusalem. Yahweh does not accept this house for the present but declares that he rather will establish a "house" (a royal dynasty) for David. This psalm remembers the story a little differently, associating Yahweh's promise of a dynasty, not with David's promise to build a house for God, but with his pursuit of a dwelling place for Yahweh and his ark as recounted in the previous chapter, 2 Samuel 6. The parallel here is not between Yahweh's "house" and David's "house" but between the oath made by David to Yahweh and the oath made by Yahweh to David.

The psalm was doubtless performed during the time of the Davidic kings at a ceremony reconfirming God's protection of the monarchy, perhaps in connection with an autumn festival celebrating (and somehow renewing?) Yahweh's kingship. At any rate, it clearly associates Yahweh's welfare with that of the Davidic family; the psalm consists essentially of a reminder of David's promise of a home for Yahweh in Zion (vv. 1-10) and Yahweh's promise of an abiding dynasty (vv. 11-18). If all is well with Yahweh in Zion, all will be well with the king.

The first part of the psalm concludes[21] with a set of three petitions to Yahweh (vv. 8-10): (1) A variant on the old cultic cry (Num 10:35f.), calling on Yahweh to go up to rest in his Temple; (2) wishes for the priests and faithful;[22] (3) a prayer for the present king. To these correspond promises of Yahweh in verses 13-18: (1) I shall always dwell in Zion; (2) I shall bless its provisions, and specifically the priests and faithful; (3) I shall provide the king with posterity and success.

Well, there's been no temple on Zion for a couple of millennia, no ark or Davidic king for two and a half millennia. And yet, long after ark and king

21. It is not quite clear whether verses 6-7 are supposed to be a continuation of David's speech in verses 3-5 or whether it is the speech of those who celebrate the feast, a kind of definition of the meaning of a procession that they are making. Quite likely it is both: the festive crowd reenacts the procession made long ago by David (2 Sam 6:12-19).

22. The Liturgy of the Hours really should read wishes ("May your priests be clothed . . . may your faithful ring out . . .") rather than affirmations ("Your priests shall be clothed," etc.) in verse 9.

were lost, the psalm was preserved. At first it was saved simply to have the hymns available when the monarchy would be restored. But as generations dragged on with no restoration, Jews came to realize ever more clearly that a king like the kings of old would not be enough; never again must they have to expect that the reforms of any good king will be undone by his evil successor. The new reign must radically and definitively restore God's people in such a way that they would never again have to succumb to their enemies. By the time of Jesus they recognized in apocalyptic circles that such a new age could be realized only by a direct intervention of God that would turn the world upside down.

Jesus announced the approach of that intervention: "Repent, for the reign of God is at hand." What a profound convulsion the world was about to witness! The disciples, of course, constantly misunderstood this, quarreling over the distribution of power in the new order (Mark 9:33-37; 10:35-40; Luke 9:46-48; 22:24-27), refusing to hear of his passion (Mark 8:31-33; 9:31), offering to defend him by violence (Luke 9:52-55; 22:35-38; Matt 26:51-54).

The marvel is that the defeat and death of Jesus, rather than destroying, confirmed their belief in the arrival of the kingdom. So deeply had Jesus changed their lives, so clearly were they convinced by their experience of his resurrection, so far was all this beyond their ability to describe it, that in their search of Scripture to find images to describe and defend him they repeatedly settled on texts about the king who would restore God's people. As all the ideals of Israel's king had fed into the expectation of a final restoring king, now the Christians' experience of Jesus came to be the true explanation of all the old images of the king. Jesus, risen from the dead and now no longer subject to death, was seen to fulfill the promise to David of a perpetually enduring kingship (Acts 7:45-46; 2:30).[23]

While we no longer see the royal psalms as predictions of Jesus, they still provide metaphors with which to express our understanding of the Christ and our allegiance to him. It is not that Jesus is a limping analogy to the long-desired messiah; on the contrary, the whole of Israel's kingship had only to the most meager extent brought about that conformity of Israel to the Lord's designs, and indeed even Israel's greatest longings fell far short of the possibilities that God wished and still wishes to accomplish in Jesus Christ.

When we chant these psalms, we join the saints of Israel and of all the ages in handing ourselves over as best we can to God's designs for the kingdom. We pray for the needs of that kingdom, for the divine presence in the

---

23. And of a "horn of salvation" for David: compare verse 17 with Luke 1:69 in a literal translation like the RSV.

midst of God's people, for the needs of all God's priestly people, and for the effective rule of David's Son. Like other royal psalms, this one becomes a great flowering of the Lord's Prayer, "Thy kingdom come."

PSALMS 51 AND 100   MORNING THIRD FRIDAY

See above, pp. 53 and 57, Morning First Friday.

PSALM 135   EVENING THIRD FRIDAY AND MORNING FOURTH MONDAY

(134) 135. A hymn of praise

¹   Alleluia!

Praise the name of the Lord,
praise, you servants of the Lord,
²   who stand in the house of the Lord
in the courts of the house of our God.

³   Praise the Lord for the Lord is good.
Praise God's name; God is gracious.
⁴   For Jacob has been chosen by the Lord;
Israel for God's own possession.

⁵   For I know the Lord is great,
that our Lord is high above all gods.
⁶   Whatever the Lord wills, the Lord does,
in heaven, on earth, in the seas.

⁷   God summons clouds from the ends of the earth;
makes lightning produce the rain;
and sends forth the wind from the storehouse.

⁸   The first-born of the Egyptians God smote,
of mortals and beasts alike.
⁹   Signs and wonders God worked
in the midst of your land, O Egypt,
against Pharaoh and all his servants.

¹⁰   God struck nations in their greatness
and slew kings in their splendor.
¹¹   Sihon, king of the Amorites,
Og, the king of Bashan,
and all the kingdoms of Canaan.

¹² God gave their land as a heritage;
a heritage to Israel, his people.

¹³ LORD, your name stands for ever,
unforgotten from age to age,
¹⁴ for the LORD does justice for his people;
the Lord takes pity on his servants.

¹⁵ The pagans' idols are silver and gold,
the work of human hands.
¹⁶ They have mouths but they cannot speak;
they have eyes but they cannot see.

¹⁷ They have ears but they cannot hear;
there is never a breath on their lips.
¹⁸ Their makers will come to be like them
and so will all who trust in them!

¹⁹ House of Israel, bless the LORD!
House of Aaron, bless the LORD!
²⁰ House of Levi, bless the LORD!
You who fear the LORD, bless the LORD!

²¹ From Zion may the LORD be blessed,
the God who dwells in Jerusalem!

Repeatedly Israeli Jews and evangelical Christians have assured me that the land of Israel belongs to the Jews because God gave it to them at the time of Moses. Muslim Arabs have told me that it belongs to the Arabs by right of the conquest that God enjoined on believers. I find one argument just as problematic as the other. Impressive as I find the Qur'an and much of Islamic piety, being no Muslim believer I seriously doubt that it is in fact God who called for extension of the blessings of Islam by the sword.

As a Christian, however, I acknowledge the inspiration and truth of Scripture, I acknowledge that God was present in the experiences of Abraham and Moses and Joshua. Still, if I am to defend the Jewish state in Palestine, in the land that was Israel in biblical times, I've got to find some other basis than the promises recorded in Scripture. Just as I can't be content to use the warnings of the prophets and of Jesus to justify persecution of Jews.

For the inspiration and truth of Scripture does not mean that every narrative of the Bible is a reliable historical record—for instance, that if the TV cameras had been there, they would always have recorded events just as they are written. Nor shall we even try to explore the mystery of what it means to hear the voice of God. There are other kinds of truth than historical information.

When Christian believers do critical biblical studies, it is because they assume that the intellect God gave us can help us better to perceive what God really meant to teach us in Scripture.

For instance, in 1 Samuel 17:41-51 David kills Goliath, the Philistine from Gath, "the shaft of (whose) spear was like a weaver's beam" (17:7). But in 2 Samuel 21:19 it is "Elhanan the son of Jaareoregim, the Bethlehemite" who "slew Goliath of Gath, the shaft of whose spear was like a weaver's beam."[24] It certainly looks for all the world as if the most natural thing in oral narrative has happened, namely, the exploit of an insignificant character has been erroneously remembered as having been done by a well-known personage. And since such inconsistencies are not uncommon in the Bible, my intellectual task is not to find ingenious ways to prove that they are not contradictions after all, but to understand what it is that the writer—and so what it is that God—is saying that does not here depend on historical exactitude.

We do well also to ask critical questions about the divine words that ancient Israelites heard. People in all ages and all nations have heard their gods giving them warnings, promises, and instructions. Israel is not unique in this. What is significant is what Israel did with their messages, the lessons God caused them to draw from them.

Israel, like other peoples, believed that their God had told them to conquer a land already inhabited, the land of Canaan. Like the story about the dog that bit a man, there's no news in that. The news is in the way they came to treat the story of God's gift of the land. "There shall not be found among you anyone who burns his son or daughter as an offering, anyone who practices divination, a soothsayer . . . or a medium. . . . For because of these abominable practices the Lord your God is driving (the inhabitants) out before you" (Deut 18:10-12). The gift of the land becomes a call to moral uprightness. For those who would make Yahweh's gift of the land the basis for arrogant confidence, Amos undermines it all: "Did I not bring Israel up from the land of Egypt? And the Philistines from Caphtor and the Syrians from Kir!" (Amos 9:7, punctuation mine). Always the remembrance of the gift of the land was at least a call to humility, and gratitude for the land that need not have been theirs.

If the occupation of Canaan was the violent conquest that Deuteronomy and parts of Joshua would suggest (Josh 6:21; 8:22-25; 11:11-14), the vio-

24. A notice that evidently dismayed the Chronicler, who reports, in exactly the same context: "Elhanan the son of Jair slew Lahmi *the brother* of Goliath the Gittite, the shaft of whose spear was like a weaver's beam (2 Chr 20:5, emphasis mine).

lence is at least fraught with moral ambiguity.[25] If God really was the strategist who ordered the massacre of the inhabitants, then God is implicated in the moral problem. But rather than a defense of Israel, we can read Scripture as God's attempt to make the best of their traditions, to bring good out of the tragic violence of desperation.

Not that the problem is unique to ancient Israel, by any means. Go back far enough and you'll find that even the finest of human achievements are based on moral ambiguities or even unambiguous crimes. The great promise of American democracy remains built on the theft of the land from its original inhabitants; Islam has given to the turbulent Arabian tribes and to much of Africa moral discipline and faith in the one merciful and compassionate God, but often by means of violence; the story of the spread and maintenance of the gospel contains hair-raising stories of compulsion, deceit, and hypocrisy. Yet the population of the United States cannot retire into the sea to leave the land to the indigenous peoples (in any event, what would one do with those who are only partially Indian?). Nor could we give the French Catholics back to the Druids.

And so we thank God for the good things God has brought out of human wickedness and folly, as one might thank God for a child conceived in adultery without endorsing marital infidelity.

It is in the sense described above that I can sympathize with the current State of Israel, beginning, as it did, better than most colonial movements, with authorization of the Turkish authorities and purchase of often marginal lands from absentee landlords, stumbling through unexpected opportunities and impelled by justified fears into autonomy. Yet at the same time I sympathize with the Christian and Muslim Arabs of Palestine, whose homeland was usurped by the Turks and the British and then given away by the United Nations, and who—sometimes, indeed, through their own desperate folly—have been thwarted in every attempt toward self-governance. At the time of the final editing of this essay, there are glimmerings of hope for a political solution of the Arab-Israeli conflict, along with abundant ominous signs from rejectionists on both the Arab and Israeli sides. Even should this conflict be fully resolved, its intellectual legacy must be to show us the necessity of a critical moral evaluation of specific attitudes attested in the Bible. Such benchmark issues lead us to recognize that the Bible provides its own correctives.

---

25. As we have noted in a footnote under our treatment of Psalm 111 (evening of the third Sunday), critical scholars are, in fact, inclined to think the occupation of the land to have been far more peaceful than such passages would indicate, if for no other reason than their doubts that Israel came into the land as a force of several hundred thousand warriors.

Psalm 135 is a good enough prayer for the likes of us. If we thank God for the death of Sihon, king of the Amorites, and Og, king of Bashan, it is only that through the survival of ancient Israel we came to learn the foolishness of casting ourselves down in worship before any but the merciful and compassionate God who finally has called us to love our enemies, to do good to those who persecute us, yes, the God who in Jesus chose to die rather than to kill.[26]

PSALM 119:145-152 AND PSALM 117
MORNING THIRD SATURDAY

See above, pp. 63 and 66, Morning First Saturday.

26. Besides the developed section ridiculing idols, the themes of this psalm differ from those of Psalm 136 in two principal ways: where Psalm 136 treats creation (vv. 4-9), Psalm 135 deals with Yahweh's power over weather (vv. 6-7); and Psalm 136 treats the deliverance from Egypt much more extensively (136:10-16; 35:8-9).

FOURTH WEEK

PSALM 122   EVE OF FOURTH SUNDAY

(121) 122. In praise of Jerusalem: a pilgrimage song

1   I rejoiced when I heard them say:
    "Let us go to God's house."
2   And now our feet are standing
    within your gates, O Jerusalem.

3   Jerusalem is built as a city
    strongly compact.
4   It is there that the tribes go up,
    the tribes of the LORD.

    For Israel's law it is,
    there to praise the LORD's name.
5   There were set the thrones of judgement
    of the house of David.

6   For the peace of Jerusalem pray:
    "Peace be to your homes!
7   May peace reign in your walls,
    in your palaces, peace!"

8   For love of my family and friends
    I say: "Peace upon you."
9   For love of the house of the LORD
    I will ask for your good.

Give us discerning eyes to perceive where it is we are standing in the temple of the Christ's Body, and let us there find all our joy and peace.

PSALM 130   EVE OF FOURTH SUNDAY

(129) 130. A prayer of repentance and trust:
sixth psalm of repentance

1   Out of the depths I cry to you, O LORD,
2   Lord, hear my voice!
   O let your ears be attentive
   to the voice of my pleading.

3   If you, O LORD, should mark our guilt,
   Lord, who would survive?
4   But with you is found forgiveness:
   for this we revere you.

5   My soul is waiting for the LORD.
   I count on God's word.
6   My soul is longing for the Lord
   more than those who watch for daybreak.
   (Let the watchers count on daybreak
7   and Israel on the LORD.)

   Because with the LORD there is mercy
   and fullness of redemption,
8   Israel indeed God will redeem
   from all its iniquity.

Now, let's not make a big dramatic production of this. So you're a sinner? What's the big deal? I mean, what do you expect—to come in as one of the Big Three? Or to be delivered from all sin like Mary?[1]

The psalm, like all the gradual psalms (Psalms 120–134), is a bit odd. It starts like a lament of the individual but never gets around to describing the dreadful state one finds oneself in, much less to explicitly asking for help. Verses 1-6 are spoken in the first person singular,[2] with verses 1-4 addressed to Yahweh in the second person. But in verse 5, as Yahweh becomes "he" in-

---

1. If you are Protestant, you can ignore the bit about Mary. (However, note that the Catholic doctrine of the immaculate conception does not mean that Mary saved herself. For even more than any of the rest of us, she was saved purely by God, in that God did not just forgive her but so blessed and sustained her from the beginning that she always recognized God's will and freely chose it rather than the elusive benefits of sin. If anything, then, this doctrine is an unambiguous assertion of the priority of grace.)

2. The Liturgy of the Hours uses first person plural forms in verses 3-4, but in Hebrew "*our* guilt" is simply "guilt," and "for this we revere you" is "for this you are revered."

stead of "you," we seem almost to slip from a prayer addressed to God into a kind of exhortation to a congregation of Israelites.

This structure would suggest that the point of the psalm is to move from personal experience to communal concerns. Such a psalm would be at home in the kind of liturgical setting suggested for Psalm 49 (evening second Tuesday and also appropriate for Psalm 32): a kind of ritual in the early synagogue that moves from personal reflection or experience to exhortation. Such a practice could be seen as a development from the ceremony of thanksgiving offerings, at which the person offering the sacrifice would often give an exhortation to the guests assembled for the sacrificial meal (Pss 30:5-6; 32:1-2, 8-11; 34; cf. the vow of Pss 22:23-27 and 51:15).

Just what the "depths" were from which the petitioner cried (v. 1) always depended on that person's experience. It could be the frustration of exile, the effects of communal strife in the attempt to restore Jewish life in Israel; it could be personal griefs or trials, indeed all the dangers and sorrows of the human condition. "Hear me," the mourner cries, "let your ears be attentive!" One asks for nothing else in the psalm. Let Yahweh only hear and he will surely do what needs to be done.

The psalm simply assumes that sin is behind all human troubles, does not protest this as unjust or cruel, but only warns God that none will survive should he demand a full account for sin. And the psalm knows that God will not call for a full account, that God does forgive "so that (he) may be feared." Surprisingly, the result of God's pardon is seen, not as thanksgiving or love, but as fear[3]—not a craven fear but the awe that knows not what to say before such power and such compassion.

And so the mourner waits for God's mercy. The idea may have its origin in some sort of ritual practice in lament ceremonies of awaiting (even overnight) an oracle or other sign of God's favor. But it has by now become a patient waiting for the help God will give. For in verses 7-8 the hope for Israel is not simply some oracle of assurance! Rather, the psalmist's confident expectation of God's pardon and help becomes a model for guilty Israel.

Originally the psalm was said or chanted by one and heard by a congregation. How we pray this psalm depends in part on whether we identify with the one who spoke or with those who heard. We can hear the psalm as still expressing the faith of those ancients who first prayed thus, recognizing ourselves as called with Israel to such humble waiting. The traditional use of the

---

3. The Hebrew term translated "revere" in the Liturgy of the Hours is a broad term like the English word "fear," covering the whole spectrum from terror to awe or respect to the effect of such awe in obedience and reverent worship.

psalm in prayers for the dead does something like this, for we speak not in our own name but in that of the deceased, leaving them open to the mercy of God, who dares not demand a strict accounting for sin, lest none be left to serve him.

And when we pray in our own name, the "depths" that we cry from express our own experience of the human condition, whether that be overwhelming guilt or the searing pain of destroyed love or the dryness of depression or the desperate recognition of our pettiness. Our words of confidence may express a strong certainty of God's care or the wrenching confession of a faith we want to believe against all evidence.

The psalm does not offer cheap assurances that everything will be all right. We wait. We wait God's good time. We trust. We trust that God's remedy, God's redemption of our sins, will be all that we need and more than we need, even if for this we must await in patience the full redemption that is greater than all our hopes and beyond all time.

PSALMS 118 AND 150   MORNING FOURTH SUNDAY

See above, pp. 70 and 74, Morning Second Sunday.

PSALM 110:1-5, 7   EVENING FOURTH SUNDAY

See above, p. 13, Evening First Sunday.

PSALM 112   EVENING FOURTH SUNDAY

(111) 112. The happiness of good people

1   Alleluia!
    Happy are those who fear the LORD,
    who take delight in all God's commands.
2   Their descendants shall be powerful on earth;
    the children of the upright are blessed.

3   Wealth and riches are in their homes;
    their justice stands firm for ever.
4   They are lights in the darkness for the upright;
    they are generous, merciful and just.

5   Good people take pity and lend,
    they conduct their affairs with honor.
6   The just will never waver,
    they will be remembered for ever.

7   They have no fear of evil news;
     with firm hearts they trust in the LORD.
8   With steadfast hearts they will not fear;
     they will see the downfall of their foes.

9   Openhanded, they give to the poor;
     their justice stands firm for ever.
     Their heads will be raised in glory.

10 The wicked shall see this and be angry,
     shall grind their teeth and pine away;
     the desires of the wicked lead to doom.

Grant, O God, that we may be counted among the compassionate and just, that sharing by faith in Christ's righteousness, we may have no cause to fear the wiles of the Enemy.

PSALM 90   MORNING FOURTH MONDAY

(89) 90. God's eternity and the shortness of life

1   O Lord, you have been our refuge
     from one generation to the next.
2   Before the mountains were born
     or the earth or the world brought forth,
     you are God, without beginning or end.

3   You turn us back into dust
     and say: "Go back, children of the earth."
4   To your eyes a thousand years
     are like yesterday, come and gone,
     no more than a watch in the night.

5   You sweep us away like a dream,
     like grass which springs up in the morning.
6   In the morning it springs up and flowers;
     by evening it withers and fades.

7   So we are destroyed in your anger,
     struck with terror in your fury.
8   Our guilt lies open before you,
     our secrets in the light of your face.

9   All our days pass away in your anger.
     Our life is over like a sigh.

10 Our span is seventy years,
or eighty for those who are strong.

And most of these are emptiness and pain.
They pass swiftly and we are gone.
11 Who understands the power of your anger
and fears the strength of your fury?

12 Make us know the shortness of our life
that we may gain wisdom of heart.
13 LORD, relent! Is your anger for ever?
Show pity to your servants.

14 In the morning, fill us with your love;
we shall exult and rejoice all our days.
15 Give us joy to balance our affliction
for the years when we knew misfortune.

16 Show forth your work to your servants;
let your glory shine on their children.
17 Let the favor of the Lord be upon us:
give success to the work of our hands
(give success to the work of our hands).

Gary Larson, the outrageously inventive creator of the "Far Side" comic strip, has a cartoon captioned "God as a kid tries to make a chicken in his room."[4] In it a somewhat overweight, dismayed Boy surveys his shattered chemistry set and a room scattered with feathers. In my youth I vaguely thought it unfair that God happened to be immortal and all-powerful, while I wasn't. Both my image of God and Larson's—the latter consciously so—are a caricature of God. God doesn't "happen to be" anything! God simply is, necessarily so, gloriously so, generously so. To resent anything about God is rather like resenting that your mother is older than you, like a rock resenting that it is not the mountain.

Still, if we are to talk to God at all, we will have to do so in terms that are as if God were one of us. The whole rhetoric of the psalms aims to please God or to convince God to intervene in our needs the only way we know how, that is, as we would please or convince a human being. Nor is that unreasonable: God, after all, has revealed God's own self to us in terms derived from human experience. Any knowledge we have of God as being powerful

4. September 24, 1986.

or compassionate or forgiving, as punishing or guiding, is reached by drawing analogies from the world around us. Even the negative designations of God—immortal, infinite—simply assume these analogies, but they try to protect their picture of God by denying the limitations we know in human experience.

Psalm 90 asks God for help precisely by appealing to the difference between God and human beings. Respectfully, but insistently, it asks God to take into account the difference between God and us. "God, you don't have to worry about death," the psalm is saying, "but we do. Your life is without beginning or end, but our life is short and miserable. Have pity, Lord, have pity!"

The psalm is rather like the gradual psalms (Psalms 120–134) in its mingling of plural forms with concerns of the individual. The prayer is not for "me" but for "us." But the psalm does not address great traumatic national issues like defeat in war (Pss 44; 74; 79; 80) or drought (Jer 14:1-9). Rather, the complaints about the brevity and misery of life and the petitions for wisdom and for relief for self and children would seem to better suit the personal needs of prayers for the individual.

Because the psalm suggests that the troubles are of long standing (vv. 10c, 15b) and because they seem to be common to all members of the community, many would date the use of the psalm to the exilic or postexilic period. Surely the psalm would be appropriate for Jews of that time, but the small farmers of the royal period, who were being dispossessed by the great landowners (Isa 5:8-10; Amos 2:6-8; 5:10-12) might just as well express much the same kind of complaint. Widespread misery was not limited to any one period.

Nor, for that matter, is misery limited to antiquity. The world is quite filled with miserable people and people who would be miserable if they allowed themselves to feel what they experience. Henry Thoreau said that "the mass of men lead lives of quiet desperation."[5] He may well have been right. For misery is not only the mother who cannot protect her children in famine, someone whose home is destroyed in an earthquake, the young person forced into addiction and prostitution; it is also individuals stuck in a job they never wanted, in a marriage they hadn't counted on, the religious—or the revolutionary—assailed by doubts about his or her cause, the pastor of an unresponsive flock, the fervent Christian seeing the community suffer from inept or self-seeking pastors, the person suppressing a story of childhood abuse or the person trying to face it, and on and on.

5. *The Variorum Walden,* annotated and with an introduction by Walter Harding (New York: Twayne Publishers, 1962) 28.

This is not to say that the desperation eats up the whole of life—there are pleasures and satisfactions as well. In 1990 a soap opera in China met with phenomenal success. It was set against the turbulent times of the Cultural Revolution, which destroyed careers, tore families apart, released a reign of terror on any who would not mouth the correct doctrines. And yet the drama is not overtly political; it is about the life of a family, their troubles and their joys; people still fell in love, a first child was born, children played in the streets.

When we pray Psalm 90 we can pray it for ourselves, or we can pray it for those we see and those we do not see around us, for the homeless, for those who have lost a spouse, for abused spouses, for unloved children, for persons laden with guilt and persons too callous to experience their guilt. Those of us who are over thirty, at any rate, know how fast this life passes, how short the time that is left; we know what a shame it is to waste this life on misery. As Christians we believe, indeed, that this short life is not the end of the tale. Still, that is no reason to squander it in futility. God made life to be lived in.

Nor is the way out always an escape from the trials. The life of Jesus was a life of conflict, sorrows, disappointments, failure. And yet it was not a life of misery or of desperation.

A rare lament this, that prays for wisdom: "Make us know the shortness of our life[6] that we may gain wisdom of heart." Often enough it is wisdom that can transform misery into peace, whether it is the wisdom to perceive and help another bear burdens, or the wisdom to recognize how we can face and surmount the trials of our own life, or finally the wisdom to accept in tranquility what cannot be changed.

PSALM 135:1-12   MORNING FOURTH MONDAY

See above, p. 164, Evening Third Friday, where the whole psalm is treated.

PSALM 136   EVENING FOURTH MONDAY

(135) 136. Litany of praises: psalm of worship

1   Alleluia!
    O give thanks to the LORD who is good,
    whose love endures forever.

---

6. An interpretative translation. The Hebrew is a more ambiguous, something like "Teach us to measure our days, that we may gain a heart of wisdom." Wisdom may well teach you that there are other ways to measure your days than by number!

² Give thanks to the God of gods,
whose love endures forever.
³ Give thanks to the Lord of lords,
whose love endures forever;

⁴ who alone has wrought marvelous works,
whose love endures forever;
⁵ whose wisdom it was made the skies,
whose love endures forever;
⁶ who fixed the earth firmly on the seas,
whose love endures forever.

⁷ It was God who made the great lights,
whose love endures forever;
⁸ the sun to rule in the day,
whose love endures forever;
⁹ the moon and stars in the night,
whose love endures forever.

¹⁰ The first-born of the Egyptians God smote,
whose love endures forever;
¹¹ and brought Israel out from the midst,
whose love endures forever;
¹² arm outstretched, with powerful hand,
whose love endures forever.

¹³ God divided the Red Sea in two,
whose love endures forever;
¹⁴ and made Israel pass through the midst,
whose love endures forever;
¹⁵ Who flung Pharaoh and his force in the sea,
whose love endures forever.

¹⁶ God led the people through the desert,
whose love endures forever.
¹⁷ Nations in their greatness God struck,
whose love endures forever.
¹⁸ Kings in their splendor God slew,
whose love endures forever.

¹⁹ Sihon, king of the Amorites,
whose love endures forever;
²⁰ and Og, the king of Bashan,
whose love endures forever.

²¹ God let Israel inherit their land,
whose love endures forever;
²² the heritage of Israel, God's servant,
whose love endures forever.
²³ God remembered us in our distress,
whose love endures forever.

²⁴ God has snatched us away from our foes,
whose love endures forever.
²⁵ God gives food to all living things,
whose love endures forever.
²⁶ To the God of heaven give thanks,
whose love endures forever.

"Nations in their greatness he struck, for his love endures forever. Kings in their splendor he slew, for his love endures forever" (vv. 17-18). Of course, the mothers of Og, king of Bashan, and Sihon, king of the Amorites, might not have been so convinced of Yahweh's love. And, while it's all right to smile cynically at this talk of love, at some point let's just let go of our own presuppositions long enough to look sympathetically at this admittedly primitive hymn. Those who used this hymn believed, according to their story, that had it not been for all these things—the deliverance from Egypt and the slaughter of the kings—they would not be there at all, they would be no nation, they would have no land. And all these things—the defeat of their enemies and the possession of their land—were not things simply for them to grab but rather the gift of Yahweh. Ideally, at least, it promoted not arrogance but humility before God's gifts.[7]

Every verse of the poem describes Yahweh's mighty works as the manifestation of his love: "For his love endures for ever," a phrase surely meant originally as a refrain to be chanted by the whole congregation. Of course, we may suppose that there was an artistic or pastoral need to have a refrain chanted by the entire congregation or by a large chorus. However, it is significant that while they could have chosen to repeat a phrase about Yahweh's power or Israel's righteousness, for instance, they chose rather to dwell on Yahweh's gracious love.

The "love" of this refrain is, of course, the Hebrew word *hesed,* a key theological term of the Book of Psalms and an idea of some importance elsewhere in the Old Testament. In secular usage the word refers to a benevolent attitude in virtue of which one does benefits to another, or else it refers to the actual benefits done, especially for one in need (Gen 20:13; 40:14; 1 Sam

7. For the relationship of the motifs of this psalm to those of Psalm 135, see the final footnote under that psalm (Evening Third Friday, p. 168 n. 26).

20:15; 2 Sam 16:17; Prov 19:22; 20:6). It is from such secular usage that the word has been taken up to refer to Israel's experience with Yahweh.

Some scholars, following Nelson Glueck, *Hesed in the Bible* (New York: Ktav, 1975), maintain that such bonds as family ties or especially covenant relationship are integral to the term *hesed;* however, that is not necessarily the case. Naturally, given human nature, people are more likely to be kind to persons with whom they have some sort of relationship. Nevertheless, in Joshua 2:12 Rahab's kindness toward the Israelite spies actually goes against her obligation to her city. Joseph asks Pharaoh's cupbearer to do him the *hesed* of interceding with the king for his release from prison (Gen 40:14). And in this psalm the very creation of the world is seen as an act of Yahweh's love, even before there existed anyone for God to have obligations to.

But certainly freedom is part of the concept of *hesed,* even if this be the free choice to live up to one's family or covenant obligations. For obligation does not take away freedom. On the contrary, if living up to one's obligations is praiseworthy, it is so only because one freely chooses to do so. Yahweh's love for Israel is characterized by the fullest freedom, for Yahweh has no obligations to Israel until he freely obliges himself through his covenant.

The psalm praises Yahweh for three great gifts: creation of the universe (vv. 4-9), deliverance of Israel from Egypt (vv. 10-16), and the giving of the lands of the nations to Israel (vv. 17-22).[8] This triad follows the core of the Pentateuch, though in the Pentateuch the land of Canaan is promised to Israel but not yet given. And of course these gifts are central to Israel's understanding of who they are before God.

These central gifts remain part of our story. How can they not be? Moses and the prophets are the foundation on which the Church is built; through Christ we are brought into the old story of God's freely given love. That story did not stop, either for Israel or for us, with the occupation of the land of Canaan. Verses 23-24, "He remembered us in our distress . . . . And he snatched us away from our foes," are not just a summary of the previous benefits but are a recapitulation of the story of Israel to the moment when the psalm is sung. And now they still continue to summarize our story, the whole story of Israel, the story of our incorporation into Israel through Jesus, the story of the survival of the gospel to our own day, the personal story of each of us as the mystery of Israel is recapitulated in our lives. In all of this we perceive God's freely given love, and in this psalm we find words to begin the praise of this love of God.

---

8. For the obviously problematic delight in the death of the Canaanite kings and the transfer of their land to Israel, see our comments on Psalm 135.

PSALM 101   MORNING FOURTH TUESDAY

(100) 101. A mirror for rulers

¹ My song is of mercy and justice;
   I sing to you, O LORD.
² I will walk in the way of perfection.
   O when, Lord, will you come?

   I will walk with blameless heart
   within my house;
³ I will not set before my eyes
   whatever is base.

   I will hate the ways of the crooked;
   they shall not be my friends.
⁴ The false-hearted must keep far away;
   the wicked I disown.

⁵ Those who secretly slander their neighbors
   I will bring to silence.
   Those of proud look and haughty heart
   I will never endure.

⁶ I look to the faithful in the land
   that they may dwell with me.
   Those who walk in the way of perfection
   shall be my friends.

⁷ No one who practices deceit
   shall live within my house.
   No one who utters lies shall stand
   before my eyes.

⁸ Morning by morning I will silence
   all the wicked in the land,
   uprooting from the city of the LORD
   all who do evil.

Though interpreters almost always explain this psalm as a solemn promise of the king pledging an honest administration, Leslie Allen has argued, correctly I believe, for a minority opinion that sees the psalm as a royal profession of innocence.[9] The protestation of innocence is, of course, a typical element of many

9. *Psalms 101–150,* Word Biblical Commentary 29 (Dallas: Word Books, 1990) 4.

psalms (16:3-4; 17:3-5; 18:21-25; 26:1-8, 11-12; 44:18-23; see Psalm 139, Evening Fourth Wednesday, pp. 193–197), usually as a motive for God to intervene to rescue the psalmist in distress.[10] Only such an understanding explains the virtual petition in the question of verse 2, "O when, Lord, will you come?"

The psalm, then, was probably part of a liturgy, one prayer in an elaborate service of petition celebrated in the royal temple in times of extraordinary need or perhaps at an annual service meant to renew the divine blessings on the king, analogous to the autumn festival in Babylon, where the feast commemorating Marduk's assumption of royal power likewise confirmed the rule of the Chaldean king. In such a liturgy the purpose of the psalm would be to convince Yahweh to intervene and help the king (and the king's people) because the king has been faithful to Yahweh.

But having said this, let us note that even if the majority are right and the psalm was, after all, a pledge of righteous behavior for the future,[11] the understanding of the nature of the king's responsibilities remains the same, despite a radical difference in the purpose of the prayer.

Formally the psalm is addressed to Yahweh, at least in the first verses; for in fact second person terms are found only in verses 1 and 2. By verse 8 Yahweh is mentioned in the third person.[12]

The first line looks rather like a hymn of praise or a thanksgiving psalm (cf. Pss 34:2-3; 103:1f.; 104:1; 145:1f.; 146:1f.), praising Yahweh for the love

---

10. While the verbs of such protestations of innocence are frequently in the Hebrew perfect tense ("I did such-and-such," "I did not do thus-and-thus"), they are almost as often in the Hebrew imperfect, as here in Psalm 101. While these two tenses often correspond to our past and future respectively, that is because the former suggests completed action and the latter action that is considered under the aspect of not being completed. But the Septuagint of this psalm actually translated the verbs in the Greek past imperfect, as repeated or continuous action in the past: "I have customarily walked with blameless heart . . . I kept disowning the wicked . . . I repeatedly silenced all the wicked in the land," doubtless sensing that the topics of these sentences corresponded to the protests of the psalmist's righteous behavior in other psalms. It is better, however, to understand them as present tense, referring to the king's customary attitudes and behavior.

11. In that case, since this psalm has no parallel in the Bible, it is only from its content that we can deduce how it was used. A good guess would be that it was spoken by the king at his inauguration, rather like the covenant between David and the Israelites (2 Sam 5:3) or the covenant of Jehoash with Yahweh and the people (2 Kgs 11:17). A somewhat similar (but specifically deuteronomic) covenant of Josiah with Yahweh is mentioned in a special ceremony of 2 Kings 23:3f. at the finding of the Law.

12. However, such third person references to Yahweh in second person contexts are not unusual, indeed are roughly paralleled in court addresses to the king. See Pss 3:9 (Heb.); 54:3-9; cf. 1 Kgs 25:24-31.

and just judgment typically attributed to him (Pss 33:5; 36:6f.; 89:15; 119:149; Jer 9:23; Hos 2:21). This hymnlike beginning is very much similar to that of Psalm 89, another text for a royal liturgy to be used like this prayer in times of distress, striving to convince God to intervene and assist the king who, despite the ancient promises to David's descendants, is in desperate trouble.

That the text is royal speech we deduce from the behavior described in verses 2-8, all of which is appropriate to the fulfillment of the king's mandate and some of which is clearly not the concern of the common householder. Thus, in verse 8 the promise to destroy the wicked from the land and from Jerusalem is the specific task of the king. And in verse 6 the term translated "shall be my friends" actually means something more like "shall be my ministers" in Hebrew, since it is used only to refer to the service given to God or to persons of great authority such as Moses and Aaron, kings, and prophets.

Nor does the rest of the promise represent a self-righteous refusal of an individual to associate with persons of inferior moral quality; rather, it is all meant to affirm honest government. Thus, the king does not have crooked retainers (v. 3), at court does not tolerate the slander that so easily subverts both justice and the ability to get good counsel, does not subject citizens to haughty officials (v. 5), recruits officials loyal to Yahweh and upright in conduct (v. 6). And finally, by holding his daily court of justice (2 Sam 15:2; Jer 21:12), the king ensures righteousness throughout the realm.

The psalm was doubtless used over a period of many reigns by scoundrels like Manasseh and Jehoiakim as well as by upright kings like Hezekiah and Josiah. But even on the lips of the worst rulers such a declaration had its value, for no matter how cynically the claim was made, no matter how misguided the king's understanding might be, still the very words kept the ideal of the king's duties alive. A powerful irony, after all, was evident in the profession of innocence made by a king whose whole royal administration belied his pious protest!

Scribes preserved Psalm 101, like other royal psalms, even after the fall of Jerusalem in 587, when there was no longer a king in Jerusalem. It was to be kept in reserve for the restoration of the monarchy, as a part of a liturgy to be done by the rulers when God would restore kings (this time righteous kings!) to his people. But the centuries stretched on, and no such restoration came. The traditional title "Psalm of David" came to be taken as an indication of authorship, and the Rabbis speculated that David had composed the psalm at the beginning of his reign as a program for his rule. Since David was the model of the ideal king, the psalm may well have come to describe the future Messiah, though the lack of allusion to the psalm in the New Testament suggests that such a reading was not important in messianic thought.

Well, not many of us are kings, so how are we to pray the psalm?[13] Even though the psalm was not traditionally understood as messianic, we can hear it as the voice of Christ, whose very title is a confession that in him are fulfilled the aspirations of Israel's kingship. However, the kingship of Christ is primarily an eschatological hope, for an honest appraisal of the real world makes it evident that all the wicked of the land have in no wise been silenced, nor are we the perfect, upright, honest, humble ministers promised by the king. Whether in Church or state, there is more than enough crookedness, arrogance, deceit, and slander to go around. It is only in the last judgment that the power of wickedness will truly be broken (v. 8).

In the meantime, perhaps it is providential that the modern reading of the text, including the Grail translation for the Liturgy of the Hours, has understood the psalm as a pledge of future behavior rather than a protest of present innocence. As such, we gratefully hear it as Christ's pledge of a day of judgment in which the power of wickedness (even within ourselves) will finally come to naught. But such hope for the coming of Christ does not exhaust the possibilities of the prayer. After all, the eschatological kingdom of peace and justice is the model of the world we are called to strive for. That kingdom defines our moral duty. And every time we hear Christ speak this pledge, we who have various ministries in Church and society are reminded of the kind of compassion, humility, and justice that Christ calls us to.

Insofar as we in any way share with Christ the ordering of the world, the prayer can become our own pledge as well. Clearly persons with civic or ecclesiastical responsibility, elected officials, bishops, superiors, pastors, must choose wisely those to whom they delegate their authority or whom they appoint to an office with its own inherent authority.[14] Those for whom they are responsible have a right to humane, honest, respectful treatment. Yet every such person of authority is well aware of the fragile stuff they have to work with; often the best one can do is to try to put the arrogant person in a position where he or she will do the least damage, to help subordinates by supportive and compassionate supervision to grow in their ability to treat others with the dignity and competence to which they are entitled.

Employers, teachers, parents have similar responsibilities. If I might express what to some economists would be heresy, an employer might express in this prayer the resolve not to subject customers to a salesperson whose

---

13. Or for that matter if you are a monarch, you are probably so limited by constitutional restraints that you cannot determine the choice of your ministers in any event.

14. The bishop or pastor, for instance, while appointed by another, enjoys (or suffers from) authority of the office itself, not simply delegated authority.

aggressive approach maximizes profits, but at the cost of the dignity of the buyer. And parents, for instance, in choosing a school are choosing the kind of persons who will strongly influence their children for life.

The psalm is not concerned only with the choice of persons with responsibility. As it was a pledge of the king's own attitudes and behavior, it can become your own promise to "walk in the way of perfection"—not some rarefied moral superiority but the earthy quality suggested by the Hebrew of simply being fully what you should be. Well, admittedly it is not as simple as this might suggest; the point, however, is that this perfection is found at the center of your responsibilities rather than in some great realm of extraordinary deeds and attitudes.

Be perfect, you are told, as your heavenly Father is perfect. Now, there is no supererogation in the perfection of the God whom you seek to imitate. God is perfect simply by being God. The perfection to which you are called is to be honest, compassionate, just, and humble as a human being, as a Christian, and in your responsibilities to whoever in any way depends on you. Each time you pray this psalm you again take up your pledge to be truly human, truly Christian.

PSALM 144:1-10   MORNING FOURTH TUESDAY

See below, p. 198, Evening Fourth Thursday, where the whole psalm is treated.

PSALM 137:1-6   EVENING FOURTH TUESDAY

(136) 137. Homesickness in exile

1 By the rivers of Babylon
   there we sat and wept,
   remembering Zion;
2 on the poplars that grew there
   we hung up our harps.

3 For it was there that they asked us.
   our captors, for songs,
   our oppressors, for joy.
   "Sing to us," they said,
   "one of Zion's songs."

4 O how could we sing
   the song of the LORD
   on alien soil?

5 If I forget you, Jerusalem,
   Let my right hand wither!

6 O let my tongue
   cleave to my mouth
   if I remember you not,
   if I prize not Jerusalem
   above all my joys!

[7 Remember, O LORD,
   against the people of Edom
   the day of Jerusalem;
   when they said: "Tear it down!
   Tear it down to its foundations!"

8 O Babylon, destroyer,
   they are happy who repay you
   the ills you brought on us.
9 They shall seize and shall dash
   your children on the rock!]

The last few kings to rule in Judah alternated between grudging acquiescence and defiant resistance to Babylonian rule as King Nebuchadrezzar replaced the Assyrians as the dominant power in the Middle East. Crushing the revolt of Jehoiakim, in 598 B.C.E. he conquered Judah and exiled thousands of the ruling class and artisans to Babylon. When the new king rebelled a decade later, Nebuchadrezzar returned, devastated the country, destroyed Jerusalem, blinded the king, and took to Babylon the great mass of those who survived, leaving only "the poorest of the land to be vinedressers and ploughmen" (2 Kgs 25:12).

This exile was a decisive time for Israel. For while some Jews intermarried with the conquerors and assimilated, others were finally able to overcome their resistance to the message of the great prophets. These had urged submission to Babylon and recognition that the disasters which befell Israel were not a sign of Yahweh's impotence before the Mesopotamian gods, but were Yahweh's punishment of his people for their rebellion, their arrogance, and their exploitation of their own Israelite brothers and sisters. Now, during the exile Jewish scholars edited the great old stories of Israel's origins, the survey of the history of the kingdom, and the speeches of the prophets in order to interpret the disasters of the nation and to find a plan for restoration through repentance.

A whole generation passed before the exiles were allowed to return, when the Persian king Cyrus conquered Babylon in 538 B.C.E. In accord with his policy of fostering the national and religious identities of his subject peoples, Cyrus permitted those who wished to do so to return to Jerusalem and reestablish the cult of Yahweh. Psalm 137 recalls this period of exile,[15] poignantly expressing the despondency and anger of those forced to dwell in a foreign land.

The waters (v. 1), the great rivers and canals, of Babylon were characteristic of that land, distinguishing it from the mountains of Israel, whose streams are filled only at times of rain. The Babylonians' appeal for song (v. 3) is not necessarily malicious, for Judah was noted for its music; a good century earlier King Sennacherib had boasted about taking singers from Jerusalem as tribute. But we cannot sing our sacred songs (v. 4) either because the foreign land is ritually unclean (Amos 7:17; Ezek 4:13) or more likely simply because our distress is too great.

The protestation to remember Jerusalem (vv. 5-6) is a typical oath, a conditional curse uttered against oneself if one breaks one's resolve (1 Sam 3:17; 2 Kgs 6:31).

At this point the Liturgy of the Hours breaks off the psalm according to the policy of omitting prayers against enemies. The psalm itself continues with a terrifying curse of Edom and especially Babylon (vv. 7-9):

Remember, O Lord,

against the people of Edom
the day of Jerusalem;
when they said: "Tear it down!
Tear it down to its foundations!"

O Babylon, destroyer,
they are happy who repay you
the ills you brought on us.
They shall seize and shall dash
your children on the rock!

Spite there was in such wishes; but more than spiteful, they were a call for justice, a hope that the nations that had brutalized us might reap appropriate pun-

15. Whether the psalm is to be dated from the Exile or after it is problematic. The oath not to forget Jerusalem (vv. 5-6) makes far better sense if spoken in exile than after the return. Nor do the past tenses of verses 1-3 indicate that the distress is being recalled at a later date, for past tenses are typical of complaints in laments (thus, Ps 22:2, 12b, 13-16a are all in the past tense, though English translations will present some verbs as present; the idea is "They have insulted me and still do so.") However, the use of the expression "there" in verse 1 would suggest that the speaker is not in the place of the experience. Perhaps the inconsistency results from the reshaping of an older text for performance after the return to Jerusalem.

ishment. For Israel, of course, had no ideal of love of enemies. Nor had they any conception of a transcendent reward or punishment: if God's justice was to be done, it must be done in the visible, historical world of here and now.

Jerusalem is in some way home for all of us, Christians as well as Jews. So much of our story, the story of the prophets, the story of Jesus centers in Jerusalem. The psalm can, then, become an expression of our concern for that troubled city. We think of our Christian brothers and sisters, who are doubly a minority, a minority as Arabs among Jews and a minority as Christians among Muslim Arabs, and who feel themselves doubly discriminated against. We remember the Jews, who sought refuge in their old land, largely in flight from the persecution of Christians, only to find themselves violently hated by those who were already there. Nor do we forget the Muslims, who like to boast of themselves as owning the land by right of conquest, but who for the most part are presumably the offspring of the old Israelites and even the Canaanites, who have lived in the land as long as anyone can remember. Millennia ago, in the centuries after the Hebrew settlement, their Canaanite and Israelite ancestors had merged in one Israelite community, and then in late antiquity many of these became Christians, and finally in the Middle Ages were converted to Islam. Like Paul's Christians sending their collection to relieve the poor of Jerusalem (1 Cor 16:1ff.), we feel a special responsibility toward the people of that tormented city, the mother of our faith.[16]

But in Christian tradition Jerusalem has also become a metaphor of the eschatological city, whose very temple is God and the Lamb, to which the glory and honor of the nations shall be brought (Heb 12:22; Rev 21:1–22:5; cf. Ezek 40–46). Called though we are to attempt to bring about in this world justice and peace like that of the kingdom of heaven, we know that the world we can make is not the ultimate kingdom, that we await a new world which is God's doing, whose peace and justice cannot be subverted by some future foolish generation but stands eternally confirmed by God.

If we try to pray the complete psalm, including its curses on the enemies (vv. 7-9), even the wishes of disaster do not make such prayer completely impossible. It is true that disciples of the One who would not call down the ready legions of angels against his murderers (Matt 26:53f.) can hardly feel at ease in wishing such vengeance even upon the worst of the enemies of God,

---

16. As this was first being prepared for publication in *Worship* in August 1993, the astonishing news broke of the historic agreement between the Israeli government and the Palestine Liberation Organization. Between the hopes aroused by this agreement and the bitter opposition of many impassioned Jews and Arabs, we have since been given plenty of opportunity for fervent prayer for the welfare of Jerusalem and in years to come will doubtless have constant call to seek its peace.

who makes the sun rise upon the evil and the good alike. However, all the language of psalmody tends to become metaphorical in our prayer. And metaphor is the only way one can pray about Babylon, since the Neo-Babylonian empire has been gone lo these twenty-five hundred years and Edom for two thousand. Metaphor also is the only way we can pray about the disasters wished upon the enemies.

Moreover, already the Book of Revelation makes Babylon to be Rome, not just as persecutor of the saints but as the one who leads the nations astray (Rev 17–18). When we pray, Edom and Babylon become on different days the Congress, the media, the Curia,[17] the satanic powers, and all that great realm of pride and concupiscence that teems in our own hearts—in short, whatever keeps us in exile from the realm of peace and justice here and now, whatever imperils our participation in the eschatological kingdom.

The wishes against the enemies, then, become metaphor. As for the desire for vengeance, we who hold so much of Babylon in our hearts would do well to leave that to God, lest in our zeal we curse ourselves. But the utter destruction of that Babylon which keeps us in exile, ah! that is another thing. Though such a prayer can be fully accomplished only in the eschaton (and all Christian petition is finally a cry for the definitive coming of Christ), even now God gives the pledges of that Last Day. These pledges may seem small: the substitution of moderately offensive legislation on criminal justice for a horrendous bill, or—in a much smaller world—the decision of a parent to seek treatment for chemical dependency.

But it is in just such concrete things that the cosmic struggle is now waged. The Rule of Benedict is engaging not in merely fanciful allegory but in true metaphor when it uses the last line of this psalm as an image to describe the monk's spiritual struggle. It pronounces a blessing on the monastic who has resisted Satan and his temptations, who has "laid hold of his thoughts while they are still young and dashed them against Christ"![18]

PSALM 138   EVENING FOURTH TUESDAY

(137) 138. A song of deliverance

1   I thank you, Lord, with all my heart,
     you have heard the words of my mouth.

---

17. One must never blame the prince for the troubles in the realm, they tell us, but rather one blames the prince's counselors.

18. Prologue, *St. Benedict's Rule for Monasteries,* trans. Leonard J. Doyle (Collegeville, Minn.: The Liturgical Press, 1948) 3.

In the presence of the angels I will bless you.
² I will adore before your holy temple.

I thank you for your faithfulness and love
which excel all we ever knew of you.
³ On the day I called, you answered;
you increased the strength of my soul.

⁴ All the rulers on earth shall thank you
when they hear the words of your mouth.
⁵ They shall sing of the LORD's ways:
"How great is the glory of the LORD!"

⁶ The LORD is high yet looks on the lowly
and the haughty God knows from afar.
⁷ Though I walk in the midst of affliction
you give me life and frustrate my foes.

You stretch out your hand and save me,
your hand ⁸ will do all things for me.
Your love, O LORD, is eternal,
discard not the work of your hands.

Despite all our frailty, all our inconstancy, your Church, O God, does proclaim your glory before all the nations by confessing how you have reached down repeatedly to deliver us from the powers of darkness. I gladly join in this great chorus, for to confess my weakness is also to acknowledge your power, which in your mercy you put at my disposal.

PSALM 108   MORNING FOURTH WEDNESDAY

(107) 108. A confident prayer for victory

² My heart is ready, O God;
I will sing, sing your praise.
Awake, my soul;
³ awake, lyre and harp,
I will awake the dawn.

⁴ I will thank you, LORD, among the peoples,
among the nations I will praise you,
⁵ for your love reaches to the heavens
and your truth to the skies.
⁶ O God, arise above the heavens;
may your glory shine on earth!

7   O come and deliver your friends;
    help with your right hand and reply.
8   From the holy place God has made this promise:
    "I will triumph and divide the land of Shechem;
    I will measure out the valley of Succoth.

9   Gilead is mine and Manasseh.
    Ephraim I take for my helmet,
    Judah for my commander's staff.
10 Moab I will use for my washbowl,
    on Edom I will plant my shoe.
    Over the Philistines I will shout in triumph."

11 But who will lead me to conquer the fortress?
    Who will bring me face to face with Edom?
12 Will you utterly reject us, O God,
    and no longer march with our armies?

13 Give us help against the foe,
    for human help is vain.
14 With God we shall do bravely
    and the Lord will trample down our foes.

See Psalm (59) 60

After firmly uniting the tribes that King Saul had held before him in a fragile union, David in the tenth century had gone on to establish a quite respectable empire, including the neighboring lands of the Philistine cities, Moab, Edom, and Ammon, and part of Syria. At the death of Solomon the tribes were divided into two kingdoms, Israel in the north and Judah, under descendants of David, in the south.

The divided nation was unable to retain control of the subject states; the Philistines and Syrians seem at once to have resumed control of their own destinies, and Ammon, Moab, and Edom followed suit in the next few decades. The Davidic kings and their court considered the emancipation of Israel (1 Kgs 12:19) and of the subject nations (2 Kgs 8:22) nothing but rebellion (cf. Ps 2:1-3). Over the centuries, whenever the Northern Kingdom of Israel was weak, their neighbors, Ammon or Syria and later Assyria, seized the Israelite territory of Gilead, vulnerably situated across the Jordan River.[19] In 721 B.C.E. the last remnants of the Northern Kingdom were absorbed into

---

19. 1 Kgs 22:3; 2 Kgs 10:32f.; 15:29; Amos 1:3, 13.

the Assyrian empire, and when Assyria collapsed toward the end of the seventh century, the Neo-Babylonian king Nebuchadrezzar incorporated Israel and finally the Southern Kingdom of Judah into his empire, deporting any potential leaders to Mesopotamia.

Israel, or at least the best of Israel, did not respond to the disaster by capitulating to Babylon's triumphant gods but by learning to interpret their defeat, not as a failure of Yahweh in the face of these gods, but as punishment by Yahweh for Israel's crimes against him, a punishment with which the pre-exilic prophets had threatened their people: "I will scatter you among the nations and disperse you through the countries . . . and you shall know that I am the Lord" (Ezek 22:15f.).

Psalm 108 is a liturgy that reflects this long period of disintegration.[20] It would seem to have been composed by combining the last verses of Psalms 57 (vv. 2-6 = 57:8-12) and 60:7-14 (= 108:7-14)[21] in order to make a prayer for a somewhat different use, emphasizing confidence in God's help rather than complaint about defeat.

The liturgy, then, begins with a jubilant thanks, modulating through verses 6-7 to a petition for help, which the ensuing verses show to be a prayer for restoration of the kingdom and the empire. Old, well-known promises of help are developed in verses 8-10,[22] apparently as a kind of motive for divine intervention, reminding God of past commitments—or else as an encouragement to the petitioner (in any case, it is apparently pronounced by a different voice).

---

20. Actually the dating is problematic. The promise of triumphant division of the Israelite cities of Shechem and Succoth (v. 8) would suggest that they are now in enemy hands, and so at least the North has fallen to Assyria. Since in the text the names of Judah (v. 9) and the northern Gilead, Manasseh, and Ephraim are sandwiched between the conquered cities on the one hand and hostile Moab, Edom, and Philistia on the other (vv. 8-10), it would seem that Judah is conquered as well. On the other hand, verse 12 suggests that we still have an army, even if it is suffering defeat. Perhaps the inconsistency reflects later revision of an older prayer.

21. It is conceivable that rather than one psalm copying from the other, all these psalms are using traditional formulas from the oral liturgy. But I could believe this more easily if only the divine saying were quoted (vv. 8-11 or 8-10). Especially because vv. 7-14 in both poems begin without invoking the divine name, it is hard to imagine them as a traditional formula that happens to be taken up in just the same form by two psalms. And Psalm 60 seems to represent the original context, since the petition of verses 60:7 follows naturally on the preceding complaint of verses 3-6.

22. Erhard Gerstenberger (*Psalms 1*, 240; cf. xvi) is surely right in suggesting that this passage shows a closer resemblance to the divine sermons of Deuteronomy and the priestly document than to prophetic speeches. The Hebrew expression of verse 8a is simply not used to introduce oracles.

Verse 11 seems to have been part of the divine speech, calling for Israelite participation in the reconquest of Edom, but perhaps the ancient prayer leader (vv. 2-4), like modern translators, understood it to be his own address to the deity. At any rate, the prayer ends with an appeal for God's assistance in restoring his people and a renunciation of confidence in any help but God's.

The political situation of the psalm is not ours. Even an ardent Irish Republican wanting to pray the psalm in reference to the northern counties must acknowledge that it requires quite a hermeneutical leap to take any promises made to David or to Israel and apply them to Ireland.

An earlier generation of Christians could naively hear the psalm as the voice of Christ announcing his triumphant passion (vv. 2-7) and his claim to the conversion of Israel (vv. 9-10) and the Gentiles (vv. 11-12).[23] If we are to pray the psalm in a similar way, at least we cannot do so with the old naiveté.

Still, the psalm can hardly become prayer for us unless it somehow comes to express our own experience. Whatever Jews may have to do when they reappropriate the psalm, Christians can hardly pray it without some reference to the Christian mystery. To pray the psalm in the hope that in Christ Gentiles and Jews alike will become God's kingdom is not necessarily to seek a fulfillment of some kind of prophetic prediction supposedly embodied in this psalm. Rather, it is to pray the old prayer for restoration of David's empire as a metaphor for the fulfillment of God's purposes in David's Son.

That this should be accomplished by compulsion or trickery, by clever manipulation of Jews or Gentiles, is impossible. The only conquest that can bring about the kingdom is the free submission of Jews and Gentiles to God, wherever God will lead us. And that is God's work, not the work of human might or cleverness. In this struggle none, Jews or Gentiles, are enemies; the only enemies to be defeated (vv. 13-14) are the satanic principalities and powers that always strive to prevent humble submission to God.

Nor need we set a date for the full realization of the kingdom. If it is God's work, God's good time is good enough for us, even if that time must await the sounding of the final trumpet.

PSALM 146   MORNING FOURTH WEDNESDAY

(145) 146. Praise of God's faithfulness

¹   Alleluia!

23. See J. M. Neale and R. F. Littledale, *A Commentary on the Psalms from Primitive and Medieval Writers,* vol. 3 (London: Joseph Masters, 1883²; reprinted New York: AMS Press, 1976) 414–420.

My soul, give praise to the LORD;
2 I will praise the LORD all my days,
  make music to my God while I live.

3 Put no trust in the powerful,
  mere mortals in whom there is no help.
4 Take their breath, they return to clay
  and their plans that day come to nothing.

5 They are happy who are helped by Jacob's God,
  whose hope is in the LORD their God,
6 who alone made heaven and earth,
  the seas and all they contain.

It is the Lord who keeps faith for ever,
7 who is just to those who are oppressed.
It is God who gives bread to the hungry,
the LORD, who sets prisoners free,

8 the LORD who gives sight to the blind,
  who raises up those who are bowed down,
9 the LORD, who protects the stranger
  and upholds the widow and orphan.

8c It is the LORD who loves the just
9c but thwarts the path of the wicked.
The LORD will reign for ever,
Zion's God, from age to age.

Alleluia!

Hear, God, the persistent cries of all who suffer, of those who are exploited, of those who helplessly see their children starving, of the vulnerable who have none to protect them. Oh show forth your power to transform the world, and we will praise the depth of your compassion.

PSALM 139:1-18, 23-24   EVENING FOURTH WEDNESDAY

(138) 139. God's knowledge and care

1 O LORD, you search me and you know me,
2 you know my resting and my rising,
  you discern my purpose from afar.
3 You mark when I walk or lie down,
  all my ways lie open to you.

⁴ Before ever a word is on my tongue
　you know it, O LORD, through and through.
⁵ Behind and before you besiege me,
　your hand ever laid upon me.
⁶ Too wonderful for me, this knowledge,
　too high, beyond my reach.

⁷ O where can I go from your spirit,
　or where can I flee from your face?
⁸ If I climb the heavens, you are there.
　If I lie in the grave, you are there.

⁹ If I take the wings of the dawn
　and dwell at the sea's furthest end,
¹⁰ even there your hand would lead me,
　your right hand would hold me fast.

¹¹ If I say: "Let the darkness hide me
　and the light around me be night,"
¹² even darkness is not dark for you
　and the night is as clear as the day.

¹³ For it was you who created my being,
　knit me together in my mother's womb.
¹⁴ I thank you for the wonder of my being,
　for the wonders of all your creation.

　Already you knew my soul,
¹⁵ my body held no secret from you
　when I was being fashioned in secret
　and moulded in the depths of the earth.

¹⁶ Your eyes saw all my actions,
　they were all of them written in your book;
　every one of my days was decreed
　before one of them came into being.

¹⁷ To me, how mysterious your thoughts,
　the sum of them not be numbered!
¹⁸ If I count them, they are more than the sand;
　to finish, I must be eternal, like you.

[¹⁹ O God, that you would slay the wicked!
　Keep away from me, violent hands!

²⁰ With deceit they rebel against you
and set your designs at naught.

²¹ Do I not hate those who hate you,
abhor those who rise against you?
²² I hate them with a perfect hate
and they are foes to me.]

²³ O search me, God, and know my heart.
O test me and know my thoughts.
²⁴ See that I follow not the wrong path
and lead me in the path of life eternal.

Protestations of innocence dominate a number of psalms and similar biblical prayers (Pss 7:4-6, 9; 17:1-5; 26:1-6, 11-12; Jer 15:15-17). But we who have learned all too well Paul's lesson that all persons, Gentiles and Jews alike, are under the power of sin (Rom 3:9-20), are likely to be put off by their apparent blanket denial of sin. These psalms, however, generally intend in fact to make a more modest claim, not that one is sinless, but that one is innocent of specific crimes of which one is accused, of charges of false worship, for instance, or of being the one primarily responsible for the enmity of one's neighbors.

Some would suggest that the occasion was a trial or ordeal to which one was to be subjected; others, that the psalm is simply a type of lament to be prayed when one is ill (and so presumed to be guilty, for is not sickness the result of sin?) or when one's enemies are causing serious trouble or danger. In either case, this psalm was, like the other psalms of innocence, meant to be used repeatedly, by anyone in more or less the same kind of trouble.

As such, it is a remarkable poem. Not that the ideas are unknown elsewhere, but in none of the psalms are they developed thus. As in other such psalms, the principal themes are the denial of guilt (explicitly expressed in vv. 21-22 and 24) and prayer against the enemies (vv. 19-20).²⁴ The rest of the psalm (vv. 1-18, 23) develops a motif found in other such psalms: the petition for God to investigate the case ("Examine me, Lord, and try me; O test my heart and my mind"—Ps 26:2), or the affirmation that God knows one's case ("You search my heart, you visit me by night. You test me and you find in me no wrong"—Pss 17:2f.; 40:10; 44:22).

But in Psalm 139 this motif inspires a remarkably vigorous and moving reflection on God's searching knowledge. Every possible attempt to escape God's scrutiny (along with one or the other impossible ones as well [vv. 8-9])

24. Omitted in the Liturgy of the Hours in accordance with the policy of suppressing anything that looks like a curse.

is considered and rejected as ineffective: neither darkness nor distance, height nor depth, hinders God's probing knowledge, which even pursues one to Sheol, the abode of the dead, which other psalmists have excluded from any contact with God's provident love (Pss 6:6; 88:6).

Apparently the psalm originally was a denial of charges of false worship, for verse 24 in Hebrew can be read, "See [i.e., observe] that I follow not the path of idols, but lead me in the path of antiquity."[25] But at a time when idolatry had become less of a problem within Judaism, even the ancient Greek translators replaced "idol" with a more ambiguous word which in Hebrew happened to be pronounced and spelled the same. Thus a formula formerly used to deny a very specific crime could be used rather as a far more general profession of loyalty to Israel's God.

We are not likely to be accused of idolatry. Still, we can pray the psalm as a profession of loyalty. Not that we can or should deny the rich abundance of our sin; apart from anything else, we are not going to deceive God on that point! But the profession of faith, the basic pledge of loyalty to God—that is quite another thing.

A story is told about the desert father Abba Agathon, who remained silent when falsely accused of pride, detraction, and fornication, but protested vigorously when accused of heresy. Asked why he had denied only the final charge, he replied that he could acquiesce to the former accusation in imitation of Christ, but the heretic, he said, "is separated from the living and true God and joined to the devil and his angels. Sundered from Christ, he can no longer pray to God for his sins, for he has totally perished."[26]

Satan, whose name means "Accuser," accuses us; yes, our very hearts would condemn us (1 John 3:20). Against this, Psalm 139 is our protest and our plea to the God who is greater than our hearts.

The prayer is as much a petition for grace as it is a profession of faithfulness. Our adherence to God is, of course, a matter of the will. We cannot pretend to be powerless to choose for God and God's will; even less can we blame our failure on a failure of God's grace. But we know the fragility of our choice, the allure of the pride, covetousness, lust, envy, anger, gluttony, and sloth that would draw us away from God's will and ultimately from God's very self. For all the confidence the psalm expresses in one's innocence, its last word is one of petition: "Lead me in the path of life eternal."

We can also hear the psalm as the declaration of him in whom all our loyalty is founded, of Jesus, who gave himself over without reservation to God

25. The Hebrew expression *olam* can refer to long ages in the past as well as the future.
26. PL 73:751–752.

and to God's will, yet was accused of impiety and subversion (Mark 2:16; 3:2, 22; 14:55ff.; etc.).[27] Of all who ever worshiped the God of Israel, none could ever pray this psalm with so much truth as the One who knew no sin but was made "to be 'sin,'"[28] so that in him we might become the righteousness of God" (2 Cor 5:21).

PSALM 143:1-11   MORNING FOURTH THURSDAY

(142) 143. A prayer in desolation:
        seventh psalm of repentance

1   LORD, listen to my prayer,
    turn your ear to my appeal.
    You are faithful, you are just; give answer.
2   Do not call your servant to judgement
    for no one is just in your sight.

3   The enemy pursues my soul;
    has crushed my life to the ground;
    has made me dwell in darkness
    like the dead, long forgotten.
4   Therefore my spirit fails;
    my heart is numb within me.

5   I remember the days that are past;
    I ponder all your works.
    I muse on what your hand has wrought
6   and to you I stretch out my hands.
    Like a parched land my soul thirsts for you.

7   LORD, make haste and answer;
    for my spirit fails within me.
    Do not hide your face
    lest I become like those in the grave.

---

27. Admittedly, the gospel tradition progressively exaggerates the opposition of the Jewish establishment to Jesus. However, if Jesus met no hostility whatever from the scribes, Pharisees, and priests, it was the first and last time in the history of the world that a great religious figure escaped his colleagues unscathed.

28. The Hebrew word *hatta't* means "sin," but it is also the technical term for the "sacrifice for sin." The play on words would not be lost on the Corinthians, with their many Jewish Christian adherents.

⁸ In the morning let me know your love
for I put my trust in you.
Make me know the way I should walk;
to you I lift up my soul.

⁹ Rescue me, LORD, from my enemies;
I have fled to you for refuge.
¹⁰ Teach me to do your will
for you, O Lord, are my God.
Let your good spirit guide me
in ways that are level and smooth.

¹¹ For your name's sake, LORD, save my life;
in your justice save my soul from distress.
¹² In your love make an end of my foes;
destroy all those who oppress me
for I am your servant, O Lord.

You know my fragility and my perversity, God; what can I say in your presence? Protect me from my enemies, of whom I am the first. I long to be truly yours: show me where you would have me walk, and give me your spirit to lead me, for what is at stake is my very life.

PSALM 147:1-11   MORNING FOURTH THURSDAY

See above, p. 112, Morning Second Friday, with Psalm 147:12-20.

PSALM 144   EVENING FOURTH THURSDAY

(143) 144. An appeal for victory and peace

¹ Blessed be the LORD, my rock,
who trains my arms for battle,
who prepares my hands for war.

² God is my love, my fortress;
God is my stronghold, my savior,
my shield, my place of refuge,
who brings peoples under my rule.

³ LORD, what are we that you care for us,
mere mortals, that you keep us in mind;
⁴ creatures, who are merely a breath
whose life fades like a shadow?

5 Lower your heavens and come down;
  touch the mountains; wreathe them in smoke.
6 Flash your lightnings; rout the foe,
  shoot your arrows and put them to flight.

7 Reach down from heaven and save me;
  draw me out from the mighty waters,
  from the hands of alien foes
8 whose mouths are filled with lies,
  whose hands are raised in perjury.

9 To you, O God, I will sing a new song;
  I will play on the ten-stringed lute
  to you who give kings their victory,
  who set David your servant free.

11 You set him free from the evil sword;
   you rescued him from alien foes
   whose mouths were filled with lies,
   whose hands were raised in perjury.

* * * * *

12 Let our sons then flourish like saplings
   grown tall and strong from their youth,
   our daughters graceful as columns,
   adorned as though for a palace.

13 Let our barns be filled to overflowing
   with crops of every kind;
   our sheep increasing by thousands,
   myriads of sheep in our fields,
14 our cattle heavy with young,

   no ruined wall, no exile,
   no sound of weeping in our streets.
15 Happy the people with such blessings;
   happy the people whose God is the LORD.

In Psalm 144 a prayer of the king (vv. 1-11) has been adapted in the postexilic period by the addition of verses 12-15 to become a prayer for the community.

The prayer for the king consisted of two parallel petitions for victory, verses 5-8 and 11, each of which is preceded by an introduction that is a little hymn of praise (vv. 1-4 and 9-10). Oddly, the translation in the Liturgy of the Hours treats verse 11 as if it consisted of indicative statements rather than the imperative petitions of the Hebrew. Thus in English verse 11 becomes a part of the reasons why I will praise Yahweh with a new song. This probably makes no great theological difference, but I note it to get a better idea of how the prayer was originally used.

The motives for praise in the first verses are very much similar to those at the beginning of the royal thanksgiving Psalm 18, Yahweh is my rock, my fortress, my stronghold, my savior, my shield, my refuge; the phrase "who trains my arms for . . . war" is found in Psalm 18:35, and something much like "He brings peoples under my rule" in Psalm 18:48. Thus, like the royal petition, Psalm 89, and the royal psalm of innocence, Psalm 101, this psalm begins with praise of Yahweh (cf. Pss 89:2-38; 101:1). This praise is completed (v. 3) with a short reflection (similar to Psalm 8) marveling at God's condescension to a mere mortal like the one who prays.[29] The king then gets to the point, praying for deliverance, drawing heavily on the kind of description of a theophany found in Psalm 18:10, 14, 16). As in Psalm 18:17f., the enemies are described as the chaotic primordial waters. All this similarity to Psalm 18 could indicate that Psalm 144 is modeled on the former, but the similarities could just as well indicate traditional language regularly applied to the king in prayer.

While the allusions in verse 8 to the perjury of the opponents could seem to limit the occasions for use of the psalm, in fact most of the enemies with whom the king would do battle belonged to nations that had at some time made treaties with the king's predecessors, a circumstance that would automatically define the present conflict as violation of earlier covenant oaths.

Verses 9-10 again give praise to Yahweh, recalling his past deliverance of Davidic kings and doubtless suggesting his responsibility to the present king. The Hebrew petitions of verse 11 surely correspond better to the original use than the indicatives found in the translation used in the Liturgy of Hours; thus the prayer "Set me free, and rescue me from alien foes," would echo and reinforce the petition of verses 5-8.

The conclusion, with its prayer for fertility, seems rather odd in a prayer before battle; and certain expressions appear to reflect postexilic Hebrew use. The best explanation is that in the postexilic period the old royal petition was taken up again and adapted for the new needs of the community. The "I" of the old psalm no longer refers to the king but is now understood metaphori-

---

29. Unfortunately the inclusive language version of the Grail translation uses plural forms here ("What are we?" etc.), thus missing the point that this is the king's reflection on the graces he has received. Better something like "What am I?"

cally of the Jewish community (cf. Isa 55:3-5),[30] which seeks redress from its foreign oppressors, a redress that is utterly beyond its own power. But to this are added the more immediate needs of a community trying to reestablish itself in the land: healthy children, good crops, and prolific herds.

It is precisely some such metaphorical reading that we do when we pray the psalm. Like the postexilic Jews, we have no Davidic king to pray the psalm. But more than that, having been formed by the gospel, we have less confidence in the usefulness of a military solution to our predicament. And often enough the needs that we experience if we are to survive are quite different from the need for fertility that these Jews recognized.

As always when the psalms pray for help in battle, we do well to heed the Pauline call to battle, "Put on the whole armor of God, that you may be able to stand against the wiles of the devil. For we are not contending against flesh and blood, but against the principalities, against the powers, against the world rulers of this present darkness, against the spiritual hosts of wickedness in the heavenly places" (Eph 6:11f.). Or with a less cosmic view we pray for help in the internal conflict in which we struggle with the passions of the flesh that war against us (1 Pet 2:11). Or again, the psalm becomes our prayer simply in the strife that is an inevitable part of preaching the gospel faithfully (2 Cor 10:3ff.; 1 Tim 1:18).

It is not unreasonable to address the needs for survival of God's people through the imagery of the psalm's prayer for fertility, whether this becomes a prayer for the spiritual health of the coming generation of Christians or a petition for seekers to join and to prosper in our religious communities and to take on with alacrity the responsibilities of ordained and nonordained ministries.

But still more, the psalm can become a prayer spoken in the name of the Son of David who met the enemy in mortal conflict in his temptation, in his ministry, and on the cross; who continues that battle in our experience of the cosmic struggle in order to bring about the coming of the kingdom; and who prays without ceasing for the welfare of his brothers and sisters.

PSALM 51 MORNING FOURTH FRIDAY

See above, p. 53, Morning First Friday.

---

30. See Leslie C. Allen, *Psalms 101–150*, pp. 288 and 290. He also understands the ambiguous Hebrew terms of verse 14bc as alluding, not to the calamities ensuing on the conquest of the city, but to natural disasters, disease and miscarriage affecting the herds of verse 14a, and their distressed bellowing.

PSALM 147:12-20   MORNING FOURTH FRIDAY

See above, p. 114, Morning Second Friday.

PSALM 145   EVENING FOURTH FRIDAY

(144) 145. Praise of God's glory

¹ I will give you glory, O God my king,
  I will bless your name for ever.

² I will bless you day after day
  and praise your name for ever.
³ You are great, LORD, highly to be praised,
  your greatness cannot be measured.

⁴ Age to age shall proclaim your works,
  shall declare your mighty deeds,
⁵ shall speak of your splendor and glory,
  tell the tale of your wonderful works.
⁶ They will speak of your terrible deeds,
  recount your greatness and might.
⁷ They will recall your abundant goodness;
  age to age shall ring out your justice.

⁸ You are kind and full of compassion,
  slow to anger, abounding in love.
⁹ How good you are, LORD, to all,
  compassionate to all your creatures.

¹⁰ All your creatures shall thank you, O LORD,
   and your friends shall repeat their blessing.
¹¹ They shall speak of the glory of your reign
   and declare your might, O God,

¹² to make known to all your mighty deeds
   and the glorious splendor of your reign.
¹³ Yours is an everlasting kingdom;
   your rule lasts from age to age.

   You are faithful in all your words
   and loving in all your deeds.
¹⁴ You support all those who are falling
   and raise up all who are bowed down.

¹⁵ The eyes of all creatures look to you
   and you give them their food in due season.

16 You open wide your hand,
 grant the desires of all who live.

17 You are just in all your ways
 and loving in all your deeds.
18 You are close to all who call you,
 who call on you from their hearts.

19 You grant the desires of those who fear you,
 you hear their cry and you save them.
20 LORD, you protect all who love you;
 but the wicked you will utterly destroy.

21 Let me speak your praise, O LORD,
 let all peoples bless your holy name
 for ever, for ages unending.

Quite a tour de force, this psalm. The poem is a well-constructed hymn despite the constraints of being an acrostic, each verse beginning with a successive letter of the Hebrew alphabet.

Like other hymns, the psalm consists of invitations to praise (vv. 1-2, 4-7, 10-12, and 21), with reasons for this praise (vv. 3, 8-9, 13-20).

The one problem caused by the acrostic form was with the call to praise, which in hymns is usually an imperative addressed to the congregation, "Praise the Lord" or the like. But appropriate verbs are few, and none begins with *aleph,* the first letter of the alphabet. So the psalm begins (like another alphabetic hymn, Psalm 111, and like songs of thanks for personal favors) with an exhortation to self, literally "May I give you glory" or "I want to give you glory," a grammatical form that in Hebrew always begins with an *aleph.* Compare Psalms 103 and 104.

The other calls are also expressed as wishes, but the third person verb, which always begins with the letter *yud,* could stand at the beginning only of the *yud* verse 10, where such a form is in fact found. Otherwise each verse is headed by a noun beginning with the appropriate letter, with the verb appearing later in the verse. Now, the less common placement of these verbs, though it was dictated by the acrostic form, has led translators to consider them to be future predictions rather than wishes, and so to translate, for instance, "Age to age shall proclaim your works" rather than "Let age to age proclaim your works."[31]

---

31. It is not unknown elsewhere in Hebrew for such wishes to be expressed in the inverted word order found in this psalm, e.g., Pss 96:12b; 149:2b, 3b.

The psalm seeks praise not only from those present: future ages (vv. 4-7) and all God's creatures (v. 10) must praise God, much as the heavens and stars, the lightning, snow, hills, and beasts are called in Psalm 148 to laud him.

Reasons given for praise are God's majesty and God's merciful works for all creatures as well as for those who know and revere him.

The outstanding characteristic of the psalm is the breadth of its view. God's greatness cannot be measured. The prayer repeats the word "all" fourteen times (seventeen in Hebrew[32])! All should praise God, for God is good to all. God's reign lasts forever (v. 13), and so the praise should last forever (vv. 1, 2, 4, 7, 21).

All those persons who composed the psalm, who kept it alive by performing it in the Jewish congregations, who incorporated it into the biblical collection of psalms, still continue to "bless God's name forever" (vv. 1f.) through our assembly. For in our days it is not only their Jewish descendants but we Christians as well who fulfill their hope that "age to age shall proclaim your works, . . . speak of your terrible deeds, . . . recall your abundant goodness." We keep their voices alive.

Yet, what odd creatures we would be to them! Not just in the clothes we wear, the buildings we worship in, the languages we use, but in our hearts and souls. Could Jews of the Persian period have understood the piety of people who would want to include among God's great works the breakdown of the stereotypes of these ancient Jews about women? Could they have identified with people like us, who have to learn to puzzle beyond our well-learned lessons of biology and meteorology if we are to recognize God as the one who feeds all creatures? Yes, what would such a Jew make of a congregation that claimed to see the reign of God realized in a Messiah who was executed by an occupying power without so much as having thought of raising an army to liberate the people?

And yet, words cannot be prayer at all unless they become our own, expressing honestly our experience and convictions. Nor could we be what we are without the Jews of the Persian period. Paul, Peter, Jesus himself, all were formed by the whole story of Israel from Abraham to their day. It was to that story that they looked in order to make sense of their experiences and their insights. The call of the ancestors, the deliverance from Egypt, the presence of God in his people, the sacrifices, the promises to David, the warnings and promises of the prophets, the deliverance from enemies, the discipline of exile, the return to the Land, the wisdom of the scribes—all this revealed the

32. Nineteen if, like the liturgical text, we restore the line for the letter *nun* after verse 13.

patterns of what happens when God encounters his people; and Jesus and his disciples recognized that it was in this same matrix that their own encounter with God was cast.

Yes, finally the disciples recognized that it was actually Christ who was the matrix, that the full revelation of God's love and justice was to be found in the Jesus whom they had known and the Lord who was to come again, and it was that which was the measure of all that Israel had ever enjoyed or suffered. But even then, like travelers studying a map to follow their route among the mountains and valleys and rivers, they found they could better understand the mystery in which they were caught up by surveying the old traditions of Israel.

And so we join in their prayers. We take them up not with the arrogance of conquerors dividing the spoil but as heirs, who know that the good land we inherit depends on the labor of our ancestors. With humility we pray their prayers in the only way we know how to pray.

And we in our turn hope that age to age will proclaim the works of God, will declare those mighty deeds. And precisely by joining in the hymn we transmit it to a new generation and through them to generations yet to come. What they will do with it, how they sing the hymn, is up to them and to the Holy Spirit, who will remain in them.

And we trust that finally we will join with all of them, with the children of Israel, with the disciples of Jesus, with the generations yet to come, in the rich harmony of the timeless, eternal hymn to the God of all splendor and compassion.

PSALM 92   MORNING SECOND AND FOURTH SATURDAY

(91) 92. Praise of God's justice

2   It is good to give thanks to the LORD,
    to make music to your name, O Most High,
3   to proclaim your love in the morning
    and your truth in the watches of the night,
4   on the ten-string lyre and the lute,
    with the murmuring sound of the harp.

5   Your deeds, O LORD, have made me glad;
    for the work of your hands I shout with joy.
6   O LORD, how great are your works!
    How deep are your designs!
7   The stupid cannot know this
    and the foolish cannot understand.

8   Though the wicked spring up like grass
    and all who do evil thrive,
    they are doomed to be eternally destroyed.
9   But, you, LORD, are eternally on high.
10 See how your enemies perish;
    all doers of evil are scattered.

11 To me you give the wild ox's strength;
    you anoint me with the purest oil.
12 My eyes looked in triumph on my foes;
    my ears heard gladly of their fall.
13 The just will flourish like the palm tree
    and grow like a Lebanon cedar.

14 Planted in the house of the LORD
    they will flourish in the courts of our God,
    still bearing fruit when they are old,
    still full of sap, still green,
16 to proclaim that the LORD is just.
    My rock, in whom there is no wrong.

In the lament Psalm 22 the suppliant vows that upon deliverance,

I will tell your name to my people,
and praise your name where they are assembled;

and in Psalm 51 the repentant sinner prays:

Give me again the joy of your help;
with a spirit of fervor sustain me,
that I may teach transgressors your ways
and sinners may return to you.

Now, the kind of instruction that is promised in Psalms 22 and 51 is just what we find in songs like Psalms 32 and 34, the latter the prayer of a penitent who has been delivered from troubles, the former a prayer for anyone who has experienced deliverance. What distinguishes these psalms from other thanksgiving songs such as Psalm 30 is their overall didactic character that goes beyond the brief reflections on God's beneficence found in more typical thanksgivings (Pss 18:31; 30:6; 116:5-6a; 118:1-4).

Some such use must explain the character of Psalm 92, which lies somewhere between the hymn and the thanksgiving song, that is, between the prayer that praises God for God's qualities and customary behavior on the one hand, and on the other the song thanking God for a specific benefit just received. It uses the verb for "praise" (v. 2) that is typically, but not exclusively, found in thank psalms, and it contains explicit first person testimony about help received (vv. 5, 11-12). However, this testimony of help received does not narrate the circumstances like Psalms 18:5-18; 30:7-12; 118:5, 10-13; rather, the bulk of the psalm is descriptive of what Yahweh is like, how God regularly deals with the world, and specifically it is a vindication of God's justice. It is almost as if the personal testimony is introduced only as an illustration of the general truth.

The psalm, then, extols God's justice. In verses 5-6 the works and designs of Yahweh allude to the governance of the world rather than the creation as the psalm title in the Liturgy of the Hours would suggest. It is this that the fool cannot understand: seeing how the wicked flourish like grass; but the psalm declares that like grass they will soon wither (Ps 102:5, 12; Isa 37:27)[33] and contrasts this with another picture of vegetation, the flourishing, perennial palm or cedar, neither of which even loses its leaves in winter.

The argument, of course, is not proof but simply declaration. The psalm only asserts that God vindicates the righteous and backs up the assertion with the testimony (vv. 11-12) that God has helped me (cf. vv. 13-16) and has destroyed my enemies (vv. 8-10).

The psalm was sung repeatedly in Israel. Its ambiguous character meant that it could be used either by an individual in a thanksgiving ceremony for a recent deliverance or by a prayer leader in communal worship. Such communal use, at least for the later period of the Second Temple, is attested by the biblical title, "A song for the Sabbath." According to the Rabbis, it was sung in the Temple at the morning sacrifice of Sabbath (Tamid 7:4). It still is prayed in the synagogue on Sabbath, and traditionally has been prayed in the Western Church at Saturday Lauds, as it is to this day in the Liturgy of the Hours.

Well, we know from experience that the righteous sometimes die unrequited and that persons who for all the world seem to be heartless, exploitative, hypocritical scoundrels sometimes die prosperous and painless at the age of ninety-two. It is doubtless some such observation that led the Rabbis to an eschatological interpretation (again in Tamid 7:4).[34] If our prayer is to be honest, it must likewise take account of the failures of justice in the world of perception, as somehow the Church always has done. After all, the monastic tradition used this psalm for the feast of martyrs, who died prematurely pre-

33. For in Israel the grass always dries up dramatically in early summer, leaving the hills parched and yellow for the rest of the year.
34. See A. Cohen, *The Psalms* (Hindhead, Surrey: Soncino Press, 1945).

cisely because of their righteousness. And it was actually Israel's encounter with martyrdom in the Greco-Syrian persecution of the second century B.C.E. that ultimately provoked Judaism to belief in a reward for the righteous in an afterlife. For it was only the heroically faithful Jews who died at the hands of Antiochus IV Epiphanes; those who apostatized or compromised got along just fine, thank you.[35]

Our confession of God's justice, as well, looks to the eschaton; our creed confesses life everlasting and the Lord who will come to judge the living and the dead. We may have trouble conceiving of what that truly means (as well we should if the mystery is worthy of God), but in simplicity we acknowledge that ultimately God will bring about the fullness of God's justice in a manner beyond anything we could imagine or hope for (thank God!). And far from the psalm's confidence in identifying one's enemies as God's enemies, we humbly pray that we, and our enemies as well, may ultimately be called to feast together at the banquet table of the Lamb!

PSALM 8

See above, p. 122, Morning Second Saturday.

---

35. All the datable passages of the Old Testament that express unambiguously belief in resurrection or immortality come from the Maccabean period or later (Dan 12:1-3; 2 Macc 7; 12:42-44; Wis 3).

Index

abstraction opens prayer to variety of experiences, 134
ambiguity, 32–3
angels, 23
Arabs and Israel, 165–8

Baal, 128–30
Baal Haddad, 21
Babylon, 188
battle, 39–40, 201
blessing, 102–4
Brueggemann, Walter, 138n
Burns, David D., 64

Canaan, occupation of, 178–9
canaanites, 133–4
Christ as King, 16
Christians and Israel, 47–8
Christians praying Jewish prayers, 204–5
christocentric prayer, 29–30, 73–4
christocentric praying, 88
Church, 183
complaint to God, 97–9
confidence, 11–2
creation, cosmic struggle of, 123, 128–30
critical biblical study, 166

David, 162–4

death, 94–6
deliverance from, 121–2, 150–1
no meaningful survival after, 79
defeat,
loyalty to Yahweh in, 78–9
prayer in, 105–7
defeat not seen as victory of other gods, 191
deliverance, 141–2, 145
Denis, the Carthusian, 57
devil, 61–2

Easter, 72–3
El, 75n
enemies,
destruction of, 178
identification of, 11
prayer against, 6–8, 43
protection from, 9–10
entrance liturgy, 27–9
eternal life, 83
ethical sensitivity, 6–7
exhortation, 94–6, 171
exile, 185–8
return from, 68
exodus, 17–9
experience as the matter of prayer, 1–3, 43–4, 59, 83, 88, 142

freedom, 130
freedom and obligation, 179

gentiles, 159
    and Jews, 190–2
God, monotheistic, 92
God's searching knowledge, 195–6
gods, 22–3
grace, 155–7
gradual psalms, 117–8
Grail Psalms, 3

helpless, the, 112
hesed, 178–9
humility, 147–8

idols, 78–9, 196
incense offering, 6–7
inclusive language, 124–5
injustice and God, 94–6
innocence, 195–6
    profession of, 180–4
intercession, 106
intercessory prayer, 25
Israel and Arabs, 165–8

Jerusalem, 46–8, 62, 115–6, 153–5,
    158–60, 187
    longing for, 81–3
Jews, 159
justice, king's duty to assure, 110

King,
    Christ as, 36
    God as, 28–9, 38–40, 128–30,
    138–9
    "knowledge"dependent on social
    factors, 137–8

Larson, Gary, 174
Law, 64–6
    of God, 85, 129–30
legalism, 64
legend, truth in, 139n
life expectancy in antiquity, 149–50
life, fragility of, 174–6

Messiah. *See* "King, Christ as"
messiah. *See* "royal psalms"

metaphor, 33–4, 141–2
metaphorical praying, 92, 106, 201
metaphorical use, 2–3
moral ambiguity, 167–8
music in the Temple, 74–5

natural law, 65

oracle, 144
Othlo, 12

poverty, human, before God, 82
praise, 114
pride, arrogance, 147–8
profession of loyalty to God, 68–70
protection, God's, 118
"punishment," 145

rain, 90–1
re-use of psalms in antiquity, 50–1
responsibility for one's own disasters,
    106
Resurrection of Christ, 69
reuse of psalms
    for new purposes. *See* "royal
    psalms"
    in antiquity, 55, 199–200
royal psalms, 15–6, 35–6, 72–4,
    86–9, 110–2, 162–4, 180–4,
    199–201

sacrifice, animal, 121 +n.
sanctuary (refuge), 24, 42
sin, 54–7, 145, 170–2
    brings death, 54
    as offering, 54–5

Temple
    liturgy, 181
    worship, 74–5
    the, 27–30, 50, 58
"text" as identification of original
    wording, 14–5
thanksgiving prayer, 49–51
thanksgiving psalms, 206–7
titles of psalms, 50n

Torah, 115–6
   Jesus as, 116
   See also "Law of God"

vow, 120 +n.
   of thanksgiving song, 81–2
vows, 10–1, 90–1

weather, 22
   modern understanding, 91–2
wedding, king's, 86–9
wisdom interpretation of history,
   133–4

Zion. *See* "Jerusalem"

Index of Psalms

Psalm 2:   3, 15, 35
Psalm 3:   82
Psalm 5:   19
Psalm 8:   122, 148, 208
Psalm 11:   23
Psalm 13:   36
Psalm 15:   26
Psalm 16:   67
Psalm 17:   195
Psalm 18:   200
Psalm 19:   84
Psalm 20:   31, 35
Psalm 21:   34
Psalm 22:   90, 98, 206
Psalm 24:   26
Psalm 25:   150
Psalm 26:   195
Psalm 27:   36, 40, 150
Psalm 29:   20
Psalm 30:   3, 48, 206
Psalm 32:   51, 55, 206
Psalm 33:   30
Psalm 34:   55, 206
Psalm 36:   37
Psalm 38:   2, 55
Psalm 40:   55, 195
Psalm 41:   59
Psalm 42:   80
Psalm 43:   81

Psalm 44:   144, 195
Psalm 45:   35, 85
Psalm 46:   60
Psalm 47:   38
Psalm 48:   45
Psalm 49:   92
Psalm 51:   53, 112, 164, 201, 206
Psalm 57:   36, 44
Psalm 59:   36
Psalm 60:   154
Psalm 62:   100
Psalm 63:   9
Psalm 65:   89
Psalm 67:   101, 146
Psalm 72:   108, 121
Psalm 74:   129, 144
Psalm 77:   96
Psalm 79:   78, 106
Psalm 80:   104, 144
Psalm 81:   107
Psalm 83:   144
Psalm 84:   135
Psalm 85:   143, 153
Psalm 86:   148
Psalm 87:   157
Psalm 88:   97
Psalm 89:   98, 144
Psalm 90:   173
Psalm 92:   122, 205

Psalm 93:   128

Psalm 96:   136

Psalm 97:   99

Psalm 98:   152

Psalm 99:   160

Psalm 100:   57, 164

Psalm 101:   180

Psalm 108:   189

Psalm 110:   13, 35, 76, 132, 172

Psalm 111:   132

Psalm 112:   172

Psalm 113:   127

Psalm 114:   16

Psalm 115:   76

Psalm 116:   116, 119, 128

Psalm 117:   66, 168

Psalm 118:   70, 172

Psalm 119:   63, 67, 168

Psalm 121:   117

Psalm 122:   169

Psalm 123:   140

Psalm 124:   140

Psalm 125:   146

Psalm 126:   153

Psalm 127:   155

Psalm 128:   157

Psalm 130:   170

Psalm 131:   146

Psalm 132:   161

Psalm 135:   164, 176

Psalm 136:   176

Psalm 137:   184

Psalm 138:   188

Psalm 139:   193

Psalm 141:   5

Psalm 142:   8

Psalm 143:   150, 197

Psalm 144:   36, 184, 198

Psalm 145:   202

Psalm 146:   192

Psalm 147:   112, 114, 155, 198, 202

Psalm 148:   130, 138

Psalm 149:   12

Psalm 150:   74, 172